Turning Two

Turning Two

My Journey to the Top of the World and
Back with the New York Mets

BUD HARRELSON
WITH
PHIL PEPE

FOREWORD BY
DARRYL STRAWBERRY

THOMAS DUNNE BOOKS
ST. MARTIN'S PRESS
NEW YORK

THOMAS DUNNE BOOKS.
An imprint of St. Martin's Press.

TURNING TWO. Copyright © 2012 by Bud Harrelson and Phil Pepe. Foreword copyright © 2012 by Darryl Strawberry. All rights reserved. Printed in the United States of America. For information, address St. Martin's Press, 175 Fifth Avenue, New York, N.Y. 10010.

www.thomasdunnebooks.com
www.stmartins.com

Library of Congress Cataloging-in-Publication Data

Harrelson, Bud, 1944–
    Turning two : my journey to the top of the world and back with the New York Mets / Bud Harrelson with Phil Pepe ; foreword by Darryl Strawberry
        p. cm.
    ISBN 978-0-312-66240-0 (hardcover)
    ISBN 978-1-4299-4139-6 (e-book)
    1. Harrelson, Bud, 1944–   2. Baseball players—United States—
Biography.   I. Pepe, Phil.   II. Title.
    GV865.H27A3 2012
    796.357092—dc23
    [B]
                                                        2011046507

First Edition: April 2012

10 9 8 7 6 5 4 3 2 1

This book is humbly and gratefully dedicated to three men who had a profound effect on my professional career:

- Glenn McKinley Harrelson, my dad and my first Little League coach, who taught me about the game of baseball at an early age.

- Don Curley, my high school coach, who converted me into a shortstop and who worked with me tirelessly, hitting to me literally thousands of ground balls to help me improve.

- Gil Hodges, who made me into a better player and, I hope, a better person. He was, is, and always will be my Hall-of-Famer.

ACKNOWLEDGMENTS

There never would have been a *Turning Two* were it not for a couple of Robs, the double-play tandem of Kirkpatrick and Wilson, the literary equivalent of Tinker and Evers.

Rob Kirkpatrick, a senior editor at Thomas Dunne Books, grew up rooting for the Mets and says he was my biggest fan. His boyhood goal was to take my job with the Mets—just what the world needed, another short shortstop—but Tim Foli beat him to it. This book was his brainchild. He conceived it and flipped it to Rob Wilson, who completed the "twin killing."

FOREWORD

I don't remember exactly when or where I first met Bud Harrelson. It was probably during spring training in St. Petersburg, Florida, in the early 1980s. I was a young player with the Mets, and Buddy was this crusty old former Met—although he never was "crusty," not then and not now, and he never was "old," not then and not now.

At the time Bud was managing in the Mets' minor league system, and he was in camp to lend a helping hand as an extra instructor. Although our paths crossed back then, Bud was there to work with the infielders and I was an outfielder, so we didn't spend any kind of quality time together. That would come a few years later.

I really got to know Buddy in 1985. I was in my third season with the Mets. Davey Johnson was our manager and Bobby Valentine was our third-base coach, but in mid-May Valentine was hired away from the Mets to become manager of the Texas Rangers. That left a coaching vacancy that the Mets filled by reaching down to Columbia, South Carolina, where Harrelson was managing their Class A team in the Sally League.

The selection of Harrelson as Valentine's replacement was a natural. For one thing, for Bud it was a homecoming, literally. After he retired as an active player, Buddy, like me a native Californian, made his home in the New York area. He still does.

For another, Bud was, and is, one of the most popular and beloved players in Mets history. His return was warmly embraced by Mets fans and the media, and it would soon also be embraced by the Mets players, including a certain tall, left-handed-hitting right fielder.

I regret I never got to see Harrelson play—his last year was 1980, which was my senior year in Los Angeles' Crenshaw High School and the year I was drafted and signed by the Mets—but I had heard a lot about him as a player. You can't spend any time around the Mets and not have heard about Bud Harrelson, the shortstop and glue of the infield on the famous 1969 "Miracle Mets," the team that defied the odds and shocked the baseball world by winning the World Series in only the eighth year of their existence, a year after they had lost 89 games and finished ninth in the ten-team National League.

A lot of tremendous players were on that team—Tom Seaver, Cleon Jones, Tommie Agee, Jerry Koosman, Donn Clendenon, Tug McGraw—but Harrelson seemed to symbolize those '69 Mets with his gritty play, his competitiveness, his baseball knowledge, and his determination. I soon found out that as a coach he had the ability to convey those qualities to players.

What set Buddy apart as a coach was his softness and kindness. He's easy to get along with. Despite the difference in our ages, I found I could relate to him and his concept of playing the game.

When I first met Harrelson, I was immediately struck by his size—or, should I say, his lack of size? He barely came up to my shoulders and he couldn't have weighed more than 160 pounds soaking wet, if that. Take just one look at him and you can't help but be impressed and appreciate his ability as a player. It's just extraordinary that a guy his size could accomplish all he accomplished at the major league level. I have tremendous respect for him for that.

Bud spent five seasons as our third-base coach, so I got to know him pretty well, and then in 1990 the Mets let Davey Johnson go and they promoted Harrelson to manager. I enthusiastically supported their choice. Now Bud was in charge, but his personality never changed. He wasn't an in-your-face manager, the kind who, if things weren't going well, would come into the clubhouse and turn over tables or throw things in anger. He was always low-key and personal. When things were going bad, he'd call a meeting and pull the team together by speaking calmly as you understood the job he wanted you to do.

Maybe because he was undersize as a player, Buddy always was more about team than individual statistics. As a player he was more interested in team than self. As a manager, that was the message he wanted to get across to his players.

That first season, the players responded to him and we almost finished first in our division. Although we were heavy underdogs, we came down to the final week of the 1990 season in a close battle for first place with the Pittsburgh Pirates. I had had a good year, but late in the season I wrenched my back, missed the last seven games, and we finished in second place. I felt bad because I would have liked to have had a strong finish and helped us win the division, not only for myself, but also for Buddy.

My last season as a Met was 1990. The next year I was gone. I had become a free agent. I wanted to stay with the Mets. I liked it there and I enjoyed playing for Buddy, but the front office was kind of pushing me out the door. In the end, I had no choice. I couldn't turn down the deal I was offered by the Dodgers, so I left. Unfortunately, the next year, the Mets fell below .500, finished in fifth place, 20½ games out of first, and Harrelson was fired as manager. I have often thought how things might have been different if I had re-signed with the Mets. I like to think I could have helped the team win in 1991 and that I might have been able to save Harrelson's job.

It's hard to believe that more than twenty years have now gone by since Bud and I were together as Mets, he as manager, me as player. The years have been good to Bud. He doesn't seem to age and he never puts on weight. He still looks as if he could go out and play a credible game at shortstop. In fact, he still puts on a uniform and hits fungoes as a part-time coach and part-owner of the Long Island Ducks in the independent Atlantic League.

I'm pleased to say that our paths have crossed more often in recent years. It seems that what goes around comes around, and Bud and I are both involved with the Mets (I played for three other teams, but I always considered myself a Met), making appearances at charity events, so we get to see a little more of each other than we used to. I run into him at various charity functions and golf tournaments around the tristate area. It's always a joy to see him.

He's a New York baseball icon, and his legacy as a Met was secured when he was elected to the Mets Hall of Fame in 1986 (I was honored to join him there, along with Frank Cashen, Davey Johnson, and Dwight Gooden, in 2010), but he remains the same Bud. He still has a bounce to his step, a twinkle in his eye, and a quip on his lips. That has never changed. He's one of my favorite people; one person you'll always remember for his outgoing personality and his spirit. He never had his head in the sky with a "Look at me, I'm a big leaguer" attitude. That was never Bud.

I love him to death. I love him for what he's meant to me in my life and for the friendship we have maintained for so many years. It's a friendship I cherish.

—Darryl Strawberry

Turning Two

INTRODUCTION

It was, by any measure, a lovely Indian-summer afternoon in October—October 8, 1973, to be exact. Temperatures had climbed into the midseventies. Humidity was low. A pleasant and gentle breeze wafted in off the bay making for a comfortable day, even in short sleeves. The sun, high in a cloudless sky, was shining brightly, bathing in a brilliant glow the area around Roosevelt Avenue in the town of Flushing, in the borough of Queens, in the city of New York.

I knew firsthand about the brilliance of the midday sun. At precisely 3:12 on the afternoon of October 8, 1973, I was looking up into that sun as I lay rolling around in the dirt, embarrassingly scuffling with another person near second base in Shea Stadium, Flushing, in full view and with the rapt attention of some 53,000 witnesses.

What was I doing rolling around in the dirt like a little kid in a sandbox? you ask.

Good question! In fact, at the time, I was asking myself the same thing.

"Why am I here?"

"How did I get here?"

"Why is a grown man of twenty-nine, a husband and a father, making a public spectacle of himself, wrestling with another grown man three years his senior with 53,967 pairs of eyes looking down upon us?"

The short answer is that I'm a battler. Always have been! It was out of necessity. As far back as I can remember, people kept telling me I was too small. I heard it when I was a kid growing up in Northern California. I heard it in Little League, in high school, in college, and many times over after signing my first professional contract.

A psychiatrist would probably say that something inside me got riled up by the doubters, the nonbelievers, and the naysayers and I was motivated to prove them all wrong. At a young age, I learned that, because of my size (I weighed 96 pounds as a high school freshman, 130 pounds as a junior, and 145 pounds when I graduated), I had to try harder and work harder than my peers, and to fight for everything I got. As small as I was, I was never afraid to stand up for myself.

That attitude was carried all the way through my professional career. I refused to be intimidated or bullied by anyone, no matter how big he was or how important. I would fight anyone that challenged me, and that included rolling around in the Shea Stadium dirt with a guy who was one of my early idols, a mentor and supporter, the superstar hit man from Cincinnati's Big Red Machine, Pete Rose, also known in baseball circles as Charlie Hustle.

It has been four decades since that October 8, 1973, dustup at second base in Shea Stadium in the fifth inning of Game 3 of the National League Championship Series.

I have been retired for more than three decades as a player, and for more than two decades as a coach and manager of the New York Mets.

It was pointed out to me that I am the only man who was in uniform for both of the Mets' two World Series titles—as a player in the Miracle Year of 1969 and as one of Davey Johnson's coaches in 1986 (I was coaching third base at Shea Stadium in the bottom of the tenth inning of Game 6 of the World Series against the Boston Red Sox on October 25, and I sent Ray Knight home with the winning run when Mookie Wilson's bouncer went through Bill Buckner's legs)—a distinction of which I am enormously proud.

Since their inception in 2000, I have been part-owner of the Long Island Ducks in the independent Atlantic League. I was their first manager and I still patrol the first-base coaching box at home games for the Ducks, who are based in Central Islip, New York.

Although I never made the Baseball Hall of Fame—I did receive one vote in 1986; I have never found out what writer voted for me (he's probably too embarrassed to admit it), but I'm going to keep searching for him and write him a check when I do find him—I am fortunate to have played 16 seasons in the major leagues, accumulated 1,120 hits, won a Gold Glove for defense, made the All-Star team twice, and played on two pennant winners and one World Series champion.

I am honored to be, along with Rusty Staub, one of the first two players inducted in the Mets Hall of Fame in 1986.

I am privileged to have known Casey Stengel (he was largely responsible for my becoming a switch-hitter), to include among my friends the incomparable Yogi Berra, and to have learned from Gil Hodges, the best manager I ever played for and have ever seen. Gil became a surrogate father to me. His death on April 2, 1972, Easter Sunday, was one of the saddest days of my life.

I am blessed to have known Tom Seaver, who not only was a teammate and a roommate, is a Hall of Famer and one of the greatest pitchers in baseball history, but has also been a dear friend for almost half a century.

It's a bit of irony that with all that I have experienced in my baseball career, I will be best remembered for rolling around and tussling with Pete Rose in the Shea Stadium dirt at second base in Game 3 of the 1973 National League Championship Series.

To this day, many people who weren't even born in 1973 ask me about the incident. When I talk to kids' groups, some youngster will invariably say, "My dad says you had a fight with Pete Rose."

"That's right," I say. "I hit him with my best punch," and that will get a reaction like "Yeah?" And then I'll say, "I hit him right in the fist with my eye."

I have no regrets about going at it with Rose. I did what I had to do to protect myself, and Pete did what he thought he had to do to try to motivate his team.

We fought and that was the end of it. It was gone right away. This was business, part of the game, nothing personal. There was no carryover, no lingering feud, and no hard feelings. We wound up as teammates with the Phillies in 1979, and years later Pete came to two Long Island Ducks games when his son, Pete Jr., played for us.

Something good even came out of the fight. In 1995, Pete and I did a card show together, and I got him to autograph a picture of the fight, which he did. He wrote, "Thanks for making me famous," and he signed his name. Here's the good thing. I didn't have to wait on a long line to get his autograph and he didn't charge me for it.

CHAPTER 1

My birthday is one of the most famous and most important dates in U.S. history!

I pause here to let the full impact of that statement sink in while you say, "Who does this guy Harrelson think he is? What an ego for a guy who was only a lifetime .236 hitter!"

Okay, let me repeat:

MY BIRTHDAY IS ONE OF THE MOST FAMOUS AND MOST IMPORTANT DATES IN U.S. HISTORY!

You see, I was born on June 6, 1944, and the reason it's such a famous date, I have to admit, is not because that's the day I was born. Students of American history and people who are old enough to remember World War II (it was in all the papers) will recognize June 6, 1944, as D-day, the day of the invasion of Normandy, the pivotal successful offensive for the Allied forces against the German army and a critical point in winning the war in Europe.

As precocious as I like to think I was, of course I remember none of this. My dad was in the service in World War II, but it was never mentioned when I was a kid that I was born on D-day. I found out about it later when I was growing up and people told me I was born on D-day. My reaction was "What's D-day?" That's when I found out that it's a big deal; the date of my birth is an honored and important one in our nation's history.

Lindsey Nelson, who, along with Ralph Kiner and Bob Murphy, comprised the Mets' radio and television broadcasting team for all the years I played for them, loved that I was born on D-day. Lindsey, who had served in the 9th Infantry Division, never failed to wish me happy birthday on the air and in person when June 6 arrived.

Recently I did some research to see which other major league players were born on June 6. I found one Hall of Famer, Bill Dickey, the great catcher for the New York Yankees in the 1920s, '30s, and '40s. Others born on June 6 were Mark Ellis, Tony Graffanino, Dave Bergman, Gaylen Pitts, Merv Rettenmund, and Carlton Willey.

I knew Carl Willey. He was a right-handed pitcher from Maine who was with the Mets from 1963 to 1965. That was before I got there, but in 1965, when I was playing for the Mets' AAA International League farm team in Buffalo, Willey was sent there by the Mets either on a rehab assignment or to work out some mechanical problem. He was a veteran nearing the end of his career, trying to hang on a little longer. Meanwhile, the Mets, desperate for pitching, were hoping Carl could add some leadership and experience to their staff.

When June 6 rolled around, Carl said to the Buffalo manager, Kerby Farrell, "Skip, I'm taking Bud out tonight. It's our birthday. We're not playing."

It was Willey's thirty-fourth birthday and my twenty-first, so we went out. Being the veteran and the class guy he was, Willey picked up the tab.

Of the major league players born on June 6, only one was born on June 6, 1944, D-day, and that was Derrel McKinley Harrelson, who entered the world that day in Niles, California, a small town in Alameda County. At one time, during the silent-film era in the early 1900s, Niles was the home of the movie industry. Many of Charlie Chaplin's films were made there.

In 1956, Niles merged with four other small communities,

Centerville, Irvington, Mission San Jose, and Warm Springs, to become the city of Fremont, which is situated almost equidistant between Oakland and San Jose, about twenty-five miles south of Oakland and twenty miles north of San Jose.

You're probably thinking, "What kind of name is Derrel? And where does the McKinley come from?"

As for the McKinley, I can only guess that it probably was because of William McKinley, the twenty-fifth president of the United States, who, coincidentally, was born in Niles, Ohio, and had some Irish blood in his family as does mine, and who was assassinated in September of 1901, in the second year of his second term as president. It wasn't uncommon back then for parents to give their sons the names of prominent Americans.

McKinley has been the middle name in my family for six generations. It started with my great-grandfather and then right on down to my grandfather, my father, and then me—my older brother missed it and I got it. I passed it along to my son, Tim, and when he had a boy, I told him, "It's up to you," but he didn't let it die, and so now the Harrelson clan has a streak of six generation of McKinleys.

Now about the Derrel! Well, how many Derrels do you know? Everybody, I'm sure, has come in contact with a Darrell, a Darryl, even a Derrell (two *l*'s), but how many know a Derrel (one *l*)? I'll print my name, D-E-R-R-E-L, and people will look at it and probably say to themselves, "He must be wrong," so they'll change it to D-A-R-R-E-L or D-A-R-R-E-L-L. People who try to pronounce it the way it's spelled will call me "Dee-rell." When I hear "Dee-rell," I know right away it's a solicitor.

In all my years, I have come across only one other person named Derrel, and that was Derrel Thomas, a little switch-hitting infielder from California who played for the Astros, Padres, Giants, Dodgers, Expos, Angels, and Phillies in the 1970s and 1980s. I guess his folks didn't know how to spell either. Or maybe the name Derrel is just "a little switch-hitting infielder from California" thing.

When the Mets moved from Shea Stadium to Citi Field and

replaced all the Hall of Fame busts with plaques, they asked us what we wanted on our plaque. Some guys, such as Jerry Koosman and Keith Hernandez, opted for just their first and last names. Koos said, "Nobody knows my middle name." I said uh-uh, I want my full name on my plaque. A lot of people know my real name. So my plaque reads DERREL MCKINLEY HARRELSON.

That's my name and I'm proud of it, and that's what I wanted on my plaque.

My old teammate Ed Kranepool is the only person who has ever called me Derrel. I don't know why, but that's what he called me the first time I met him, and that's what he still calls me to this day. Nobody else calls me Derrel. Nobody ever has. At home I was always Bud. I was told that came about because my brother, Dwane, who is two years and two months older than me, called me Bubba because he couldn't say *brother* and that evolved into Bud. I was Bud, never Buddy. My dad had a relative named Buddy, so I became Bud to distinguish between us.

That reminds me that another Mets teammate, Clarence "Choo-Choo" Coleman, called me Bub, but then Choo-Choo called everybody Bub, probably because he didn't know their names.

Ron Swoboda once challenged Coleman, saying, "Choo-Choo, I bet you don't even know my name."

Coleman is said to have replied, "You're number four."

Somebody once asked Choo-Choo what his wife's name was and he said, "Mrs. Coleman."

So Choo-Choo called me Bub, but at least he was close, and it sounded like Bud.

Not until I came to New York and was playing with the Mets did people begin calling me Buddy. Tom Seaver started it, and some others picked it up. Now some people call me Bud and some call me Buddy. I don't have a preference, and I'll answer to either one, but for the record, I sign autographs Bud.

In school, my nickname was Buddo. The first time I went back with the Mets to play in San Francisco, I heard someone in the stands yell, *"Buddo."* I knew exactly where that guy was from.

My ancestry is English-Irish-Dutch-Swedish–Cherokee Indian. My folks were typical Middle Americans, Mom and Dad both "Grapes of Wrath" migration: my mom, Rena, from Merkel, Texas, my dad, Glenn, from Wewoka, Oklahoma (which might account for my affinity with Mickey Mantle, also an Oklahoman). Mom and Dad had three children. My brother, Dwane, is the oldest, I'm in the middle, and my sister, Glenna, is the baby.

We didn't have money for extra stuff when I was growing up. Dad was a mechanic/car salesman. Mom was a homemaker when I was young. Later, she got her real estate license. My dad worked his butt off to provide for us, and he and my mom were always involved in the lives of us children. We'd go camping and boating, and from a young age, we children were very involved in all sports. My mom and dad were always in favor of our sports, always supportive.

Both my father and mother were athletes. Mom was a hurdler. Dad was a good football player. He also played baseball and basketball. Who knows how far he could have gone athletically, but he dropped out of school in the tenth grade because he had to go to work. My dad was my first Little League coach. When I talk to Little League groups, I tell this story, embellishing it only slightly:

"When I got to be old enough to play Little League, I was smaller than all the other kids, and when the coaches selected their teams, I was picked by another coach, not my father. I was disappointed.

"'You didn't choose me?'" I said.

"'No,' my dad said. 'Somebody took you before I got the chance. I took your brother first, and when my turn came up again, you were gone.'

I had one talent when I was nine years old. I could cry. So I cried. My tears obviously got to my mom because she told my dad, "Oh, that's terrible, you have to do something." Through tears I was saying, "I wanted to be on your team, Dad."

That did the trick. The next thing I knew, my dad was on the phone with the coach who picked me. My dad made a trade and threw in some cash to complete the deal, and that's how I got to play on my father's team.

Niles was in the Hayward school district, and I started at Hayward High along with about a thousand others that made up my freshman class. When I was a freshman, my brother, Dwane, was a junior, and he was a stud, a big-deal athlete, a star baseball, football, and basketball player. I idolized him. In baseball, he was a shortstop/catcher. He had a great arm, good power, and he could run.

In his junior year, a Washington Senators scout told him, "If you have a good senior year, we'll sign you." Dwane didn't have a good senior year, so instead of signing, he went to Coalinga Junior College, a rich oil school down in the Central Valley toward Fresno. One day he was playing shortstop and he got wiped out on a double play. He would have been better off if his leg was broken. Instead, he got his ankle twisted, and he was never the same after that. He was sidelined a long time. He couldn't play sports so he dropped out of school, got married, and that was the end of his athletic career.

It's sad because Dwane was the athlete in the family. In high school, I was the "little" Harrelson.

The area in and around Hayward was growing rapidly, and Hayward High was so crowded that they built a new school, Sunset High, and redistricted all the students. I was sent to Sunset for my sophomore year. My class would be Sunset High's first graduating class. The schools in the area were integrated, and Sunset got most of the blacks and Hispanics. However, they decided to keep Hayward High's senior class intact so they would graduate together, and my brother, Dwane, who was a senior, stayed at Hayward High. As a result, for that one year, my brother and I attended different high schools.

Moving to Sunset proved to be fortunate for me for my athletic career. In the beginning, Sunset had only two classes, freshman and sophomore. It didn't field a varsity baseball team, so I was still playing jayvee ball as a sophomore.

Throughout my high school years, my dad was my biggest booster. He was always positive. And he never interfered. He wasn't one of those fathers who would try to coach me or come to the games and yell at the umpires or complain to the coach if he thought I deserved more playing time than I was getting. I'd never see him sitting in the stands, but I always knew he was there. His business was near the high school, and he'd come up and sit in his car in the parking lot and watch the game.

If I made an error or didn't get a hit, he wouldn't try to correct me, even though he could have because he knew the game. If he saw something I did that was wrong, he wouldn't say, "You looked bad" or "You should have done so-and-so," nothing like that. He'd never say anything negative. He was always positive and always supportive. Throughout my professional career, my dad was the most proud guy.

In my junior year, Sunset fielded a varsity baseball team, and I came to a turning point in my life. I got to play against some good competition, such people as Ed Sprague, who pitched for four major league teams, and George Mitterwald, who caught for 11 seasons with the Twins and Cubs. And I started playing shortstop.

Until then I had never played shortstop. Not ever. I didn't play much at any position my first year of Little League. When my dad did put me in a game, I played a deep right field. Later, I moved to the infield: a little second base, a little third, but never shortstop.

The man who gets the credit (or blame) for making me a shortstop was my high school baseball coach and mentor, Don Curley. "You're the fastest player on the team and you have the best arm," he told me, and moved me from third base to shortstop. I wore him out hitting me ground balls. He must have hit me thousands. He'd hit me ground balls in practice, and when practice was over and the rest of the guys were packing up and getting ready to leave, I'd say, "Mr. Curley, would you hit me some more ground balls?"

I had a good junior year, made all-league, and the scouts started coming around, from the Cubs, the Cardinals, the Yankees, and the Mets. Dolph Camilli was the area scout for the Yankees. He was a big name in baseball and a local hero. Born in San Francisco, he was a two-time All-Star for the Dodgers when they played in Brooklyn. He led the National League in home runs and RBIs and was voted the league's Most Valuable Player in 1941, helping the Dodgers win their first pennant in twenty-one years. He seemed eager to sign me. He gave me his card and told me the Yankees would be willing to send me to college.

As a kid I was a Yankees fan. California had no major league team at the time, so the only major league baseball I got to see was the "Game of the Week" on television, and that usually meant the Yankees against somebody. To me, the Yankees were gods and Mickey Mantle was my favorite player. Later, when the Giants moved to San Francisco, I became a Giants fan, and Willie Mays replaced Mickey Mantle as my favorite player.

About the time I was beginning my senior season of baseball at Sunset High, the New York Mets were beginning their first season in the National League. I couldn't follow them because they were never on television in California, but like most people at the time I thought they were laughable because they were so bad. Yet there's a fatalistic symmetry in that the Mets came into existence the year I graduated from high school. Colliding as they did, those two events might indicate that the stars were aligned to make me a New York Met.

While I had been mildly aware that the National League was expanding from eight teams to ten, and that one of those new teams would be playing in New York, that didn't consume my attention or capture a great deal of my interest. I was not jumping on the Mets' bandwagon and becoming a fan of the fledgling team, something that I later learned was a trend for young people in and around New

York at the time. I was eighteen years old, and like any other high school senior I had enough going on in my life to occupy my thoughts without concerning myself with something that was happening three thousand miles away.

Whatever knowledge I had about the Mets came from the Giants having come to California from New York, where they had played their home games in a place called the Polo Grounds, which, coincidentally, was where the Mets played their home games in their inaugural season of 1962.

I had a great senior year and was all-league again. That really boosted my confidence. It also boosted my confidence that I got offers to sign out of high school. It was tempting, and flattering, but I thought I should go to college instead.

At Sunset High I had played baseball, basketball, and football on a team that had 150-pound tackles. In football, I was the lone kickoff receiver, the lone punt returner, the safety on defense, and a 140-pound running back. The only time I left the field was for extra points.

In basketball I was a guard, fast and quick. I could drive, but I wasn't a good shooter. I would take two guys with me to the basket, then dump the ball off to an uncovered teammate for an easy basket. I got a lot of assists. I'd take one guy to the basket and a bigger guy would come up, and that's when I'd dump it off. We played against some good competition, such as the famous McClymonds High from Oakland, which had produced Bill Russell and Paul Silas in basketball and Frank Robinson, Vada Pinson, and Curt Flood in baseball. They had guys five feet eight that could dunk. I was five-ten and I could rebound and touch the rim, but I couldn't dunk. McClymonds kicked our butts. They beat us warming up. We saw these little guys dunking the ball in warm-ups, and we were beat before the game started.

I didn't have any college offers. I knew I was too small for football, but I thought I could play basketball and eventually get a scholarship at San Francisco State. So that's where I went, but when I got there, I decided I didn't want to play basketball. I wanted to play baseball. I went out for the baseball team as a walk-on. When I told one of the varsity players that I was trying out for the team, he asked me what position I played. When I said shortstop, he said, "Not here. We have a senior at shortstop and he's the coach's pet."

I asked him what position I should try out for and he said, "Third base. They don't like him."

So I tried out for third and I made the team.

I didn't play at first, but then the coach stuck me in the lineup and I was on fire. I kept hitting and the coach kept playing me, and eventually the other third baseman quit the team. I was starting at third base on the varsity, and at the same time they were working me out at shortstop with the jayvee. I was so busy there was no time to study.

My hard work soon paid off. I had a good freshman season at San Francisco State. We played a top-notch schedule against schools such as Stanford, and soon the pro scouts were putting the rush on me. I decided it was time to take advantage of that and give pro baseball a shot. I had eliminated the Cubs and the Cardinals and narrowed my choices down to the Yankees and the Mets. New York fascinated me because of its long tradition and history in baseball and because the city is the world capital in finance, entertainment, and culture. My mom tried to talk me out of signing with a New York team.

"You're going to get killed," she said.

"Mom," I said, "you watch too much TV."

Later, after I signed my contract, my mom and dad came to New York and I showed them areas in and around the city to try to convince them that even if you work in the city, you don't have to live in the city; there are some beautiful areas in the New York suburbs.

There was no free agent draft in those days, and no agents. The only indication a young baseball player had of his worth was based on the offers of the teams interested in signing him, and I was getting my share of calls from major league scouts in my area.

"They keep calling you and making you offers," my dad said. "If I were you, the next time they call, I would tell them to make you a final offer." And that's what I did. The Yankees' offer was $16,500. The Mets' was $13,500. I thought at the time it was all the money in the world, but after I bought a car and a new wardrobe, there wasn't much left, so I was forced to get by on my salary of $500 a month. Even though the Yankees offered more money, they were scary to me. I still looked upon them as gods. I was overwhelmed and somewhat intimidated by their tradition, their many championships, and their legendary players. I wondered if I was good enough to make it with the Yankees. I was afraid if I signed with them, I'd be stuck in the minor leagues forever. I had pretty much made up my mind from the beginning that I was going to sign with the Mets because I was little and because the Mets were brand-new. The team was just being organized so I figured my advancement to the major leagues would be quicker with the Mets than it would be with the Yankees.

Another reason I leaned toward signing with the Mets was their scout that followed me. His name was Roy Partee and he had been a backup catcher for the Boston Red Sox in the 1940s. He was a wonderful man, someone I trusted, and he became a friend.

Although it wasn't a condition of signing with the Mets or the reason I chose them, it didn't hurt that I was going to start my professional baseball career in Salinas in the Class A California League, just about sixty miles from home. Coincidentally, in 1962, the Mets had operated a California League team in Santa Barbara, which is almost all the way down to Los Angeles. However, in 1963, the year I turned pro, that team would be moving to Salinas, practically in my backyard. I considered that an omen.

The year I signed, the Mets also signed Dick Selma, who would join me at Salinas and who was from Fresno, about seventy-five miles east of Salinas. In 10 seasons in the major leagues with the Mets, Phillies, Padres, Angels, Cubs, and Brewers, Dick would win 42 games and save 31 more.

Since I signed after the school year, the California League

season was already under way when I joined the Salinas Mets. To make room for those of us who signed late, some players had to be released. I felt bad about that because one of the players they released was a guy I got to know and like when I worked out with the team.

At Salinas, I got into 36 games, had 136 at bats, batted a cool .221, and began a streak in which I hit a home run in five consecutive professional seasons.

If the minor leagues are supposed to prepare you for the major leagues, playing for Salinas certainly did just that. The 1963 Salinas Mets won 49 games and lost 91, so you can see I was totally prepared to play with a team that lost 397 games in my first four major league seasons.

CHAPTER 2

"Hey, you swing pretty good left-handed. I like it. Why don't you try it?"

The gruff, gravelly voice was unmistakable. If you've heard it once, you never forgot it, and I had heard it more than once; a lot more. That voice belonged to the one and only Charles Dillon (Casey) Stengel.

This was Huggins-Stengel Field, the New York Mets' spring training facility in St. Petersburg, Florida, early one morning, practically the crack of dawn, in the spring of 1966. Stengel was there not as the manager of the Mets (he had announced his retirement the previous August) but as an adviser and an interested spectator.

Dating back to his playing days, which spanned 1912 to 1925 with five teams, the Brooklyn Dodgers, New York Giants, Pittsburgh Pirates, Boston Braves, and Philadelphia Phillies, Stengel was one of the most unforgettable and most colorful characters in baseball history. As a player, he was underrated in baseball lore, but not in his time. Born in 1890 in Kansas City (thus the nickname Casey), he was a lifetime .284 batter in 14 seasons and a .393 hitter in three World Series.

Later as a manager, he was a disaster. In nine years at the controls of the Dodgers and Braves (known at the time as the Bees), he had one winning season and never finished higher than fifth place. When the Bees fired him in 1943, Stengel went back to the minor leagues to manage, first for Milwaukee and Kansas City in the American Association, then to the Oakland Oaks of the Pacific Coast League, where he finished second, fourth, and first in three seasons.

In 1949, the Yankees shocked the baseball world by naming Stengel their manager. He was fifty-eight years old and came with a reputation as a clown (he once came to bat, lifted his cap, and a sparrow flew free), yet he stayed for twelve years as manager of the Yankees, won ten pennants and seven World Series, and then was let go after the 1960 season for, as Casey said, "making the mistake of turning seventy years of age."

When the Mets entered the National League as an expansion team in 1962, they named Stengel their manager. He was obviously there to provide name value and as a promotional distraction since the fledgling Mets were going to be a woefully inept team.

I thought the way the Mets went about stocking their team in 1962 was brilliant. Expansion teams were stocked differently then than now. Back then, expansion teams were in a no-win situation. They were getting other people's rejects. What the Mets did made sense, selecting players with major league résumés, recognizable names, and some connection to New York, even if those players were past their prime. But it meant the Mets were going to put a team on the field that had no chance to be successful, and Stengel understood that better than anybody else.

If Casey was a failure as a manager with the Mets, he was a rousing success as a salesman, promotional tool, and pitchman. He became a renowned and tireless ambassador for baseball, calling attention to the Mets they would otherwise never have attracted. He knew he had a bad team (they would finish with a record of 40-120, a whopping 60½ games out of first place), but Casey portrayed the Mets as lovable losers by referring to them as "the Amazin' Mets" and by employing his unique form of double-talk, which came to be known as Stengelese.

This obfuscation was skillfully used when Casey wanted to

deflect attention from the team's ineptitude. Trust me, as a manager talking to his players, Stengel's message always was crystal clear, and he never left any doubt about what he was trying to get across.

I remember one encounter with him at Al Lang Field in St. Petersburg, Florida, in the spring of 1967. Stengel was still on the Mets payroll as an adviser, and the Mets brought him back for spring training to promote the team, entertain the writers, and just to have him around.

On this particular day, it wasn't Tom Seaver's turn to pitch, and I was given a breather and told I could do whatever I wanted.

After we had completed our workout, Tom and I got dressed in our street clothes and wandered out into the stands at Al Lang Field to watch the exhibition game. When we noticed Casey sitting alone in the more-than-half-empty stands, we went over and joined him. We knew Stengel enjoyed having company, somebody he could talk to, and Tom and I liked spending time with him and listening to his stories. As usual, we weren't disappointed as Stengel, obviously catering to Seaver, who had played baseball at the University of Southern California, went into a lengthy dissertation about all the coaches and players that had come out of USC. Stengel, who lived in Glendale, not far from the Southern Cal campus, had clearly kept up with USC's baseball program. I was in awe of how he could remember all the players that had come through USC and how he could recount some anecdote about every one of them.

He went on and on, making perfect sense until this older man meandered over and sat down next to us. The guy was just a fan, we had no idea who he was, but he apparently saw Stengel holding court and out of curiosity decided to come over and listen in.

As soon as the stranger hit the seat, Casey went into his mumbo-jumbo act. One moment he was speaking lucidly about players from USC, and the next moment he was talking gibberish and not making any sense; not one word. He just went rambling on. Befuddled and not understanding what Stengel was saying, the frustrated eavesdropper got up and walked away. Once he did, Stengel went right back and picked up his conversation about USC alumni where he had left off. He didn't miss a beat. And I'm thinking, "You sly old son of a gun; you didn't want that stranger listening in on your conversation so you went into your double-talk act to get rid of him without insulting him."

I actually met Stengel briefly before I even signed with the Mets, in the fall of 1962. Roy Partee, the scout that eventually signed me, was hustling me pretty hard, and he invited me to the seventh game of the World Series between the Yankees and Giants. I wound up sitting right behind Stengel. Roy introduced me to him, saying something like "Casey, this is a young man we hope to sign and be the Mets' shortstop of the future." Casey said something that I can't remember, probably because at the time I couldn't understand what he was saying.

Stengel was sitting right in front of me, and the thing I remember is that he had the biggest ears I'd ever seen on a human being. It was like sitting behind Dumbo. At times I missed plays on the field because Stengel's ears kept blocking my view. I kept shifting to the left and to the right to try to see around those ears. We were at the famous game in which Willie McCovey hit that vicious line drive to Bobby Richardson for the final out of the game with the tying run on third and the winning run on second. I never did see Richardson catch McCovey's line drive. Stengel's ears were in my way.

In 1964 I had my first encounter with Stengel as a manager. I had just completed my first season of professional baseball, 36 games for Salinas in the Class A California League, and I was invited to the Mets' minicamp for their top prospects. I had broken my arm, and I guess they got good reports from my manager about my play at shortstop. I was only a right-handed hitter at the time, but I could run, so I figured they wanted to take a look at me at camp.

I don't remember how many prospects were there. Some major league guys who either needed to work on something or, like me, had been injured were also there.

The camp was in St. Petersburg, the Mets' spring training home. They put us up at the Colonial Inn on the beach. My first night there I was sitting in the hotel lobby when this guy came up to me and said, "You a ballplayer?"

"Yeah. Bud Harrelson."

"Okay. You're coming with me."

He took me to the dog track. I had never been to a dog track before. The guy was Tracy Stallard, a right-handed pitcher who just three years earlier had thrown the pitch that Roger Maris hit for his 61st home run. The Mets had acquired him from the Boston Red Sox in a trade prior to the '63 season.

The following day the minicamp got under way. We were put through a series of drills, most of them conducted by Stengel, seventy-three years old at the time. When we got in the batting cage, we'd have to take a few swings, bunt a few, hit-and-run, and then, after our last swing, run to first base. At first base, we would have to react to what the next batter did—a bunt or a hit-and-run. We'd run hard to second base, then round the bag, ready to go to third if the opportunity presented itself. All the while Casey was on the field paying close attention to what was going on.

One time, I was on first base and suddenly old Casey was hustling to second base. He pulled the base out of the ground, held it over his head, and started shouting, *"Harrelson's trying to steal second, Harrelson's trying to steal second."*

Stengel had a routine that he followed in minicamp—and I know from talking to guys who came before me and after me that he did this regularly. He would gather all the players—pitchers, catchers, everybody—at home plate, and he had something to say to them there. Then he took them around the diamond, to first base and to second base and to third base, and at each stop he had some advice or piece of strategy to impart. It might be picking up the pitcher's motion from first base in order to steal second, or getting a good jump at second so you could score on a single, or trying to distract the pitcher when you're on third base to get him to balk; little strategy sessions at every stop. That was Casey. He loved to talk baseball at any time in any place, and he liked teaching young players.

Although I got to know Stengel and spend a lot of time in his company—early in my career when, as a minor leaguer, I was invited to the Mets' minicamp, in spring training as a major leaguer, and later after he had retired—I regret that I never had the opportunity to play for him in a regular-season major league game. I missed out on what I'm sure would have been an interesting, enlightening, and instructive experience.

When I was first called up by the Mets late in the 1965 season, Stengel was recuperating from a broken hip. As part of their annual Old Timers Day celebration, the Mets had planned a party in Toots Shor's restaurant on July 24, in honor of Stengel's seventy-fifth birthday six days later. The exact details have never surfaced, but the best guess was that either in the men's room at Shor's or getting in or out of a car, Stengel fell, fractured his hip, and was hospitalized.

From his hospital bed, Stengel selected coach Wes Westrum to manage the team in his absence, which he said would be temporary. But on August 30, Stengel reluctantly but realistically came to a difficult decision. He was retiring for good.

"I got this limp," he explained, "and if I can't walk out there to take the pitcher out, I can't manage."

So when the Mets called me up in the late summer of 1965, Wes Westrum, not Stengel, was my manager. I was playing for Buffalo and we were in Rochester when my manager, Sheriff Robinson, called me and Dick Selma into his office and told us, "You two guys are being called up to the Mets." Roy McMillan had injured his shoulder, and I was going up to take his place as the Mets' shortstop. Selma had a car, so we drove from Rochester to Shea Stadium.

Life was beautiful. I was twenty-one years old and I was a major leaguer earning whatever the percentage was for the few weeks I was there based on the major league minimum salary of $6,500.

I made my major league debut on September 2 against the Houston Astros in Shea Stadium when I was sent in to pinch-run for McMillan in the bottom of the eighth and replaced him at shortstop in the top of the ninth. I didn't come to bat and had no plays in the field. These were the starting lineups for Houston and the Mets on that "historic" day:

For the Astros: Lee Maye, left field; Joe Morgan, second base; Jimmy Wynn, center field; Rusty Staub, right field; Bob Aspromonte, third base; Jim Gentile, first base; Ron Brand, catcher; Bob Lillis, shortstop; Larry Dierker, pitcher.

For the Mets: Ron Hunt, second base; Roy McMillan, shortstop; Ed Kranepool, first base; Charley Smith, third base; Johnny Lewis, center field; Ron Swoboda, left field; Joe Christopher, right field; John Stephenson, catcher; Jack Fisher, pitcher.

I made my first start four days later in the second game of a doubleheader against the Braves in Milwaukee and popped out in my first at bat in the third inning. The next time I was due to hit, in the fifth, Westrum sent Danny Napoleon up to pinch-hit for me.

I was hitless in my first eight major league at bats. Then, on Sunday, September 19, against the Cubs in Wrigley Field, I started and batted second. In my first at bat, I hit a single to left off left-hander Bob Hendley for my first major league hit. By my reckoning it was a wicked, solid, frozen-rope line drive blistered to left field—and there's nobody around to prove that it wasn't. After that impressive bit of hitting, I still to this day can't understand why Westrum removed me for a pinch-hitter in the sixth inning. I finished the season, and my first tour of major league duty, by starting each of the final 13 games at shortstop.

By the spring of 1966, I had moved up on the Mets' minor league depth chart; two years at Salinas in the Class A California League, followed by a year at Buffalo in the Class AAA International League. I was earmarked to return to the International League that season with the Jacksonville Suns, who had replaced Buffalo as the Mets' top farm team, and I had been invited to spring training with the big club. It was clear to everyone, including me, that I was still in the Mets organization because of my glove. It certainly wasn't because of my bat.

At Salinas I had batted .221 in my first year and .231 in my second. Despite my low batting average, I was nonetheless rated the top shortstop prospect in the entire Mets minor league system. In Buffalo, I got my average up to .251, but when I was called up by the Mets for 19 games in 1965, I batted an anemic .108 (4 for 37). I knew that to get to New York—or any other major league city—to stay, I was going to have to hit. Consequently my top priority in the spring of 1966 was to work on my hitting. I also knew that, as a rookie in camp, if I was to work on my hitting, I had to be the early bird that catches the worm.

Huggins-Stengel had one field and one batting cage, and because I was a rookie, I was low man in the pecking order. If I wanted to work on something, I had to get there early, before all the other guys showed up. If I waited, when the veterans got there, they'd chase me out of the cage in a heartbeat.

Fortunately, I had driven to camp in the 1964 Chevrolet Chevelle that I bought with my bonus money. Since I had my car at my disposal, if I wanted to work on something, I'd wake up early, jump in my car, drive over to Huggins-Stengel, and get there before anybody else arrived. That's what I did this one morning in the spring of 1966. I got to Huggins-Stengel at the crack of dawn, got in my workout clothes, went to the batting cage, loaded up the pitching machine, and started hitting. I hit right-handed, my natural side, for a while, and then I turned around and was taking a few swings left-handed. That's when I heard the voice. I turned around and there was Casey.

I didn't even know he was there. I was tending to my own business, I wasn't thinking about him. I knew he had an office on the premises, but I didn't bother checking to see if he was in his office. He might even have slept in his office for all I knew.

"Hey, you swing pretty good left-handed. I like it. Why don't you try it?"

And that's how I started switch-hitting.

A few days later, I found myself coming to bat left-handed for the first time in an exhibition game against the St. Louis Cardinals. On the mound was Hoyt Wilhelm, he of the famous knuckleball, so not only was I going to bat left-handed in a game for the first time, I was going to have to do it against the game's greatest knuckleball pitcher. First pitch! A knuckleball! I bunted it down the third-base line. Base hit! Hey, this switch-hitting isn't so tough!

Although I was surrounded by and learning from such veterans as McMillan, Ken Boyer, Chuck Hiller, Eddie Bressoud, Dick Stuart, and Ron Hunt, and beginning to feel more like a big leaguer, McMillan was healthy again so I knew I was going to be sent out. I remembered back to spring training the year before when I arrived in the clubhouse, went to my locker, and there was no uniform for me. The clubhouse guy came to me and said, "Skip wants to see you."

Now, a year later, I arrived in the clubhouse late in spring training, went to my locker, and there was no uniform hanging there for me. So I opened the bottom of my locker, took out my bag, and started packing.

The guy next to me looked at me throwing stuff in my bag and said, "What are you doing?"

"I'm getting sent out. Do you have a uniform in your locker?"

"No."

"Start packing."

Sure enough I was sent to the minor league camp in Homestead, Florida, to continue spring training with the Jacksonville Suns. Being assigned to play in Jacksonville was a break for me. I like to think it was fate because my manager at Jacksonville, Solly Hemus, had spent 11 seasons in the major leagues with the Cardinals and the Phillies as a left-handed-hitting infielder. Although he hit 51 major league home runs, Hemus was a little guy, about five feet nine inches tall and 165 pounds, who primarily just slapped the ball around. He had 736 hits and a career batting average of .273. He was a tough, hard-nosed, heady player and a student of the game who had been a player/manager for the Cardinals in 1959.

At Jacksonville, Solly worked with me tirelessly to improve my left-handed swing and helped me become a switch-hitter. I owe a lot to Hemus. He taught me the inside-out swing—how to take the inside pitch and hit it to left field by staying inside the ball. From hitting right-handed, my righty swing was strong, but I needed to strengthen my lefty stroke and that's where Hemus helped me the most. I learned to foul off pitches or to stop my swing and take the pitch instead of swinging at the breaking ball that wasn't there. As a result, I got a lot of walks (633 in 16 seasons) for a guy that was a .236 hitter. I wasn't a great hitter, but I must have done something right according to a lot of the pitchers I faced that didn't call me by my name unless they thought my name was "You little son of a bitch, hit the ball fair!"

On September 11, 1970, when I broke the Mets' all-time single-season walks record against the Cardinals at Shea Stadium, Bob Gibson walked me in my first three at bats. All three times I took him to 3-2. I have always said I'll take God to 3-2 and take my chances. I might foul two off before He gave me ball four.

On the third walk, Gibson threw me a 3-2 slider. I started to swing but checked it and took it for ball four. If you've never seen Gibson pitch, let me explain that he had a violent pitching motion and follow-through in which he fell off the mound toward first base, and that he was a mean and unrelenting competitor. I started jogging to first base with my walk, and Gibson fell off the mound toward first base and continued walking menacingly toward me, looking as if he wanted to do to me what you do to your Thanksgiving turkey wishbone. At the time, he was pitching a 3-hit shutout and leading us, 4–0, but that didn't soften him one bit.

"Dammit," he snarled. "You have to swing at that pitch."

"But, Bob," I said. "I can't hit it."

He couldn't help himself. He just laughed. What else could he do?

(Editor's note: In his career, Bud Harrelson faced Hall of Famer Bob Gibson 76 times and had 20 hits in 60 official at bats, a .333 average, the fourth-highest average against Gibson by a batter with at least 60 at bats, and a higher average against him than Willie Mays, Hank Aaron, Roberto Clemente, Frank Robinson, Pete Rose, or Joe Morgan. His 20 hits off Gibson included 3 doubles and 1 triple. He also drove in 5 runs and had more walks, 14, than strikeouts, 3. In 1968, when Gibson recorded an earned run average of 1.12, the lowest in baseball history, Harrelson batted .364 against him with 4 hits in 11 at bats.)

I was with Hemus from the beginning of the 1966 season until August 12, when the Mets called me up. They gave me 99 at bats. I didn't do that great. I had batted .221 at Jacksonville and I batted .222 in those 99 at bats with the Mets, but I was still a work in progress as a hitter, and I was just beginning to get the hang of switch-hitting. Fortunately, I always could run, and I took advantage of being a few steps closer to first base batting left-handed by putting the ball in play on the ground or dropping down bunts and beating out infield hits.

With the Mets, Whitey Herzog, who was a coach, worked with me every day on my bunting. I also owe a great deal to Whitey. He'd take me down to the left-field corner or the right-field corner at Shea Stadium, pitch to me, and I'd drag-bunt or push-bunt down the line.

I have often thought about that morning in the batting cage at Huggins-Stengel Field in the spring of 1966 and wondered, what if I didn't go to the field that day?

What if I had slept late?

What if Stengel had not been there to see me in the batting cage?

What if I had not turned around and taken a few swings batting left-handed when Stengel was watching?

Would I ever have become a switch-hitter?

And if I never became a switch-hitter, would I have been a victim of platoon baseball, playing only against left-handed pitchers?

Would I have hit enough as a strictly right-handed hitter to remain the Mets' starting shortstop for 11 seasons?

Would I even have been given the chance to be the Mets' regular shortstop?

Those questions will never be answered. All I can say for certain is that I must have been thinking about batting left-handed or I wouldn't have turned around in the cage and taken a few swings from the left side. I can remember thinking at the time that Don Kessinger of the Cubs had started switch-hitting that spring, and that Maury Wills had come up to the Dodgers a few years earlier at the age of twenty-six and begun switch-hitting. I was only twenty-one years old, still young enough to make changes, so the thought of switch-hitting must have been on my mind. But what if Stengel hadn't been there to see me and offer his encouragement?

When I started switch-hitting and Stengel saw me hitting left-handed, he said, "Yeah, you got it, man. You're looking to right field and you're hitting to left."

After that, whenever Casey saw me, he would invariably say,

"Ahh, I shoulda kept you." I like to think that what he meant was that back in '64, when I was only twenty years old and he first saw me in the minicamp, he should have made me the Mets' shortstop right then, which is a wonderful tribute from one of baseball's true legends.

CHAPTER 3

Spring training, 1966! Homestead, Florida, a suburb of Miami on Florida's east coast: a quiet, lazy, blue-collar town of about twenty thousand. In the first six years of the Mets' existence, it was in Homestead, across the state from their major league training base in St. Petersburg, that the Mets' minor league teams got ready for the upcoming season.

I had played the previous season for Buffalo, the Mets' top farm team in the AAA International League, but the Mets had switched their International League affiliation from Buffalo to Jacksonville, and I was now listed on the roster of the Jacksonville Suns.

We had been in Homestead only a few days when one morning we sensed a buzz of excitement in camp. A group of us were in the batting cage taking our swings when we noticed a flurry of activity and a strange commotion. Out of the clubhouse, heading for the field, had come an entourage of writers, photographers, coaches, spring training instructors, and front-office executives all seeming to be escorting this young guy as if they were the Secret Service and he was some head of state.

The young guy obviously was a player, but not one any of us recognized. He was wearing—or I should say flaunting—a purple, woolen University of Southern California shirt.

Homestead, Florida, armpit of the world, is all the way down the state, almost to the Florida Keys. The temperature there reaches one hundred most days at that time of year, and the humidity is stifling. Yet this clown was wearing a woolen USC shirt like some Southern California nerd. One word entered my mind: pompous.

We determined he had to be a prospect and, judging from the horde around him, a hot one. We knew he was somebody special not only because of the entourage but because he wasn't being marched over to some rookie league or Class A team; he was being brought to the triple-A team, the top minor league affiliate in the Mets' farm system.

We couldn't help noticing all the attention this dude was getting. We soon figured out who he was. We had heard through the baseball grapevine that the Mets had signed this blue-chip pitching prospect named Tom Seaver from USC. His story, by now, is well-known.

After his sophomore year at USC, Seaver was drafted by the Los Angeles Dodgers, but when he asked for a $70,000 signing bonus, the Dodgers backed off. The Atlanta Braves jumped in and signed him to a $50,000 contract, but the signing was voided by baseball commissioner William Eckert because by the time the Braves signed him, Seaver's USC team had played two exhibition games. No matter that Tom hadn't played in either of those games. He was on their roster, and therefore that invalidated the signing according to the rules of major league baseball.

Reluctantly, Seaver seemed to accept the ruling and was prepared to return to USC. But the NCAA stepped in and ruled that since he had signed a professional contract, Seaver no longer had college eligibility. Now Tom was left in limbo, damned if he did and damned if he didn't. Major league baseball said his Braves contract was invalid because his college team, not Tom, had played two exhibition games; the NCAA said he couldn't go back to play in college because he had signed a professional contract. It didn't matter to the NCAA that major league baseball had voided that contract.

Seeing the inequity in all of this, Tom's father, a prosperous

California businessman and a former member of the US Walker Cup golfing team, threatened to sue major league baseball. He claimed that his son had to be a collegian or a professional, one or the other, and he was being denied both.

The threat of a suit brought major league baseball to its knees. Eckert reacted by stating that any team except the Atlanta Braves was free to sign Seaver simply by matching the Braves' offer of $50,000. When three teams—the Cleveland Indians, Philadelphia Phillies, and New York Mets—came forward with matching offers, Eckert decreed that the only fair way to break the deadlock was a lottery. The names of the three teams would each be written on a piece of paper and the papers placed in the proverbial hat. Eckert would then draw out one paper, and the team drawn would own the rights to Seaver's services.

The Mets, who up to that time hadn't won anything, won the lottery. So that led to all the fuss in Homestead in the spring of 1966, even though, at the time, nobody could have predicted that the Mets' unusual good fortune would have such a profound effect on baseball in the 1960s and 1970s.

We watched as they marched this hotshot to the side and warmed him up. He started throwing to a catcher with the coaches observing him intently, and a cadre of writers and photographers recording the momentous event for posterity. When he was sufficiently warmed up, they brought him over to where we were hitting and sent him to the mound. We were told he was going to pitch batting practice.

"Oh, yeah, batting practice my ass," I thought. "He's the new kid on the block. All the coaches are here and some of the front-office brass. He's going to want to make an impression on them; he's not going to care about helping us get ready. This isn't going to be batting practice; it's going to be a one-man pitching recital, him blowing us away while we're made to look foolish swinging feebly at his stuff."

Seaver started throwing and what I saw next surprised me:

POW! A long drive to left.

BAM! A deep shot to right.

CRACK! A shot off the wall.

BANG! A rocket over the fence.

I couldn't believe my eyes. Suddenly, I had a different opinion of this Southern Cal prima donna.

"I like this guy," I thought. "I like his attitude."

We players had an immediate respect for him. He wasn't trying to make an impression at our expense. He wasn't trying to show off. He was trying to get ready for the season. He got all that money and all that attention, but he wasn't big-timing us. We guys were probably going to be his teammates that season, and he wasn't going to embarrass us by blowing us away with his best stuff.

From that time and all throughout his career, no matter how big he got, how many games he won, what honors he received, how many Cy Young Awards he collected, Tom treated spring training the same way every year. He wasn't out there to impress anybody. He was out there to work on his timing. He didn't throw a lot of breaking balls. He moved his fastball around. He wouldn't over-throw the ball. He was a seasoned pro from day one.

Of the thirty-nine players who got into a game for the 1966 Jacksonville Suns, thirty-four of them got some time in the major leagues, three made a major league all-star team, and one was elected to the Hall of Fame. Despite all that talent, we finished 11 games under .500 with a record of 68-79 and in seventh place in the eight-team International League, 15 games out of first. We were young and inexperienced, seventeen of us twenty-three years old and younger, and many of us were in over our head.

Remember, the Mets had started from scratch just four years earlier and hadn't had enough time to build up their farm system, and what prospects they did have they tended to rush. Many of those 1966 Jacksonville Suns should probably have been playing in

Class A or AA, Seaver included. But the Mets either wanted to force-feed them or they simply didn't have enough AAA-caliber players.

On the other hand, just three years later, five of those '66 Suns would make a contribution to the Mets' first World Series championship.

I escaped Jacksonville in August when Roy McMillan reinjured his shoulder and the Mets called me up. I played pretty much every day and batted .222 in 99 at bats. Seaver stayed in Jacksonville the entire season and was 12-12, which may not seem like anything special until you consider he was pitching for a team that was 11 games under .500. He had an earned run average of 3.13, he struck out 188 batters in 210 innings, and he was only twenty-one years old and playing at the highest minor league level in his first year as a professional. Pretty impressive.

In 1967, Seaver and I both went north with the Mets. We opened the season at home against the Pirates on April 11 and lost, 6–3. I was the opening-day shortstop and was hitless in 4 at bats. Tom started the second game of the season, two days later. He pitched 5⅓ innings, allowed 2 runs, and struck out 8. When he left the game, the score was tied, 2–2. We scored a run in the bottom of the eighth and won, 3–2. Seaver got a no decision, but he had made a positive impression in his major league debut, witnessed by only 5,005 spectators.

After the brief 2-game home stand, we were scheduled to take our first road trip, a short one to Philadelphia and Pittsburgh. In those days, only the longtime superstar veterans such as Mickey Mantle and Willie Mays had a single room, so they asked Seaver whom he wanted to room with—nobody bothered to ask me. Seaver got a lot more money than me and a lot more publicity, so he was pampered. Tom said, "Harrelson. He's the only guy I know."

We had hung out a little in Jacksonville, but we weren't close. Still, it made sense that we would wind up rooming together. We were about the same age—Seaver is five months and eleven days younger than me—and we were both from Northern California.

Even though we grew up only about 120 miles apart (Tom in Fresno, me in Niles) and were close in age, we had never met and I had never heard of him before he showed up in Homestead in the spring of 1966.

We didn't have much else in common and were sort of an odd couple as roommates. He pitched once every five days and I played every day. He couldn't sleep on airplanes, he couldn't sleep when he first got into a room, and he couldn't sleep unless the TV was on. I could fall asleep at a Wagnerian opera and could sleep through a tornado.

We would room together for ten and a half years and become as close as brothers.

Watching him pitch from the very beginning, I said, "This *kid* knows what the hell he's doing. He knows how to *pitch*."

I watched him win 16 games in 1967, with an ERA of 2.76, 18 complete games, 2 shutouts, 170 strikeouts in 251 innings, and be voted National League Rookie of the Year.

Through the years, people have told me that I always played better behind Seaver than I did behind any other pitcher.

Maybe I did. If so, it was mainly because of him. With Tom, if he was supposed to throw a slider away, he threw a slider away. If he was supposed to throw a fastball in, he threw a fastball in. Nolan Ryan was different. He had great stuff, but the catcher would set up inside, and more often than not, Nolie would throw it outside.

Not Seaver. From day one, I was telling people, "This guy is a great self-analyzer. He immediately analyzes what he's got and what isn't working, and he will get by with what he has until he could get all his stuff together."

We had this thing going on between us. He'd come in from the bullpen and I'd say, "Roomie, what have you got today?" He might say, "I've got shit. Get over in the hole." I knew what that meant. Right-handed hitters were going to pull him and it was up to me to be there between third and short to take away base hits. Then, in-variably along about the fourth inning, he'd look out at me and he'd pick up the rosin bag and toss it back down on the mound, all the while still looking at me. I knew that meant he had his stuff together and I could go back to my normal positioning.

Hall of Famers are consistent. Do they get beat? Yeah, they get beat. Do they have off days? Yeah, they have off days. Do they make mistakes? Yeah, they make mistakes. But Tom was generally consistent. And a little flaky, except when he was pitching. Then he was all-business. But when he wasn't pitching . . .

He could be impish. We'd be in a crowded elevator in our hotel in Chicago, say, or St. Louis, and at the top of his voice, Tom would say, "Did you see Seaver today? Boy, did he stink." And he'd kind of sneak a look around the elevator to see if he could rope somebody into agreeing with him and get a debate started.

Or he might nudge me and say, "Roomie, you and me tonight," and I'd think, "Oh, no," because that meant he wanted to go out to some Polynesian restaurant where he'd order mai tais for the two of us. This usually came after he had pitched, knowing he wasn't going to have to pitch again for four days. But I had to play the next day. So he'd order two mai tais. The waitress would put them down and I'd slide mine over to him. After a few minutes, Tom would tell the waitress, "Two more mai tais," and the waitress would come back, put them down, and I'd again slide mine over to him.

Except for the day he was scheduled to pitch, Tom was always pretty flaky and funny. He liked to cut cartoons out of a newspaper and put them up in the room or leave notes taped to the walls. One time he left a note for me written on one of those phone-message sheets you get in a hotel. It said, "Please call Mr. G. Raff," with a phone number. So I called the number and asked for Mr. G. Raff. How was I to know the number was for the Bronx Zoo?

CHAPTER 4

If it's true, as conventional wisdom suggests, that you have to take a step back before you can take two steps forward, then the New York Mets were right on schedule in 1967. After finishing dead last in the ten-team National League in each of their first four seasons, the Mets, under manager Wes Westrum, escaped the cellar and jumped up to ninth place in 1966. If it was not cause for celebration, at least it was progress.

But alas, in 1967, it was back to the basement as the Mets slipped from 66 wins the previous year to 61 wins. I have always maintained, and still do, that the decline in the Mets' win total in my first year as their regular shortstop was merely a coincidence.

In fact, I was pleased with my production in my first full season in the majors. I got into 151 games, 144 as the starting shortstop, fielded .963, was third in the league in assists by a shortstop, and now a full-time switch-hitter, I batted a respectable .254.

I liked Wes Westrum a lot. He was low-key, a nice man, and very professional. And he gave me a chance to play every day. I got 603 plate appearances that season.

I remember one game in particular, Sunday, July 9, against the Braves at Shea. I had hits in each of my first 4 at bats, a single, a double, and a bunt single batting left-handed against Ken Johnson and a single batting right-handed against Dick Kelley, but we went to the bottom of the ninth trailing, 4–3.

Jerry Grote led off the ninth by striking out, and Cleon Jones, batting for Hal Reniff, grounded to second. Two outs, nobody on, we're down by a run, and it was my turn to hit. Westrum asked me, "Can you hit a home run?"

"Have you ever seen me hit one?" I replied.

He hadn't. Nobody had. I had never hit a home run in the majors. So Wes sent Jerry Buchek up to hit for me, and the fans booed. I had no problem with Westrum removing me for a hitter in that situation. I got pinch-hit for in key situations a lot. But these fans in New York are savvy. They know their baseball and they love the home team. They wanted to see me try to get 5 hits. Only two Mets had ever had 5 hits in a game up to that point, Jim Hickman and Dick Smith, both in 1964.

The Mets were losing a lot of games in those early years from 1962 to 1967, and if your team is losing games and a guy is 4 for 4 and he's taken out for a pinch hitter, the fans are going to boo. That's just the way fans are, especially in New York.

Kelley got two strikes on Buchek, then Jerry hit one over the fence in right-center field. That tied the score. After that Tommie Reynolds walked, Tommy Davis singled him to third, and the Braves walked Ed Kranepool to load the bases. Ron Swoboda then walked with the bases loaded and we won the game, 5–4.

About five weeks later, I hit my first major league home run. Like all seven of my home runs, my first one came batting right-handed, but it was the only one of the seven that did not leave the yard. It came off Juan Pizarro on August 17 in the first game of a doubleheader against the Pirates in Pittsburgh. The great Roberto Clemente must have been injured because I remember him sitting in the bullpen and in his place in right field was Al Luplow, who had been sold to the Pirates in June after starting the season with us.

With the score tied, 4–4, in the top of the eighth inning, I hit a line drive down the right-field line. Luplow tried to make a shoe-string catch but missed it and lost his balance. His momentum carried him across the foul line into the Pirates' bullpen. He bounced off the wall and so did the ball, which ricocheted toward center field. Matty Alou, the center fielder, obviously didn't expect the ball to carom to him because he didn't break over to back up the play. I always could run, so it was easy for me to circle the bases with my first major league home run.

None of that might have happened if Clemente was in right field instead of Luplow. As great as he was, Clemente would probably have made the shoestring catch. He would at least have retrieved the ball much quicker, and with his great arm, he might have thrown me out at home . . . or at third.

Nevertheless, it went into the books as a home run; however, because it was inside-the-park, I was deprived of the thrill of standing in the batter's box watching the flight of the ball as it disappeared into the seats, getting high fives or a series of handshakes from my teammates as I crossed the plate. Also, because it came on the road, I was deprived of what I fully expect would have been a curtain call.

Oh, well, I'd just have to wait for my curtain call until I got back home at Shea Stadium and hit one there. How was I to know I would have to wait almost three years before I hit a home run at Shea Stadium? It came against Grant Jackson of the Phillies on April 17, 1970, and it was the *only* home run I ever hit at Shea.

Funny thing is, while I hit only one home run at Shea, it was there where I came closest to hitting my only home run batting left-handed. I hit one deep down the right-field line that got out of the park (I can't remember who the pitcher was, but I doubt he lasted in the majors for long), but it hooked foul.

On the home runs I hit out of the park right-handed, I'd run around the bases as if I were being chased or as if I were trying to leg out a triple. I'd sprint all the way into the dugout, where my teammates would be lying on the floor in mock shock.

Not only did all my home runs come batting right-handed, they all came on the same pitch, down and in. I was a low-ball hitter right-handed and a high-ball hitter left-handed, which is unusual.

Most left-handed hitters are low-ball hitters, and most right-handed hitters are high-ball hitters, but I had an inside-out swing left-handed. That means I liked to wait for the ball to travel deep in the strike zone and stay behind the ball and hit it to left field.

You're probably not going to believe this, but I swear I once won a home-run-hitting contest. In the major leagues! It happened in Philadelphia in 1977. The Phillies staged a "reverse" home-run-hitting contest, so they paired me and Felix Millan of the Mets, who would hit 3 home runs between us that season, against Larry Bowa and Ted Sizemore of the Phillies, who combined for 8 homers that season, and we beat them.

The players from both teams were in the dugout watching, and razzing us, saying things like "This is a home-run-hitting contest in which nobody hits a home run," but we fooled them. I hit two out, right-handed, of course. I had an old bat in my attic and I brought it to Philly and used it in the contest. It was my version of Robert Redford's "Wonderboy" from *The Natural.* It had good wood. Felix and I won $500 each.

In his first full year as Mets manager, Westrum improved the team by 16 games and moved them out of last place, but when the team regressed the following year, many felt a change at the top was needed and was inevitable. Westrum, however, thought he would be given a new contract, but when one was not offered with less than two weeks remaining in the season, Wes marched into the front office and submitted his resignation, thereby setting off a flurry of rumors, predictions, and suggestions over the identity of the next manager of the Mets.

The name mentioned most prominently as Westrum's likely successor was Gil Hodges. The mere mention of his name brought a wave of excitement and eager anticipation from the sportswriters that knew him and the fans that idolized him.

Through the years, M. Donald Grant, the Mets' chairman of the board, has received more than his share of criticism as a Wall Street executive who made important decisions for the team with no background in, and little knowledge of, baseball. But to his credit, Grant targeted Hodges as the one and only candidate to succeed Westrum. Grant may not have recognized Hodges's ability as a manager, but he understood his appeal to fans and the media.

Behind closed doors, Grant told his people he wanted Hodges as the team's next manager and charged them to do whatever it took to make it happen. He made it clear that he would not accept anyone else.

I didn't know Hodges, had never met him, but I'd certainly heard a lot about him, all of it positive. When you come to New York to play baseball, even for a little while, you learn that the Dodgers were here and the Giants were here and that the Mets replaced both of those teams.

If you were interested in baseball history and you followed the game in the newspapers, as I did, you heard about John McGraw and Mel Ott and Bill Terry and Jackie Robinson and Pee Wee Reese and Duke Snider and Gil Hodges. Hodges was one of the most popular players on those great Brooklyn Dodgers teams of the 1940s and 1950s, a big, right-handed, power-hitting first baseman who played 18 major league seasons, hit 370 homers, 30 or more six times, and drove in 1,274 runs, including 7 straight seasons with at least 100 RBI. If he wasn't the best defensive first baseman of all-time, he might have been the best *right-handed* defensive first baseman ever. He was the strong, silent type, a former decorated U.S. Marine who fought in the Pacific Theater during World War II and was awarded a Bronze Star.

Off the field, his reputation was impeccable. The strong, silent type, Hodges was a God-fearing native of Indiana and a devoted family man who had married a Brooklyn girl, Joan Lombardi, and further endeared himself to the Flatbush Faithful by making Brooklyn his permanent home.

In keeping with their plan to cater to their anticipated fan base by stocking their expansion team with as many familiar names as possible, especially players who had been members of the newly

departed Brooklyn Dodgers and New York Giants, the Mets had selected Hodges off the roster of the Los Angeles Dodgers for $75,000
in the 1962 expansion draft. At the age of thirty-eight, his best
years behind him, Hodges appeared in 54 games for the first-year
Mets in 1962, batted .252, hit 9 homers, and drove in 17 runs.

The following year, Hodges was batting .227 without a home
run and only 3 runs batted in when, on May 23, 1963, he was traded
by the Mets to the Washington Senators for Jim Piersall. The Washington Senators were in their second incarnation. The "original"
Senators left in 1961 to become the Minnesota Twins. At the same
time the "second" Washington Senators arrived as an expansion
team to replace the departed.

Those expansion Senators were a ragtag collection of has-
beens and never-weres, not unlike the original Mets. In their first
two seasons, they won 121 games and lost 201 and finished last in
the American League both years. When they lost 26 of their first 40
games in 1963, the team's ownership fired manager Mickey Vernon
and made Hodges their manager. They saw in Hodges a man with
the sort of leadership potential that could direct them out of the
baseball wilderness.

Hodges had never managed before anywhere on any level, so
you can say he got on-the-job training in Washington and soon
gained a reputation as an excellent manager by improving the Senators every year and moving them up from last place to sixth. That
did not escape the notice of the Mets, their executives, and their
fans. If Hodges could so dramatically improve one expansion team,
the Senators, why couldn't he do likewise for another expansion
team, the Mets?

For his managerial skills, his ties to New York, his popularity,
and his desire to return home, Hodges was the perfect choice to become manager of the Mets. But there was a problem. Hodges had a
few years remaining on his contract, and the Senators were reluc-
tant to let him go.

In the end, because of Grant's insistence, the efforts of Mets assistant general manager Johnny Murphy, and Hodges's exemplary reputation, a deal was consummated. The Senators graciously acceded to Hodges's request that he be allowed to return to his New York home, but only after the Mets agreed to compensate them in the form of a player, pitcher Bill Denehy, and a check for $150,000. To the Mets, it was well worth the price. So, too, was Hodges's three-year contract, $60,000 per year. It was more than he ever made as a top-drawer player and eight-time All-Star.

So many rumors had linked the Mets and Hodges that nobody was surprised when the deal was announced in Boston on October 11, 1967, just a few hours before the start of Game 6 of the World Series between the Red Sox and the Cardinals. Because of everything I knew about Hodges, I was thrilled when I heard the news.

As much as Hodges wanted to come to New York, he made it clear to the Mets that he would take the job only if he had a free hand. In effect he said, "If you want me, things are going to have to be done my way." He was one of the first managers to wield that sort of power. He was the manager, and in a sense, when it came to decisions on player deals, he also served as the general manager.

One of his demands before he accepted the Mets' offer was that he be allowed to select his own coaches. The Mets agreed, and Hodges brought with him three from his Washington staff, all with ties to New York: Rube Walker, his pitching coach, who had been a catcher and a teammate of Gil's with the Brooklyn Dodgers; Joe Pignatano, another former Dodger and a Brooklyn native; and Eddie Yost, who had been an all-star third baseman for the Senators but who was born in Brooklyn, raised on Long Island, and went to college at New York University.

Those coaches fit right in with us, and the players took an immediate liking to them. Talk about loyalty! I've been around baseball, on various levels, for almost half a century and I've never seen a manager and coaches as close as Hodges, Pignatano, Walker, and Yost. Sometimes, when you become a manager, two of your coaches want your job. Not with these guys. Gil's coaches admired him. They would do anything for him, and I never heard one of them indicate he had any more ambition than to simply work with Hodges and help him succeed.

The fourth coach was Yogi Berra, who was held over from the regimes of both Stengel and Westrum. Although Gil inherited him, Yogi was warmly welcomed by Hodges. In addition to his keen baseball mind, Berra, who had been a longtime rival of Hodges's in six World Series between Yogi's Yankees and Hodges's Dodgers, in 1947-49-52-53-55-56, knew the National League and the Mets' personnel, knowledge that Hodges lacked.

Hodges put his stamp on the Mets almost immediately. In the weeks following his return, the Mets acquired outfielder Art Shamsky from Cincinnati, and catcher J. C. Martin, outfielder Tommie Agee, and infielder Al Weis from the White Sox—all deals recommended by Hodges, who knew and respected Martin, Agee, and Weis as American League rivals.

In time, Agee would prove to be a great addition, but not right away. In his first at bat as a Met, in our first exhibition game of 1968, Agee was hit on the head by a pitch from Bob Gibson, and it would affect him all season. Just two years before, Agee had batted .273, hit 22 homers, and driven in 86 runs for the White Sox and been voted American League Rookie of the Year. That was the player Hodges remembered from his days as Washington manager and the player he thought the Mets were getting. But after getting beaned by Gibson, Tommie was kind of gun-shy at the plate. He batted only .217, hit 5 homers, and drove in a mere 17 runs.

Hodges was no dummy. He knew what Agee could do because he had seen him in the American League, so after Tommie was beaned, Gil never lost faith in him. He stayed with Agee in the belief that he would once again be the player he was in Chicago, and in 1969, he was that player and then some.

Tommie was a breath of fresh air, a guy who could cover a lot of ground in center field and who could steal a base and hit the ball out of the park. He was a great teammate, a good guy in the club-house, well liked by everybody. Agee in center and Cleon Jones in left were a good match, two guys from around Mobile, Alabama, the area that produced the great Hank Aaron.

I met Gil Hodges for the first time at the Mets' 1967 Christmas party. He had been the manager for only a few weeks, and what I remember most is that when he put out his hand and I stuck out mine, his hand just engulfed mine. I never saw anybody with bigger hands.

Hodges took me by surprise when he asked me, "Can you play center field?"

I kind of hesitated and mumbled, "Yes." I had never played center field anywhere at any time, but I wasn't going to tell that to my new boss. If he wanted me to play center field, I'd play center field. If he wanted me to wrestle alligators, I'd do that, too. But I was relieved when, only a few days later, the Mets announced the trade that brought Tommie Agee, a center fielder, to New York.

Right from day one of spring training there was a new feeling around the Mets. Camp was different from any I had attended before. It was more businesslike. There was more instruction. Spring training was kind of like a marine boot camp with Hodges in charge as the drill sergeant.

While he didn't say much, when Hodges did talk, he had everyone's attention. There was never any doubt that he was in charge, involved in every aspect of the game. He missed nothing. He had come through the Dodgers system, where, dating all the way back to the days of Branch Rickey, fundamentals were stressed. Consequently, Hodges was a stickler for details and ingrained fundamentals into us from the start.

Hodges seemed to enjoy imparting his discipline and his teaching to players, and we were willing students, young guys who craved discipline and had a thirst for the knowledge Hodges was feeding us.

Hodges didn't have a lot to say during the 1968 season. Mostly, he just observed. He spoke softly but carried a big stick. Having been in the American League for the previous five years, Hodges spent most of that first season familiarizing himself with his players and evaluating them: who do I want to keep and who do I want to get rid of?

Hodges didn't do a lot of crazy stuff when he took over the club. Whatever your opinion of players, he didn't want to know. He wanted to judge for himself, and that's what he did in that first year. He pretty much stayed with the same regulars that had played the year before, making only a few subtle changes. The only new guys who were regulars for Gil were Ken Boswell, who replaced Jerry Buchek at second base, and Agee, who took over in center field, with Cleon Jones, who had played center the year before, moving to left.

Cleon was a bit of an oddball because he threw left-handed and batted right-handed. That's a rarity. He also tended to be a little lazy. But he wasn't a bad guy.

Cleon didn't hit a lot of home runs—never more than 14 in 11 major league seasons—and he wasn't a big run producer—his high was 75 in 1969—but he could hit. Man, could he hit. He might have been the best pure hitter the Mets have ever had; certainly he was the best up to that time. His .340 average in 1969 is the second highest in Mets history (John Olerud's .354 in 1998 is the highest). He could run. And he had occasional power. I witnessed his power when I played with him in Buffalo in 1965.

Cleon was an inside-out hitter. Some real good hitters have been inside-out hitters. They stay inside the ball. In Buffalo, we played in the old War Memorial Stadium, where they filmed the baseball scenes in the movie *The Natural,* with Robert Redford. War Memorial was built for football. There was a net in right field, which was a short distance from home plate, so pitchers would throw Cleon inside to keep him from taking the ball to the short porch in right field. That was a mistake. They'd have been better off pitching him away.

With his inside-out swing, Cleon wanted them to pitch him inside. He'd get up on top of the plate and they'd come inside, and the farther inside they came, the farther he'd hit it over the net. Fastballs he'd hit to right field. If they threw him a breaking ball, then he would pull it because he was on top of the plate and the breaking ball was right in his swing.

In Jones, Hodges saw that he had a key man that he could use at the top of his lineup. Another of Gil's pet projects was Jerry Grote, a young guy who seemed to have a perpetual chip on his shoulder and a scowl on his face. He could be surly with the writers and surly with the fans. Once we were in a restaurant after a game and some fans came over and asked for autographs. A guy comes up to Jerry and says, "I hate to bother you," and Grote looked at the guy and growled, "Then don't."

Grote could be difficult, but he was a competitor and a gamer. The Mets got him after the 1965 season in what was a minor trade with Houston when Jerry was only twenty-three years old. Houston had a few other young catchers, such as John Bateman and Ron Brand, that they apparently liked better than Grote, so Jerry was expendable.

I got to know Grote pretty well and got to see the curmudgeon in him. He lived near me on Long Island, and I would pick him up and drive him to the ballpark. I'd purposely park near the Press Gate because he wouldn't sign autographs and fewer fans were near the Press Gate than near the bullpen, where the players normally parked. Jerry would wait in the car while I signed autographs, and I knew that the longer he had to wait, the surlier he became. Once, he was really irritated when I signed autographs for everyone. I got in the car and he said, "I ought to kick your ass." I said, "You ought to, but you won't." Apparently Hodges, who had started his professional career as a catcher, recognized that in Grote he had a superior defender behind the plate with a great arm, a fierce, if abrasive, competitiveness, and the innate wisdom and savvy to help bring along a young pitching staff.

Because of his defense, Grote was going to be our number one catcher, but if he was going to play every day, Hodges knew it was important for Jerry to improve his offense. He told Grote, "You don't hit that many home runs. Shorten your swing and try to make better contact."

So Jerry shortened his swing and improved from a .195 average in 1967 to .282 in 1968, from 67 hits to 114, and from 23 RBI to 31, while hitting only one fewer home run, 3. He continued to provide exceptional defensive skill and leadership for the young pitchers.

That Hodges put such a high priority on defense might have saved my job. My average fell off 35 points to .219, but because of problems with my knee I played in only 111 games and was scheduled for surgery after the season.

Early on, I had noticed something about Hodges. When you're playing and you're observing and stuff starts to happen quickly in the game, such as a walk and a double by the opposition, it pops into your mind, "Hey, we better get somebody up in the bullpen." At that moment, I'd look at the bullpen and see that somebody was warming up. When I thought about a move, it was already happening, so it impressed me how much Gil was on top of things.

When he needed to talk to a player, Hodges would do it quietly and privately, behind closed doors in his office rather than in front of the whole team. He did it with me several times. Coach Joe Pignatano would come to me and say, "Skip wants to see you in his office."

I'd go in and Gil might say something like "I was just wondering what you were thinking when you tried to steal home."

"I wanted to tie the game," I said.

"I appreciate that. But why shouldn't you have done that?"

"Well, I got thrown out."

"No, no. That's not why it was a bad play. The reason it was a bad play is that our best hitter was at bat. There was a good chance he was going to get that run in anyway, so there was no reason to risk getting thrown out there."

After a while I came to understand why he called me into his office. It wasn't to chastise me. He never put me down or chewed me out. He was making me smarter, getting me to think. He always said the difference between winning and losing is knowing what you should do and what you should not do, and when you should do it and when you should not do it.

He'd call you in and, without accusing or reprimanding, ask, "What were you thinking?" He knew he had good players; he just wanted them to think more. He wanted them to anticipate what might happen. "When you're in the on-deck circle, if such and such happens, what do you think you should do?"

He made me think I was the only one he called into his office. Later I found out that he did that with most of the guys, but nobody knew that. That was one of Gil's gifts. He made you feel that you were special. With me, he was always positive, always complimentary, and always protective. I'd show up in spring training and step on the scale and the needle would come to rest at 147 pounds and Gil would say, "You're the strongest 147-pound player I've ever seen."

Little things Hodges did impressed me. There would be a day off and Gil would say to me, "We have an afternoon game tomorrow and we're off on Monday. You're not playing. I don't want you to take ground balls. I don't want you to do anything."

I'd argue with him because I hated not playing. I tried to convince him I was fine and that I wanted to play, but he wouldn't hear of it. He'd say, "We played Saturday. You're off Sunday, you're off Monday, and we're playing Tuesday night. I'm giving you almost three days off. You'll come back strong as an ox."

He was right. It's not that I wanted to come out, but he gave me a reason why he was sitting me. It would help me in the long run. It made sense. He also platooned guys and was consistent with it. You knew when you were going to play.

When I was fulfilling my military obligation in the late 1960s, serving in the Army Reserve—two weeks of summer camp and meetings—Gil helped me arrange to do my time at Fort Totten in Bayside, Queens. I'd go to my reserve meetings and come back to the ballpark for a night game. The clubhouse had a little office for the team doctor, with a couch and a table. Gil would say, "I know you had to get up early for your meeting and you had a full day, so I don't want you taking batting practice. I want you lying down. I want you to go in and get your rest. If you fall asleep, I'll be the one to come in and wake you up and get you ready for the game.

People have asked me if I was Hodges's pet. I don't know about that. Maybe I was. Gil's widow, Joan, tells me he really liked me. The feeling was mutual. My personality was to always run when on the field—hustling out and running back, making an out at first base and running back to the dugout. I think Gil liked that, but he didn't expect me to be the guy on the dugout bench watching for the sign from the television crew to take the field and, when they did, shouting, "Let's go." Nothing like that. He didn't insist on any of that stuff, and I wasn't doing things to impress him. It just came naturally to me. It's the way I was. It's what I always did, all the way back to when I was a kid.

Hodges was a father figure to me. He said all the right things even when I did something wrong. My father was alive and well at the time and I kept seeing my dad in Hodges. Even though Hodges scared me sometimes—just because of who he was, this big physical specimen, this icon—I loved him. I truly loved him as a person.

Mostly, Hodges accomplished his goals with compassion and a gentle hand and attained discipline simply by being such an imposing physical specimen. He rarely lost his temper, but on the few occasions that he did, you can bet he got our attention.

He had one confrontation with Ron Swoboda about something Ron said that was quoted in a newspaper. Gil thought Swoboda was out of line, and he let Ron know it in no uncertain terms. Another time we lost a game on the road and Gil didn't like something that had happened on the field. After the game we came into the dressing room, and as usual the clubhouse guys had set up this postgame buffet. Gil was so angry he took the table and turned over the spread. All of a sudden, the room got quiet and looks on the players' faces said, "What did we do?"

As successful as he was in his time, Hodges was a throwback and might have had a hard time managing today's players. Although I believe he had the ability to adjust, I also believe he would be angry a lot more today than he was back then. He wouldn't tolerate guys not hustling, guys half-assing it, guys not protecting each other. There's a certain kinship on a team: get along, don't talk behind your teammates' backs, respect the manager. All that was part of the success of the '69 Mets, but I'm not sure today's players have those qualities.

Although he didn't say much in his first season as manager of the Mets, Hodges's silence spoke volumes. He exuded strength, leadership, stability, control, patience, confidence, and hope. He also brought a sense of stability to the team by streamlining it. Under Westrum in 1967, we had used 54 players, 27 of them pitchers. In 1968, Hodges used 34 players, 14 of them pitchers.

We didn't exactly set the National League on its ear in Hodges's first year as manager, but we made progress, improving from 61 wins to 73 and moving up from tenth place to ninth.

We were getting better, and we were young. Of our eight starters, excluding pitchers, only third baseman Ed Charles was over thirty. The seven others were all twenty-five years old or younger

Of our six top starting pitchers, only Don Cardwell was over thirty. The other five were all 25 years old or younger.

Jerry Koosman, twenty-five, came up from Jacksonville and won 19 games with a 2.08 earned run average, 17 complete games, and 7 shutouts. He was second in the Rookie of the Year balloting by one vote to Johnny Bench.

Tom Seaver, twenty-three, won 16 games for the second straight year and had an ERA of 2.20, 14 complete games, and 5 shutouts.

Dick Selma, twenty-four, won 9 games; Nolan Ryan, twenty-one, won 6 games and struck out 133 batters in 134 innings; and Jim McAndrew, twenty-four, won 4 games.

Playing for Hodges had energized us, and we looked forward to continued improvement in the next few years, but our enthusiasm would be dampened on September 24, with just five games remaining for the season. The team was in Atlanta, but I wasn't with them. I had been shut down and sent home a couple of days earlier because I needed an operation on my right knee. (Even though I missed games with assorted broken bones in my arm, my hand, my sternum, and other areas of my body, that was the first time I was operated on. I would have four operations, all on the same knee.) The Mets lost the first game of a 2-game series to the Braves in Atlanta, and when they returned to the clubhouse after the game, Hodges was nowhere to be found. The team was told that he had been taken to a hospital. Later, they learned that he had suffered a heart attack.

I found out about it when I got a phone call at home. I don't remember who called me, but I was told, "Your boss had a heart attack."

I said, "Mrs. Payson?"

"No. Gil Hodges."

The news hit me like a lightning bolt. You mean Superman had a heart attack? I couldn't believe it. To look at him, Hodges was the last person you would expect to have a heart attack. He was Man Mountain Dean, six feet two inches tall and 210 pounds with not an ounce of fat on a powerful and muscular physique. And he had a calm outward demeanor. Although he had his occasional moments, he was not often given to fits of rage or anger. But now this giant of a man, this tower of strength, was in a hospital, and we all couldn't help thinking the unthinkable.

Doubt crept into our minds; questions to which we had no answers.

Would Gil survive?

If he survived, would he be able to manage again?

If he was able to manage again, would he be ready at the start of spring training?

And, perish the thought, what if his doctors forbid him to manage?

Would that halt our progress?

And who would the Mets bring in to replace him?

All of those questions, and more, were on our minds going into the 1969 season.

CHAPTER 5

I can do something Henry Aaron can't do. Neither can Barry Bonds, Willie Mays, or Alex Rodriguez. I can list every home run I ever hit in the major leagues along with the dates of the homers, the ballparks where they were hit, and the poor guys that threw the pitches.

Here's the list:

DATE	OPPONENT	PLACE	PITCHER	INNING	RUNNERS ON
August 17, 1967x	Pirates	Forbes Field	Juan Pizarro	8	0
April 17, 1970	Phillies	Shea Stadium	Grant Jackson	1	0
May 1, 1972	Giants	Candlestick Park	John Cumberland	3	0
May 27, 1974	Reds	Riverfront Stadium	Fred Norman	5	1
May 11, 1976	Braves	Fulton Co. Stadium	Roger Moret	8	0
May 29, 1977	Phillies	Veterans Stadium	Jim Kaat	5	0
June 18, 1980	Brewers	Arlington Stadium	Jerry Augustine	6	1

x—inside the park

Notice that all of my home runs were hit off a left-handed pitcher, which means that all of them were hit right-handed, the way I batted in Little League, high school, college, and the minor leagues, all the way up to 1966 when I started switch-hitting.

You might also notice these oddities:

- I never hit more than one home run in any season (I also hit 7 home runs in the minor leagues, but in only four seasons, and in my second season as a pro, 1964, I hit three dingers while playing for Salinas in the California League).
- I hit all my home runs, except the last one, as a Met (I hit the last one as a Texas Ranger).
- I hit only one home run in Shea Stadium even though I played almost half of my 1,533 games there.
- Four of my 7 home runs came in the merry month of May. I never hit a home run in July or September.
- From 1970 to 1976, I hit a home run in alternate years.
- I hit one home run for every 677.7 at bats. Babe Ruth hit one home run for every 11.8 at bats, Henry Aaron one for every 16.4 at bats, Willie Mays one for every 16.5 at bats, and Barry Bonds one for every 12.9 at bats.
- I hit more home runs than Sandy Koufax and Whitey Ford, and as many as Christy Mathewson, and all three of them are in the Hall of Fame.

As for the seven pitchers (I never got any pitcher twice) that served up my home runs, there isn't a pushover in the lot. Combined, those seven guys, who are linked primarily by being my victims, pitched 95 years in the major leagues, appeared in 2,651 games, pitched 11,864⅔ innings, won 664 games, and, in addition to my 7, allowed only 1,080 other home runs.

The victims:

Pizarro: Born Juan Ramon Pizarro Cordova in Santurce, Puerto Rico, pitched for eight different major league teams over 18 seasons. He won 131 games, lost 105, and pitched for the American League in the 1963 All-Star Game.

Jackson: Pitched in three World Series with the Orioles

(1971), the Yankees (1976), and the Pirates (1979). In 18 seasons, he won 86 games and saved 79.

Cumberland: After a 6-year career with the Yankees, Giants, Cardinals, and Angels, in which he posted a record of 15-16, he served as bullpen coach and pitching coach for the Boston Red Sox and pitching coach for the Kansas City Royals.

Norman: He was in the starting rotation for the Cincinnati Reds' Big Red Machine that won back-to-back World Series titles in 1975 and 1976. In 1972, pitching against the Reds for the Padres, Norman struck out 15 batters. He had a career record of 104-103.

Moret: In 9 seasons with the Red Sox, Braves, and Rangers, he won 47 games and lost only 27, a winning percentage of .635. With the Red Sox, he twice led the American League in winning percentage, in 1973 when he was 13-2, a winning percentage of .867, and in 1975 when he was 14-3, a winning percentage of .824. His career ended tragically in 1978 after an incident in which he was seen in the Rangers' clubhouse in a catatonic state, his arm extended holding a slipper, and was taken to a psychiatric facility.

Kaat: The possessor of one of the longest and most distinguished careers in baseball history, he played 25 major league seasons (only Cap Anson and Deacon McGuire, who began before the turn of the twentieth century, Nolan Ryan, and Tommy John played longer) and pitched in his last game at forty-four years, seven months, and twenty-four days. His playing career spanned the administrations of seven US presidents (Eisenhower, Kennedy, Johnson, Nixon, Ford, Carter, and Reagan). He's ranked 31st all-time in wins (283), 24th in games (898), 25th in innings (4,530⅓), and 33rd in strikeouts (2,461). He is a 16-time recipient of the Gold Glove for fielding excellence by a pitcher. Only Greg Maddux has won more Gold Gloves.

Augustine: A Wisconsin native, he spent his entire 10-year major league career with his hometown team, the Milwaukee Brewers, and posted a record of 55–59.

CHAPTER 6

On January 12, 1969, the New York Jets, 16½-point underdogs, pulled off one of the biggest upsets in sports history when they beat the powerful Baltimore Colts in Super Bowl III. Professional athletes are a superstitious lot, and I'm a member in good standing in that club. Probably because it was so close to home, some of us, me included, looked upon the Jets' shocking victory as some sort of omen.

To add to the thought that the stars might have been aligned in the Mets' favor, we found ourselves ahead of the game before the 1969 season even started. The National League had voted to expand from ten teams to twelve, with new franchises awarded to San Diego and Montreal. At the same time, the league also voted to split into two divisions of six teams each, forming the National League East and the National League West.

The teams that finished first in each of the two divisions would square off in best-of-five-games play-offs with the survivor being the National League pennant winner and the league's representative in the World Series.

The Mets would compete in the NL East along with the Philadelphia Phillies, Pittsburgh Pirates, and the expansion Montreal Expos, which made sense, plus the Chicago Cubs and St. Louis Cardinals, which didn't make sense.

The NL West would comprise the expansion San Diego Padres, Los Angeles Dodgers, San Francisco Giants, Houston Astros, and for some strange reason the Cincinnati Reds and Atlanta Braves.

I admit I never was good in geography, but I couldn't help scratching my head as I contemplated a map in which St. Louis and Chicago are located in the eastern half of the United States and Cincinnati and Atlanta are located in the western half.

Of greater interest to the Mets and their fans, however, was that because there would now be two divisions of six teams each, never again would the Mets be relegated to finishing in tenth place, or even in ninth place. The lowest we could finish now, and forever, was sixth.

Despite all this good feeling, as far as the '69 Mets were concerned, to Las Vegas oddsmakers nothing had changed. We were listed as 100-to-1 shots to win the National League pennant. Perfect! All the better to sneak up on our opposition.

We were left pretty much in the dark, with little information about Gil Hodges's condition during the downtime between the 1968 and 1969 seasons. After his heart attack, Gil had spent most of the time in Florida, recovering and relaxing. We had no contact with him. We didn't know if his doctors were going to allow him to return to such a stressful job as managing a major league baseball team, and a chronic losing one at that.

Happily, when we reported to St. Petersburg for spring training, Hodges was there to greet us. Seeing him was comforting and reassuring. He was tanned. He looked well rested. He appeared eager to go to work, and he left no doubt that he was still the man in charge.

Hodges went right to work in 1969. On the first day of spring training, Gil told us he believed we were better than our 1968 record of 73-89 indicated. He pointed out that we lost 37 games by one run in '68 (we won only 26), and that if we won just eight of those games, *just eight,* we would have been a .500 team and moved up from ninth place to fourth.

I can still hear him saying, "We've got good defense, we've got pitching. Just think, if you have a positive attitude when you get into those close games, you could win many more games."

He was so upbeat and so positive you couldn't help agreeing with him. I never felt I had anything to do with the early days, the image of a team that lost and everybody laughing at them losing. I wanted to disassociate myself from that team and those days. I felt, as Hodges did, that losing isn't fun; that losing is unacceptable.

Hodges constantly preached the importance of each player doing his job, not worrying about what the next guy was doing. If each player just did his job, he reasoned, the whole team would benefit. Everything changed in 1969 because of him. Until Hodges arrived, a defeatist attitude pervaded everyone on the Mets, from the players to the front office. We expected to lose.

I can remember one game against the Giants. We had a 1-run lead in the ninth inning, and Willie Mays came up and the thought that entered my mind was "Oh, this game's tied." Everybody on the field was probably thinking the same thing. Nobody wanted the ball hit to him in that situation. That all changed when Hodges came. Then everybody wanted the ball hit to him. He was a winner and he made winners out of us. Where we once took the field expecting to lose, we now had an attitude of "Yeah, we can be contenders."

Hodges was telling us we were a good ball club and we bought into it. He was so upbeat it changed the culture of the team. Because of Hodges's optimism, instead of being the chronic and laughable losers of the Mets' first five or six years we began to think of ourselves as winners.

Tom Seaver would be pitching and we'd get a run early, and inevitably somebody on our bench would crack, "All right, Tom, you've got your run." We were confident that with Seaver pitching and with our defense, one run was all we needed to win. That was the sort of positive thinking Hodges instilled in us, and when we started to win, it was because of him. We would win 41 games by one run and lose only 23 in 1969, an improvement in 1-run games of 14½ games over the previous season.

Spring training in 1969 went smoothly. We treated the exhibition games as an extension of the regular season. We won 14 spring training games and lost 10 and arrived in New York brimming with hope to open the season on Tuesday, April 8, against the expansion Montreal Expos. Even Mother Nature cooperated, providing us with a perfect spring day, bright sunshine and temperatures in the upper sixties that brought out a huge Shea Stadium crowd of 44,541.

The game was historic, the first in major league history to be played between teams representing two different countries. However, what transpired over the next few hours was still frighteningly familiar.

For the second straight year, Tom Seaver drew the opening-day starting assignment (he would be our opening-day starter every year from 1968 through 1977). The Expos' starter was Jim (Mudcat) Grant, who had won 21 games for the American League champion Minnesota Twins in 1965, was traded to the Dodgers two years later, and selected by the Expos in the expansion draft.

The Expos jumped on Seaver for 2 unearned runs in the first inning, but we came back to knock Grant out in the second and score 3 runs to take the lead. I drew a walk and scored in the 3-run rally.

The Expos tied it with a run in the third and took the lead in the fourth when Dan McGinn, who had replaced Grant on the mound, hit a home run off Seaver. It would be McGinn's only home run in 92 major league plate appearances.

We rallied for 3 more runs in the fourth to go ahead, 6–4, which was the score when Seaver left for a pinch hitter in the bottom of the fifth. At the time, he was the pitcher of record on the winning end, but the bullpen failed to hold the lead. The Expos tied it with 2 runs in the sixth, took the lead with a run in the seventh and added 4 in the eighth, including a home run by Rusty Staub (he wasn't my friend at the time, and if he kept that up, he wasn't going to be!), which gave the Expos an 11–6 lead.

We made a bid in the bottom of the ninth when we scored 4 runs and had runners on first and second, but Rod Gaspar struck out to end the game and we were beaten, 11–10.

The bad news is that here was an expansion team that came into our home and beat us in the first game in the history of their franchise, and here we were, in our eighth year, and we still had not won on opening day.

The good news was that even though we were down by 5 runs in the bottom of the ninth, we refused to quit and rallied to make it close. I attribute that to the positive attitude Hodges had instilled in us.

We bounced back to win the next 2 games, but then lost 4 in a row. After our first 10 games, we were 3-7 and in fifth place, already six games out of first, and people were saying, "Same old Mets."

On April 19 in St. Louis, Seaver went mano a mano with Bob Gibson and got us moving in the right direction. We pushed across 2 runs in the third inning when Tom drew a leadoff walk and I sacrificed him to second. Ken Boswell walked and Amos Otis struck out, but back-to-back singles by Cleon Jones and Ed Kranepool scored Seaver and Boswell.

Seaver held the Cards scoreless until the eighth, when they got 1 run but stranded runners on first and second. Seaver struck out Steve Huntz looking to end the eighth and went to the ninth inning protecting a 2–1 lead. In those days, there were no ninth-inning bullpen specialists, or closers, and nobody was paying attention to pitch counts. Pitchers finished what they started, and Tom finished this one by retiring the Cardinals in order for his first win of the season.

Seaver would win 4 more games over the next four weeks,

and then, on May 21 in Atlanta, he dueled knuckleballer Phil Niekro. Cleon Jones singled home 2 runs in the first inning, and that was all the scoring until the eighth, when I came to bat with the bases loaded and hit one over the head of Braves' center fielder Mike Lum for a 3-run triple. Tom allowed just 3 hits, all singles, for his 8th career shutout. The win evened our record at 18-18, the latest in the season the Mets had ever had a .500 record. Even though we were still 5½ games behind the first-place Cubs, we were feeling pretty good about ourselves because we had moved up to third place in the National League East.

The good feeling of so lofty a perch was short-lived, however, as we finished the road trip by getting hammered the next night in Atlanta and then being swept in a 3-game series in Houston. That left us in fourth place, 4 games under .500, and 9 games behind the Cubs, who were beginning to look as if they would run away with the division. To make matters worse, we were going home to face the three West Coast teams for 8 straight games.

You have to understand that in their first eight years, the Mets had won only 79 games and lost 173 home and away against California teams, which, until 1969, meant only the Dodgers and Giants. Now there was a third California team, the expansion Padres, but the West Coast jinx still seemed in force when we lost the first game of the home stand 3–2 despite outhitting the Padres, 12–9. Here we go again. Same old Mets. Or was it? What happened next was nothing short of miraculous and, in my mind, the first indication that the Mets had turned the corner and put their bumbling, laughingstock past in the rearview mirror. Our loss to the Padres dropped our record to 18-23 and left us in fourth place in the National League East. It was only May 27 and we were 9 games behind the Cubs already. But the next night, we beat the Padres, 1–0, in 11 innings, and if you're looking for signs, that might have been the date that signaled the turnaround. It wasn't only *that* we won, but *how* we won that inspired us.

For nine innings, Jerry Koosman and San Diego's Clay Kirby

had hooked up in a scoreless pitchers' duel. Kirby left for a pinch hitter in the tenth, but Koos continued. He worked the top of the tenth, then left for a pinch hitter in the bottom half. He had allowed only 4 hits and struck out 15, but when we failed to score in the bottom of the tenth, Koosman had nothing to show for his tremendous effort.

We went to the bottom of the eleventh still scoreless when Cleon Jones led off by reaching base on an error by the shortstop. Ed Kranepool struck out, but Ron Swoboda singled to center off reliever Frank Reberger to send Cleon to third base with the winning run. The Padres then walked Jerry Grote intentionally to load the bases and set up a force at any base. They were no doubt hoping they would be able to entice the next batter to hit into a double play.

And who was the next batter? you ask. None other than "Sluggo" Harrelson, at the time a career .239 hitter. I bore down, tried to concentrate on making contact, and lined a single to center field. Cleon scored the winning run and the guys poured out of the dugout to engulf me and pound me in celebration. There's no way to adequately describe your exhilaration when you get a game-winning hit and your teammates mob you to congratulate you.

As exciting as that win was, it was only against the expansion Padres. We would have the next day off, then the real test would come for us when the Giants and the Dodgers would arrive at Shea Stadium for 6 games.

We began the Giants series on Friday night, May 30, in front of a crowd of 52,272, which shouldn't be taken as an indication the fans were beginning to believe we were a contender. No, most of the capacity crowd no doubt came for a chance to watch Willie Mays back in New York where he began.

Those who came to cheer for Willie had to be disappointed when he got only 1 hit, a single, and struck out twice in 4 at bats, but if they stayed long enough, they wound up cheering for the home team. Trailing, 3–1, in the bottom of the eighth, our first two batters were retired, Amos Otis on a fly ball to left, me on a fly ball to that man Mays in center. But then Rod Gaspar belted a home run, and we got four consecutive singles, from Agee, Jones, Swoboda, and Duffy Dyer, a pinch hitter. We had scored 3 runs and taken a 4–3 lead. Ron Taylor pitched the top of the ninth. He struck out Mays looking and Willie McCovey swinging before Ken Henderson singled. Taylor, who would later go to medical school and became the Toronto Blue Jays team physician, then retired Bobby Bonds, Barry's father, on a pop to me, and we had our second straight win. Maybe the biggest win in Mets history up to that time.

Beating the Giants seemed to energize us. The next day we beat them again, 4–2, as Gary Gentry and Tug McGraw combined to outpitch Gaylord Perry. The day after that, we went to the bottom of the ninth tied 4–4 when I led off with a walk, moved to second on Agee's sacrifice and to third on a ground out. Jones was walked intentionally to bring up Otis. But when Cleon stole second and first base was open, the Giants walked Otis to load the bases for Swoboda, who also walked to force in the winning run, and we had swept the Giants.

Next came the Dodgers, but we were on a roll. Koosman was brilliant again as he held the Dodgers to 5 hits, struck out 8, and beat Claude Osteen, 2–1. It was our 5th straight win and it evened our record at 23-23. And we still weren't finished.

The next night, Seaver struck out 8 and beat the Dodgers, 5–2, on a 3-hitter, and the night after that it took 15 innings, but we beat the Dodgers again, 1–0, and I had the satisfaction of starting the winning rally with a walk. Agee forced me, but Wayne Garrett followed with a single to center, and when the ball got past the Dodgers' center fielder, Willie Davis, Agee came all the way around to score the winning run.

Our winning streak was seven and we had done something no Met team had ever done before: swept the Giants and Dodgers in consecutive series.

Suddenly, the atmosphere in our clubhouse was different. It was like "Wow! Nothing like this has ever happened before around here." We were winning games with late rallies. We were winning close games. We were winning games in which the lead went back and forth. We never won those kinds of games before. In the old days, the feeling was "Who's going to screw this up?" Now, all of a sudden, the feeling was "Who's going to get the big hit to win this game for us?"

We were flying high, so high we probably didn't need a plane to get to the West Coast, where we continued our winning streak, stretching it to 11 straight by sweeping a 3-game series in San Diego and winning the first game of a 2-game series in San Francisco. It left us with a record of 29-23 and we had moved into second place, but we'd managed to lop only 2 games off the Cubs lead during the streak and still trailed them by 7 games.

Even though we lost 3 of the last 4 games in San Francisco and Los Angeles, we had turned a corner and built up a head of steam that boosted our confidence. And we had gotten the California monkey off our back by completing a stretch of games, home and away, against the three West Coast teams by winning 12 of 16. The final game of that stretch was a 3–2 defeat to Don Drysdale and the Dodgers on June 15, which proved to be a significant date in the Mets' chronology.

All the way back to the start of spring training, Hodges had been saying that the team needed one more bat, a veteran presence and a run producer, and Gil had apparently hounded the front office to find somebody he could stick in the middle of his lineup. At one point, the Mets were supposedly close to a deal with the Braves for Joe Torre, who had fallen in disfavor with Atlanta's general manager, Paul Richards.

Torre seemed like the perfect guy to fill what Hodges saw as a huge void. In a three-year span, 1964–66, with the Braves, Joe had batted .321, .291, and .315, hit 83 home runs, and driven in 290 runs. He became expendable when, in the next two seasons, he slipped to .277 and .271, hit only 30 homers, and drove in 123 runs. But he was still only twenty-eight years old, so the Mets figured he had a lot left in his bat. Besides, in keeping with a policy of acquiring players with New York roots that the Mets had followed since their inception, Torre had to be attractive to them because he was a Brooklyn native.

When Richards insisted that the Mets include both Amos Otis and Nolan Ryan, two of their brightest prospects, in any trade for Torre, the deal fell through, and Torre was sent to the Cardinals for Orlando Cepeda. That left the Mets still on the hunt for the bat Hodges coveted. Torre eventually became a Met, but it was six years later when he was thirty-four and on the decline. Two years after joining the Mets, he was named their manager, a position in which he failed miserably. It was his first try at managing and some twenty years before he would become a Hall of Fame manager with the Yankees.

On the June 15 trading deadline, the Mets acquired the run producer they had been seeking. Donn Clendenon was a thirty-three-year-old veteran in his ninth major league season, the first eight with the Pittsburgh Pirates, for whom he had batted .280, hit 106 home runs, and driven in 488 runs. Just a few years before, he had two outstanding seasons in Pittsburgh—1965, when he batted .301 with 14 homers and 96 RBI, and 1966, when he batted .299 with 28 homers and 98 RBI.

Clendenon's production fell off in the next two seasons, so the Pirates left him unprotected and therefore eligible for the expansion draft. He was snapped up by the new Montreal franchise, but Clendenon refused to report to the Expos, saying he had no desire to play in Canada. It forced the Expos to trade him and Jesus Alou to Houston for Rusty Staub.

After first agreeing to play in Houston, Clendenon changed his mind and announced he was leaving baseball to accept a management position with the Scripto Pen Company. That left the Astros holding the bag. They had given up Staub and had only Alou to show for it, so they asked recently elected commissioner Bowie Kuhn to void the deal. Kuhn denied the request, properly ruling that to do so would be unfair not only to the Expos, who had dealt in good faith and were happy with Staub, but also to Staub, who had no wish to return to Houston.

Both sides agreed to abide by any decision Kuhn made to resolve the problem, and he ordered the Expos to send pitchers Jack Billingham and Skip Guinn to the Astros. A few weeks later, Clendenon, apparently influenced by certain inducements, "unretired" and joined the Expos. In 38 games with Montreal, he was batting .240 with 4 home runs and 14 RBI when the Mets acquired him for infielder Kevin Collins, pitcher Steve Renko, and two minor leaguers who never would get into a major league game.

Collins played one season with the Expos and two with the Tigers and then was out of baseball. Renko had a long and fairly productive career of 15 years with seven teams. He won 134 major league games and twice won 15 for the Expos.

Clendenon's situation was similar to Tom Seaver's. The Mets got lucky that both of them just kind of fell into their lap. They got Seaver when Commissioner Eckert pulled their name out of a hat, a one-in-three chance that could just as easily have gone against them; and they got Clendenon after he went from Pittsburgh to Montreal and made it clear he was unhappy in Canada and wanted out.

When the deal for Clendenon was announced, my first thought was "Wow! We got a guy who could turn a game around with one swing."

Clendenon proved to be the run producer Hodges was looking for. Gil platooned him at first base with Ed Kranepool. Clendenon started slowly, driving in only 1 run in his first 8 games as a Met, but then he drove in 14 runs in his next 8 games and continued to get big hits throughout the season and beyond.

Some guys complained that he jabbered too much and that turned them off, but I liked him a lot; I really did. He carried us many times in '69, but I remember one time he came up in a big situation and struck out, which deflated a lot of guys. Clendenon came back to the bench and saw all those long faces, and he said, "You're all waiting for me to be good today? I'm horseshit today. C'mon, get your asses out there and pick me up."

Clendenon was "good" in the World Series, batting .357, hitting 3 home runs, driving in 4 runs, and being named World Series Most Valuable Player. He had another big year for the Mets in 1970 and a not-so-big year in 1971, after which he was released. He played one season with the Cardinals in 1972, then retired and enrolled in law school. To his credit, he became a lawyer. Sadly, Donn died of leukemia in 2005 at the age of seventy.

Clendenon helped us stay close to the Cubs, but while we remained in second place, as June ended we were 7 games out of first. By July 8, we had trimmed the lead to 5 games, with the Cubs coming to Shea Stadium for a 3-game series, without a doubt the most important series in Mets history to that point.

That brought a crowd of 55,096 to Shea on a typically hot and humid July afternoon in New York, and they were treated to a dramatic come-from-behind victory. Trailing future Hall of Famer Ferguson Jenkins going into the bottom of the ninth, we rallied for 3 runs—a double by Ken Boswell, a pinch-hit double by Clendenon that was misplayed by center fielder Don Young, a double by Cleon Jones, and a two-out, game-winning single by Ed Kranepool—and a 4–3 victory that sent the fans into hysteria.

That generated another sellout crowd the following night when 55,709, 613 more than the previous day, showed up to watch Tom Seaver hook up with Ken Holtzman. We scored a run in the first, two in the second, and one more in the seventh, but the big story was Seaver. Going into the ninth inning, he had faced 24 Cubs batters and retired them all, 11 by strikeout.

Randy Hundley started the ninth by hitting back to Seaver, and it was 25 Cubs up and 25 Cubs down. Seaver was two outs away from a no-hitter, and a perfect game to boot. The next batter was a rookie, Jimmy Qualls, playing in only his 18th major league game. He had been to bat 48 times in the big leagues with 11 hits, but he lined a clean single to left center.

Seaver would call it the best game he ever pitched and "the game I'll never forget."

The irony is that the only reason Qualls was playing was because Don Young had botched Clendenon's double the day before, and manager Leo Durocher benched Young in favor of Qualls's defense. Suppose Young had caught Clendenon's drive! Would Durocher have played him against Seaver? Would Tom then have completed his perfect game?

Seaver was not only the best pitcher in Mets history, he was their best player, "The Franchise," the first (and to this date the only) full-fledged Met to be elected to the Hall of Fame. Unfortunately when he reached his two greatest pitching milestones, pitching a no-hitter and winning his 300th game, they came with other teams.

In 11½ seasons, Seaver won 198 games as a Met, pitched 171 complete games and 44 shutouts, but he never pitched a no-hitter with them. No pitcher did. Tom eventually pitched his no-hitter against the Cardinals on June 16, 1978, as a member of the Cincinnati Reds. He would return to the Mets for one season, in 1983, and leave with 273 career wins. And he would win his 300th game with a 6-hit, 7-strikeout, 4–1 win against the Yankees as a member of the Chicago White Sox on August 4, 1985. To make it even more hurtful for the Mets and their fans, he would do it in Yankee Stadium in the Bronx, some fifteen miles away from Shea Stadium.

After Qualls's hit, Seaver retired the next two batters to complete the 4–0, one-hit shutout, but the Cubs salvaged the final game of the series with a 6–2 win. Nevertheless, we had taken two out of three from them, trimmed their lead to four games, and had made a statement. For the first time, we were being taken seriously as pennant contenders.

A week later, we went to Chicago for a 3-game series July 14, 15, 16. We lost the first game 1–0 when Seaver was outpitched by Bill Hands, but we came back to win the next two, 5–4 and 9–5. I missed the series because I was away fulfilling my military obligation; Al Weis played shortstop in my absence.

We had obtained Weis from the White Sox after the 1967 season in the deal that also brought us Tommie Agee. Hodges knew Agee and Weis from the American League and pushed for the trade. I was coming off a knee operation and I also had to fulfill my military obligation and would miss a weekend a month during the season, so Weis was acquired to play shortstop when I wasn't available.

Weis was six years my senior, a six-year veteran, and a terrific guy. I liked and respected him a great deal. In addition to shortstop, he played a lot of second base for us in 1969 and even one game at third. He had surprising power that he would occasionally unleash, usually in big spots. Against the Cubs in that 3-game series in Wrigley Field in July, he hit a 3-run home run in the second game of the series, then hit a solo home run the next day. Here's a guy who had hit only 4 home runs in more than 1,000 major league at bats, and he hits home runs in back-to-back games. It was that kind of year. We left Chicago just 3½ games out of first place.

On July 20, while we were splitting a doubleheader with the Expos in Montreal, astronaut Neil Armstrong became the first man to walk on the moon, commemorating the occasion with the words "That's one small step for man; one giant leap for mankind." Moments later, his partner Buzz Aldrin became the second man to walk on the moon.

This historic event coming when it did was not lost on us. We began to take flights of fancy. Perhaps unreasonably, we began to speculate that if Joe Namath and the New York Jets of the upstart

American Football League could beat the heavily favored Johnny Unitas and the Baltimore Colts in the Super Bowl, and men could walk on the moon, then it was not too far-fetched to believe that the New York Mets could win the National League pennant in only the eighth year of their existence.

After splitting the doubleheader in Montreal, we came home and split 4 games with Cincinnati. Then the Astros came to Shea for 3 games, a doubleheader on July 30 and a single game on July 31.

We trailed 5–3 going into the ninth inning of the first game of the doubleheader when the Astros hit 2 grand slams, exploded for 11 runs, and beat us, 16–3. It was an embarrassing defeat in front of almost 30,000 of our home fans, but we had another game to go and could save the day by gaining a split of the doubleheader.

Neither team scored in the first two innings, but in the third, the roof fell in. The Astros started hitting and didn't stop. With 7 hits, 3 walks, an error, a wild pitch, and a stolen base, the Astros scored 10 runs. So they had an 11-run inning and a 10-run inning on the same day. I could just imagine Hodges doing a slow burn in the dugout.

Seven runs were already in when Johnny Edwards, who had started the whole barrage with a single, hit a ball to left field. Cleon Jones went after it halfheartedly, and when he retrieved it, he lobbed the ball lackadaisically to the infield. It had rained and the field was getting sloppy, but that was no excuse. I looked up and here came Hodges out of the dugout. My first thought was that he was coming to remove the pitcher, Nolan Ryan, but he walked past the mound and he seemed to be heading straight for me. I had no idea why. I pointed to my chest as if to say, "Me?" and Gil shook his head and pointed to left field.

Gil went past me and continued to left field, walking slowly and deliberately, on the tip of his toes as he always did, and I went out there with him, walking right behind him.

When he got to left field, Gil said to Cleon, "Are you hurt?"

Cleon, who had had knee surgery earlier in the season, said, "Yes."

Gil said, "Come with me."

The next thing anyone knew, here was Hodges heading back to the dugout, walking deliberately, on the tip of his toes, and Cleon was walking right behind him.

From what has been said and written about the incident, the perception was that this was some sort of rebuke by Hodges for Jones's lackadaisical play. Based on what I witnessed and what I heard, that wasn't the case at all. When he got to left field, Hodges wasn't ranting and raving. If you watch replays of the incident, Gil wasn't emotional or mad at Cleon. He was calm. But it has been depicted as Gil taking a stand against our best player (at the time, Cleon was batting .346) and as a turning point in our season.

If Hodges was upset with Jones and this was his way of reprimanding Cleon, Gil had made his point. And he did it in his own typically quiet and subtle manner.

Although the incident with Cleon didn't produce immediate results—Gil sat him the next day and we lost, 2–0; over the next 14 games we played .500 ball ending with another damaging 3-game sweep by the Astros, this time in Houston, and fell into third place, 9½ games behind the Cubs—it would eventually become a galvanizing point in our season.

Once again a stretch of games, home and away, against the three West Coast teams would propel us in a run at the Cubs. In 20 games against the Padres, Dodgers, and Giants from August 16 to September 3, we won 15 of them and closed to within striking distance of first place, just 5 games behind. That stretch invigorated us and got us believing that we could pull off this miracle.

Back home, we split the first two games of a 4-game series with the Phillies, then ran off 10 straight wins. The Cubs came into Shea on September 8 for a 2-game series, leading us by 2½ games.

In the first game, Jerry Koosman outpitched Bill Hands for a 3–2 victory. Koos struck out 13, and Tommie Agee hit a 2-run homer in the third. In the sixth, Agee doubled and scored the go-ahead run on a single by Wayne Garrett.

Tom Seaver, a 20-game winner, and Ferguson Jenkins, a 19-game winner, both of them future Hall of Famers, squared off in the second game of the series on September 9. We jumped on Jenkins for 2 runs in the first, 2 more in the third on a 2-run homer by Donn Clendenon, 1 in the fourth, and 1 more in the fifth on Art Shamsky's solo homer. Seaver allowed 5 hits and we won the game, 7–1, to close to a half game out.

At one point, someone (not me, honest) released a black cat onto the field. It hovered around Ron Santo, in the on-deck circle, then pranced over and stared into the Cubs dugout before being chased away. Baseball players being superstitious creatures, the Cubs believed they were jinxed by a spell cast by the cat. Maybe they were.

The Cubs left town and went to Philadelphia the next day and lost, while we swept a doubleheader from the Expos and moved into first place for the first time in Mets history.

Having captured first place with an impressive uphill surge from 9½ games behind, we were determined not to give it up. And we didn't. We continued to keep the pedal to the metal, and the Cubs continued to fade. On September 18 we were 5 games ahead. And against the Cardinals in Shea Stadium on September 24, in front of an overflow crowd of 54,928, we reached the Promised Land.

Gary Gentry, who joined the team that year and had a sensational rookie year, winning 13 games and fitting right in behind Seaver and Koosman in our rotation, got the start against 17-game-winner Steve Carlton. Just nine days earlier, Carlton had pitched against us in St. Louis and struck out 19 (he got me twice), but this time we jumped on him right away.

Gentry retired the Cards in order in the top of the first, and when we came to bat in the bottom, the crowd, eager to witness the division clincher, began chanting and clapping as I stepped in the batter's box to lead off. The clapping and chanting grew louder when I looped a single to center. Tommie Agee then walked, and after Cleon Jones struck out, Clendenon, who had gotten so many big hits in our second-half drive, blasted a long home run over the center-field fence to give us a 3–0 lead. Now, the crowd was going crazy.

Before the inning was over, Ed "the Glider" Charles had hit a 2-run homer to give us a 5-run lead. In the fifth inning Clendenon hit another homer, his 12th for us in 190 at bats, to make it 6–0. The way Gentry was pitching, we were feeling secure. From that point on, you could feel the excitement in the stadium as the crowd was just bursting to explode in celebration.

A steady buzz filled Shea Stadium when the Cardinals came to bat in the ninth. The crowd was on its feet, but a momentary nervous hush followed when Lou Brock and Vic Davalillo started the inning with back-to-back singles, only the third and fourth hits off Gentry. But Gary struck out Vada Pinson, and that brought to the plate Joe Torre, the guy the Mets had tried, and failed, to acquire.

I wanted the ball hit to me. I always wanted the ball hit to me in clutch situations because I had confidence in my ability, especially on the routine plays. I was sure-handed. If I botched a play, it was more likely to be on a throw than on fielding a ground ball, so with the game on the line I was always thinking, "Hit it to me." I believe in positive thinking. I believe you have to want the ball. If you don't want the ball hit to you because you're afraid you'll screw it up, invariably you *will* screw it up. I especially wanted a ground ball hit to me in this situation because Torre hit the ball so hard and didn't run that well. I knew if he hit it to me, we could turn the double play, clinch the pennant, and make history.

And that's exactly what happened. Torre hit a smash to me at short and I'm thinking, "Don't screw up the throw; don't rush it." I knew I could catch it. I just wanted to be sure to make a good, firm throw right at the chest of Al Weis at second base. I tossed it to

Weis and he turned it over to Clendenon at first for the double play, and we had won the Mets' first title. We were the first champions of the National League East. The scoreboard clock read 9:07 p.m.

Gentry had held the Cardinals to 4 singles and beat them, 6–0, for our 96th win of the season, 23 more than we had won the year before, and the first time a Mets team had won more games than it lost. It had taken only seven years, and Gil Hodges, for the Mets to go from lovable losers to champions.

When the final out was recorded, all hell broke loose. As fans poured out of the stands onto the field, we players made a mad dash for the clubhouse. Outside, the fans were going wild. For almost an hour they ran rampant over the field, tearing up patches of sod, grabbing anything they could for souvenirs.

In our clubhouse, the players were just as wild, running amok, dumping champagne on everybody with Seaver and Koosman leading the charge.

Hodges retreated to his office to meet with the press. He was emotionally drained, but happy. Only a year ago, he had suffered a heart attack, his baseball future in doubt, but now he was enjoying the most satisfying achievement in a distinguished professional career. But while he was happy, he also was cautious.

"I really didn't think we'd come as far as we have as fast as we have," he told the writers. "But now that we're here, I see no reason to stop."

Because we were descended, and only a few years removed, from Casey Stengel's lovable losers, nobody took the 1969 Mets seriously as pennant contenders, let alone World Series champions, even after we won 100 games and came from 9½ games behind on August 13 to overhaul the "runaway" Chicago Cubs and win the National League East by 8 games. But if you put aside the perception of the Mets as baseball's laughingstock and looked dispassionately at the statistics, we deserved to be favorites over the Atlanta Braves in the first best-of-five championship series in the ninety-four-year history of the National League.

We never slowed down after we clinched the division. We continued to win, extending our winning streak to 9, and wound up winning 9 of our last 10, and 38 of our last 49.

The strength of our team was pitching. Tom Seaver and Jerry Koosman combined for 42 wins, 34 complete games, and 11 shutouts. Seaver won his last 10 decisions to finish 25-7 with a 2.21 earned run average. Koos won 9 of his last 10 decisions to finish with 17 wins. Our pitching staff had 28 shutouts.

Another factor in our favor was the play-off schedule. We would be the visiting team in the NLCS for the first two games, but the next three would be at Shea Stadium, where we had a record of 52-30.

During the regular season, we had won 8 out of 12 games against the Braves, champions of the NL West, but even though we were confident going into the NLCS, by no means were we taking the Braves lightly. They had finished their season as hot as we were with 10 wins in their last 11 games and 17 wins in their last 21.

The Braves were led by the magnificent Henry Aaron, who had batted .300, hit 44 home runs (to that point he had 554 career homers and would hit another 201 before he retired as baseball's all-time home-run champion), and driven in 97 runs; Rico Carty, who batted .342; and Orlando Cepeda, who had 22 homers and 88 RBI. Their pitching staff was led by the knuckleball guru Phil Niekro, who was 23-13.

The first game of the series was played in Atlanta on Saturday afternoon, October 4. In a way, it was just as well that we opened the NLCS on the road and that our last 5 games of the regular season also were on the road. It had been ten days since we'd clinched the NL East in Shea Stadium. The field was in such terrible condition after the fans ravaged it, we couldn't have played at home in the days that followed. The field might not even have been ready if the first play-off game had to be played there.

Considering the pitchers chosen to start—Seaver for us and Niekro for the Braves had won 48 games between them during the regular season; combined, they would go on to pitch for 44 seasons, appear in 1,520 games, post 629 wins, pitch 476 complete games and 106 shutouts, strike out 6,982 batters, and both would be elected to the Hall of Fame—and that the first pitch was scheduled for a little after 4:00 p.m. when shadows would have begun to fall around home plate, thereby making it difficult to for batters to pick up the ball, Game 1 of the NLCS figured to be a pitchers' duel with runs hard to come by. But as so often happens, when you expect a pitchers' duel, you get a slugfest, and when you expect a slugfest, you get a pitchers' duel. What we got in Game 1 was a 9–5 seesaw contest with the lead changing hands four times as Seaver and Niekro surprisingly yielded 14 runs and 17 hits between them. What was even more surprising, since in our 49-game stretch run we had scored as many as 9 runs only twice, was that we were the team with the 9.

We jumped out in front in the second inning when we scored 2 runs on a single by Art Shamsky, a walk to Ken Boswell, an RBI single by Jerry Grote, and a passed ball. The Braves scored a run in the second on a double by Carty, an error, and a sacrifice fly by Clete Boyer. They took the lead with 2 in the third on consecutive doubles by Felix Millan, Tony Gonzalez, and Aaron.

We regained the lead with 2 runs in fourth to go up, 4–3. With two out, Kranepool singled and Grote walked. Then I hit a ball inside first base past Cepeda and down the right-field line into the corner as Krane and Grote scored and I went all the way to third.

Again, the Braves came back. A home run by Gonzalez tied it in the fifth and a home run by Aaron put the Braves ahead in the seventh. After his shaky start, Niekro had settled down and held us to 1 hit through the fifth, sixth, and seventh. The Braves and Niekro had taken control and needed only 6 more outs to win Game 1.

But in the eighth, we got 4 hits, capitalized on 2 Braves errors and scored 5 runs, 4 of them unearned, to take a 9–5 lead. Ron Taylor pitched a perfect eighth and a scoreless ninth and we had won the first game. With Koosman ready to start Game 2 and the last three games on our home field, if needed, we were in great shape.

The outcome of the second game of the series was just as surprising as the first. Most experts had predicted that the only chance we had was if our pitching shut down Atlanta's offense, but if the series turned into a high-scoring affair, it would favor the Braves. Few thought we could win in a slugfest matched up with Aaron, Cepeda, Carty, & Co.

It might not have been too big a surprise that the Braves scored 5 runs against Seaver in the first game and 6 against Koosman in the second game (after all, they had the great Hank Aaron and he hit 2 home runs and drove in 5 of those runs), but it was a shock that in the first two games we scored 20 runs and banged out 23 hits, including 4 doubles, 1 triple, and 3 homers.

We beat Niekro in Game 1 and we knocked Ron Reed out in the second inning of Game 2 and continued our assault against Paul Doyle and Milt Pappas. Going into the bottom of the fifth, we had a 9–1 lead. With Koos on the mound, we figured we were home free. But the Braves showed what they were made of by scoring 5 runs in the bottom of the fifth, all after the first two batters were retired. Ron Taylor and Tug McGraw combined to hold the Braves to 2 hits over the last 4⅓ innings and we won Game 2, 11–6, and went home the next day needing one more win to become National League champions.

In Game 3, Aaron hit his third home run of the series and Cepeda hit his first, but we got home runs from Agee, Boswell, and Wayne Garrett and jumped out to a 7–4 lead after 6 innings. The turning point actually came in the third inning with the Braves ahead, 2–0, and threatening to break the game wide-open when Gonzalez led off with a single and Aaron doubled him to third.

Here was another of those times when Hodges jumped the gun on me by making a move that I had been thinking about. I thought we needed to warm somebody up, and when I turned to look in the bullpen, Nolan Ryan was already warming up. Then after Aaron hit his double, I thought we needed a pitching change, and sure enough, here came Gil out of the dugout, heading for the mound. He signaled for Ryan, who came in to replace Gary Gentry.

Nolan struck out Carty and Hodges ordered an intentional walk to Cepeda to load the bases, a gutsy decision because Ryan was notorious for his inability to consistently throw strikes (he had walked 53 batters in 89⅓ innings during the season). Gil's gamble and his confidence in Ryan paid off when Nolan struck out Clete Boyer and got Bob Didier to fly to left, stranding 3 runners. That seemed to take a lot of the fight out of the Braves. Ryan held them to 2 runs and 3 hits over seven innings, while we rallied for 7 runs in the third, fourth, fifth, and sixth innings and completed the 3-game sweep.

When Tony Gonzalez hit a ground ball to third baseman Wayne Garrett with 2 out in the top of the ninth, and Garrett threw across the diamond to Ed Kranepool, we were National League champions, setting off another wild celebration as fans once again overran Shea Stadium and pandemonium erupted in the victorious clubhouse.

In only the eighth year of their existence, the Mets were going to the World Series.

CHAPTER 7

Not many gave us a chance to win the 1969 World Series. We were decided underdogs against the Baltimore Orioles, American League champions under Earl Weaver in his first full season as manager. The Orioles had steamrolled the American League, winning 109 games, the most in the majors, finishing a whopping 19 games ahead of the Detroit Tigers in the American League East, then winning the American League Championship Series in a 3-game sweep of the Minnesota Twins, managed by Billy Martin.

The Orioles were a solid, well-rounded team with pitching, power, and defense. Their offense was led by first baseman Boog Powell (37 homers, 121 RBI), right fielder Frank Robinson (32 homers, 100 RBI), third baseman Brooks Robinson (23 homers, 84 RBI), and center fielder Paul Blair (26 homers, 76 RBI). They had three outstanding starting pitchers in Mike Cuellar (23-11), Dave McNally (20-7), and Jim Palmer (16-4). And the two Robinsons, Blair, shortstop Mark Belanger, and second baseman Davey Johnson (yes, *that* Davey Johnson) were among the best in baseball defensively at their positions.

They were the names and we were the nobodies. All this talent made the Birds kind of cocky, a few of them even predicting a 4-game sweep over these upstarts from the National League who needed a comeuppance.

Frank Robinson, the Orioles' outspoken, fearless, and fearsome superstar right fielder, set the tone when he chanted, "Bring on Ron [*sic*] Gaspar! Who the hell is Ron Gaspar?" Either inadvertently, but more likely intentionally, Robinson was demeaning us by combining the names of *Rod* Gaspar and *Ron* Swoboda. The ultimate put-down came when Robinson went on television as a guest of Johnny Carson and said he never heard of most of our players.

Everybody was impressed by the Orioles, including the odds-makers, who installed them as 8-to-5 favorites to win the World Series. When the experts compared the two teams, they gave the Orioles the edge at virtually every position—Powell over Donn Clendenon/Eddie Kranepool at first base, Johnson over Ken Boswell at second, Brooks Robinson over Ed Charles/Wayne Garrett at third, etc. We didn't mind. We were getting used to being underrated. We liked the role of underdogs. We felt we had everything to gain and nothing to lose.

We looked at those comparisons and just said, "Okay, what else is new?" We were loose. We weren't nervous. And certainly we were not intimidated by the Orioles, their reputation, and the backs of their baseball cards. That attitude flowed from Hodges, who remained upbeat, calm, and confident. Gil didn't have anything special to say to us before the World Series. When he called us together for a team meeting, it wasn't for a pep talk or any rah-rah kind of thing; it was simply to go over the scouting reports. All Gil did was write out the lineup card and send us out to play.

One thing Hodges did that would help us in the play-offs and the World Series was to play everybody on the roster during the season. Consequently, every player on the team was ready to be in a World Series, not just nine guys. He rested guys to keep them fresh and gave the extra men enough playing time to keep them sharp.

At first base he platooned Donn Clendenon and Ed Kranepool. At third base he platooned Ed Charles and Wayne Garrett. In right field he platooned Art Shamsky and Ron Swoboda. Our backup catcher, J. C. Martin, played in 66 games. Rod Gaspar, a spare outfielder, was in 118 games. Al Weis, a utility infielder, got in

103 games. For the most part, I avoided the platoon and played in 123 games mainly because I was a switch-hitter.

The only regulars that played in more than 124 games were Cleon Jones and Tommie Agee. The Orioles had seven regulars that played in 142 games or more. Seaver and Koosman led our staff with 35 and 32 starts, respectively. For the Orioles, McNally started 40 games and Cuellar 39.

The World Series of 1969 started off badly for us. The first game was to be played on the afternoon of Saturday, October 11, so we arrived in Baltimore the night before. The next morning we got up and most of us went down to the restaurant for breakfast, and only one person was waiting on tables. Here it is the morning of the first game of the World Series, the hotel is housing the visiting team, and they're not prepared for us. So we went to the ballpark without breakfast, and when we got there, we had to get the clubhouse guys to order us some food.

The game started and was barely ten minutes old when it appeared that all of the experts' predictions were right on the mark. We went down quietly in the top of the first when Cuellar got two ground balls to third, then, after a single by Jones, struck out Clendenon.

In the bottom of the first, Don Buford led off for the Orioles and smacked Seaver's second pitch over the right-field fence. As he rounded second base, I could hear Buford, with a sneer of defiance in his voice, say, "You guys ain't seen nothing yet."

The first inning of the first game and this prima donna is popping off like that. I know he might not have been representing the whole team, but that remark did seem to typify their cocky, superior attitude.

In truth, we were a little shaken up by this sudden turn of events but reminded ourselves that there was still a long way to go. Were we rationalizing? Probably.

That sort of start never bothered Seaver. He just shrugged off Buford's homer and kept the Orioles hitless until there were 2 outs in the fourth, but then he gave up single, walk, single, single, double, for 3 runs and a 4–0 Baltimore lead. In the sixth, Tom was removed for a pinch hitter.

Meanwhile, Cuellar was sailing along, holding us scoreless through the first six innings. In the seventh, we loaded the bases with one out, but all we could get was 1 run on a sacrifice fly by Al Weis. And that's how the game ended, a 4–1 victory for the Orioles, who made it look so easy many people were expecting them to get the 4-game sweep some of their players had predicted.

Even though it was only one game, the Orioles had used a familiar formula of timely hitting, excellent pitching, and great defense such that we couldn't help feeling we'd be in big trouble if we didn't come up with something special.

We got that "something special" from Jerry Koosman in Game 2. For 6 innings, he held the Orioles hitless, which was exactly what we needed to boost our confidence. Clendenon homered off Dave McNally leading off the fourth and Koos protected his slim 1–0 lead into the seventh, when Paul Blair led off with a single to break up the no-hitter. Koos got Frank Robinson on a line drive to center and Powell on a pop to short. With the Orioles' two best hitters retired, Blair stole second and scored on Brooks Robinson's single to center, which aroused the more than 50,000 fans in Baltimore's Memorial Stadium.

You could sense that after the way Koosman had pitched, Brooks's hit had shifted momentum back to the Orioles. If they were able to push across the winning run and take a two games to none lead in the Series, most people figured that would signal our demise. But we scored a run in the ninth on consecutive singles by Ed Charles, Jerry Grote, and Al Weis off McNally after he had retired Clendenon and Swoboda.

It was fitting that what may have been our most important rally of the year would be accomplished by Grote, a .252 hitter, and two platoon players, Charles, who played in only 61 games and batted .207, and Weis, who appeared in 103 games and batted .215. But that's what we had done all season, role players and part-time players coming through time and again with big hits, all a tribute to Hodges's plan of using all his players.

Now Koosman, with a 2–1 lead, needed to get 3 outs in the bottom of the ninth to even the Series at a game apiece. He retired the first two batters easily—Buford on a pop to short right, Blair on a ground ball to short—but the third out proved to be elusive. With Frank Robinson at bat, Hodges employed one of his unorthodox bits of strategy that we had become accustomed to seeing. He moved second baseman Weis to the outfield, thereby giving us four outfielders and only three infielders. With the move, Hodges, in effect, was conceding Robinson, a dangerous power hitter, an easy single if he wanted to take it, but he was going to try to prevent him from hitting one in the gap for an extrabase hit that would put the tying run in scoring position.

It was a wise but futile move, as Koosman walked Robinson on a 3-2 pitch. No problem. It brought up Boog Powell, a left-handed batter against the left-handed Koosman. But Boog also walked, putting the tying run on second and the winning run on first, with Brooks Robinson, who had singled in the only run off Koosman, coming to bat. Hodges had no choice. Even though Koosman had allowed only 2 hits, he was removed in favor of Ron Taylor, a right-handed pitcher against the right-handed-hitting Robinson.

The move almost backfired. Taylor fell behind in the count 3-1, but Brooks swung at the next pitch and bounced it to third baseman Charles. At first, "Glider" thought he could simply run to third and touch the bag to retire Frank Robinson on a force out for the final out. But when Charles saw Frank barreling down to third and thought he might not be able to beat him to the bag, he fired to first instead. The throw was in the dirt, but Clendenon scooped it for the final out, and we had won Game 2.

Some pessimists were relieved with the knowledge that, at

least, the Mets would not be swept in this World Series. That wasn't what I was thinking. My thought was "We're even and we're going home for the next three games. We can beat these guys."

Game 3 would prove to be the turning point in the Series. Buoyed by drawing even with the Orioles and supported by 56,335 of our fans, we jumped on Jim Palmer early. We scored a run in the first when Tommie Agee copied Don Buford's Game 1 act and led off with a homer, and 2 in the second on a walk to Grote, my single, and a 2-run double by pitcher Gary Gentry, of all people.

From that point on we were emboldened by a series of events that added to our mystique and convinced us we were destined to be world champions. In the top of the fourth, the Birds put runners on first and third with two outs, and then Elrod Hendricks hit a rocket to left center. When it left the bat, it looked like a certain double, probably scoring 2 runs and putting the Orioles back in the game. But Agee caught up with the ball, reached out, and snared it just as he smashed into the wall. It was an amazing catch, but maybe even more amazing was that after crashing into the wall and sprawling on the ground Agee still held on to the ball in the webbing of his glove.

Aided by Agee's catch, Gentry took his shutout into the seventh inning. Through the years, I have come across several of those Orioles and talked to them about that World Series. Most of them still insisted they were the better team and they should have won the Series. I guess it's predictable that they would believe that. Another thing they seemed to agree on was that their biggest problem was that their reports on Gary Gentry were all wrong. They underrated him and he surprised them with his stuff.

After disposing of the first two batters in the seventh, Gentry suddenly had a streak of wildness. He walked Mark Belanger, pinch hitter Dave May, and Buford to load the bases and bring up Paul Blair. Here, Hodges made another bold decision. He removed Gentry and once again called for Nolan Ryan in a situation in which he had to throw strikes.

At the mound, Gil said to Ryan, "Bases loaded and two outs. Here's the ball. You're familiar with this situation."

In a sense, the remark was made to lighten the moment, but at the same time it was a compliment to Ryan and a reminder that he had been there, done that before, and come through. Nolie came in throwing heat, and strikes, and quickly got ahead of Blair, 0–2. Ryan's next pitch was over the plate, and Blair put a vicious swing on it and drove a shot to the gap in right-center. Again, it looked like a bases-clearing double or triple when it left the bat. And again Agee took off with the crack of the bat, caught up with the ball as it was about to land on the warning track, dived, skidded along the ground, and came to a stop with the ball in his glove. It was his second miraculous catch in 4 innings, depriving the Orioles of at least 5 runs.

When the Orioles came to bat in the ninth, they were behind 5–0, but they had one more rally left in them. After getting the first two batters on fly balls to right, Ryan loaded the bases on two walks and a single. Again Blair came to bat with a chance to do some damage. Hodges stayed with Ryan and Nolie struck Blair out looking to end the game. We had taken a 2–1 lead in the World Series and were determined not to relinquish it.

We pressed our advantage in Game 4 with a 2–1 win in 10 innings that included an outstanding effort from Tom Seaver, who took on Mike Cuellar and three relievers and outpitched them, and another spectacular, miraculous catch in a critical situation by a Mets outfielder. It also included a bit of controversy revolving around Seaver that would have unnerved most people, but not someone as strong-willed as Tom.

Even back then at the age of twenty-four, Seaver was outspoken, opinionated, and a political activist. He had made known his opposition to the war in Vietnam and publically urged the United States to get out of Vietnam, information that, on the day he was to pitch Game 4 of the World Series, was printed on leaflets and disseminated outside Shea Stadium by a group of citizens against the war. In that day's edition, *The New York Times* carried a page-one story that mentioned Seaver's opposition to the war and noted that he was to be the Mets' starting pitcher that day.

I was concerned that this incident would be a distraction, but knowing Tom to be single-minded and rather stubborn, I kept my opinion to myself.

It was mind-boggling enough that Seaver was able to pitch a World Series game with all that controversy swirling around him, and even more mind-boggling that he would pitch so well under those conditions.

Clendenon got us going with a home run leading off the bottom of the second. That run was all Seaver was going to get for 9 innings—"All right, Tom, you've got your run"—but the way he was pitching, it looked as if that was all he was going to need.

Through 8 innings, he had allowed just 3 hits, all singles, and struck out 5. He protected his 1–0 lead into the ninth, when, with one out, Frank Robinson singled and Boog Powell followed with a single that sent Robinson to third with the tying run.

Brooks Robinson, the next batter, hit a sinking line drive to right field. By all the dictates of fundamentally sound baseball, Swoboda should have played it safe, let the ball drop, conceded the tying run, and kept the go-ahead run from advancing to third. But the 1969 Mets were not about playing it safe.

Daringly, Swoboda dived for the ball face-first and made an unbelievable catch. Frank Robinson tagged from third to score the tying run, but Swoboda probably saved the game with that catch. Agee had burned the Orioles with two catches the day before, and now Swoboda had done them in with another spectacular play. By this time, the Orioles should have gotten the message that we truly were a team of destiny.

We failed to score in the bottom of the ninth and Seaver continued on, pitching the tenth, in which the Orioles put runners on first and third with two outs. But Seaver struck out Blair and we had survived another threat.

In the bottom of the tenth, Grote got a double on a bloop hit to left field that was misplayed by Buford. Weis was intentionally walked. With Seaver due to bat, Hodges sent up J. C. Martin to hit for him with instructions to bunt. The bunt was fielded by pitcher Pete Richert, whose only play was at first base. When Richert's throw hit Martin on the wrist and ricocheted into right field, Rod Gaspar, who had gone in to run for Grote, scored from second base with the winning run.

We were up in the Series, 3–1, and wonder of wonders, the onetime sad-sack New York Mets, "the Amazin' Mets," were one win away from winning the World Series.

Our confidence was sky-high for Game 5, but we knew if we lost, we'd have to go back to Baltimore for Game 6 and, if needed, Game 7. So it was sort of imperative that we not let the Orioles up and closed them out in our own park, in front of our home fans.

Unfortunately, things weren't going right for us in the early innings. Jerry Koosman, so brilliant and practically unhittable in Game 2, was a little ragged at the start. In the third inning, he gave up a single to the eighth-place hitter, Mark Belanger, followed by a home run to pitcher Dave McNally, and then another home run to Frank Robinson, and we were down, 3–0.

Koosman decided enough was enough; the Orioles would get nothing more against him. He was almost true to his promise as he held the O's to just one single over the last 6 innings.

Meanwhile, we did little against McNally until the sixth, when we benefited from more gamesmanship from our manager. Our first batter in the inning was Cleon Jones, who took a ball in the dirt. Plate umpire Lou DiMuro of the American League called the pitch a ball, and the baseball was retrieved and tossed into our dugout and out of the game. Moments later, Hodges was out of our dugout, walking slowly on his tippytoes as he usually did and heading to home plate. In his hand was a baseball, which he calmly showed to DiMuro.

"I want you to check this ball," Gil said calmly. "This is the ball that came into the dugout."

The ball had a shoe-polish smudge on it, which Hodges insisted proved that the ball McNally threw in the dirt had to have hit Cleon's shoe. Whether the ball Hodges showed DiMuro was actually the one McNally had thrown or Gil had another baseball with a shoe-polish smudge stashed away for use when he needed it, I can't say for certain. But a God-fearing, churchgoing, honorable man such as Gil wouldn't lie about such a thing, would he? Whom are you going to believe, Weaver or Hodges? The reputation helps. One guy (Weaver) got kicked out of games all the time. The other guy (Hodges) walked out slow, holding a baseball and saying to the umpire, "I want you to check this ball." The way he did it, never mad, never ranting and raving, you had to believe him.

DiMuro bought Hodges's argument and changed his ruling, awarding Jones first base. Clendenon followed with a blast off the left-field auxiliary scoreboard for his third home run in the World Series, and we had cut Baltimore's lead to 3–2. We would tie the score an inning later when Al Weis, who hadn't hit a home run in Shea Stadium all season, hit one off McNally.

Momentum had shifted to our side, and we refused to let go of it. In the eighth, we scored 2 more runs on doubles by Jones and Swoboda, who later scored when the Orioles made two errors on Grote's line drive to first base.

With a 5–3 lead and only 3 outs away from wrapping up the world championship, the Shea Stadium crowd of 57,397 was buzzing in eager anticipation as Koosman went out for the kill in the top of the ninth. Some uneasy moments followed when Koos walked Frank Robinson and had to face slugger Boog Powell, he of the 37 regular-season home runs and 121 RBI, representing the tying run. But Powell never hurt us all Series. He had only 5 hits, all singles, and did not drive in a run. This time he hit a weak ground ball to second baseman Weis, who tossed to me to force Frank Robinson.

The next batter was Brooks Robinson, also a home run threat with 23 during the season. He, too, had been held in check in the

Series with 1 hit, a single, in 19 at bats, and 2 RBI. He flied out to right.

We were one out away and the batter was Davey Johnson. How ironic that the final out of the 1969 World Series should be made by the man who, seventeen years later, would manage the Mets when they won their only other World Series. Davey hit a lazy fly ball to left field that Cleon camped under. The ball settled softly in Cleon's glove for the final out. We've all seen the picture hundreds of times, Cleon kneeling on one knee after the catch as if genuflecting in gratitude.

Over the years many people have asked me what I was thinking as the ball was settling in Cleon's glove. I can tell you that I wasn't thinking of the winners' World Series share, which was $18,338.18, more than my salary for the season. No, when that last out was made, all I could see was the World Series ring, not dollar signs; just the ring. My mom and dad had come to New York from California for the Series, and I was proud and happy for them as much as for myself.

As Jones tucked the ball safely in his mitt, the clock on the Shea Stadium scoreboard showed 3:17 p.m. The Mets were world champions. It was a miracle. The Miracle Mets! The Impossible Dream come true!

With the final out, the crowd erupted and stormed the playing field. By then it had become a familiar, almost mandatory, scene, the fans tearing up Shea Stadium. Let them tear it up; we weren't going to need it for another six months. The horde of humanity poured down from the stands and overran Shea Stadium like bulls in Pamplona, trampling anything in their path. They tore the bases out of the ground and scooped up dirt from the field.

Cleon Jones in left field and Tommie Agee in center weren't taking any chances. They raced straight for the bullpen gate in right center, got off the field and out of harm's way, and headed for the clubhouse by way of a runway under the stands.

I clutched my glove tightly with one hand, grabbed my cap in my other hand, and took off on a dead run for the dugout as if I were going for a triple. The feeling of joy that swept over me was like nothing I had ever experienced. Hardly any of us had. The only player on our team who had so much as even been in a World Series was Ron Taylor, who got in two games for 4⅔ innings with the Cardinals against the Yankees in the 1964 Series.

Our clubhouse was pandemonium, overrun by players, Mets front-office workers, friends, family, the media, politicians, and assorted celebrities big and small. Cases of champagne were yanked open with little of the bubbly going down throats and most of it being sprayed around the room and on humans.

Holding forth in one corner of the room was that well-known Mets fan New York mayor John V. Lindsay. Coincidentally, ongoing at the time was a hotly contested and contentious mayoralty race among Lindsay, the incumbent, and his rivals Mario Procaccino and John Marchi. Lindsay had lost the Republican primary to Marchi and was on the ballot as the Liberal Party candidate. But most polls had Procaccino the winner, with Lindsay running a well-beaten third through most of the summer.

With the election scheduled for November 4, the month of October was critical, "the ninth inning," so to speak, for the candidates. Mayor Lindsay, who had previously evidenced no great affection for baseball, suddenly began showing up in Shea Stadium during our push for the National League East division title, the National League pennant, and the World Series championship.

Sociologists and political pundits have theorized that when citizens are euphoric because of outside forces—peace, the economy, the weather, the success of their sports teams—it bodes well for an incumbent in any election. In 1969, New York sports fans were euphoric. In January, the New York Jets had won Super Bowl III. The New York Knicks were embarking on a magical ride that would lead to their first NBA championship. And the New York Mets were performing miracles in Flushing.

Nineteen days after Cleon Jones cradled Davey Johnson's fly

ball to left field in his glove for the final out of the World Series and knelt on the ground, New Yorkers went to the polls and produced another upset: they reelected John Lindsay mayor by a margin of almost 200,000 votes over Mario Procaccino.

The political pundits attributed Lindsay's upset victory in part to the Mets' World Series victory.

Maybe Lindsay would have been elected even if we finished at the bottom again.

But maybe he wouldn't.

In another corner of the clubhouse, surrounded as usual by a gaggle of New York press, what he liked to call "my writers," was the old man, Casey Stengel, as pleased and proud of this victory as if he were still wearing a uniform and calling the shots.

"This club doesn't make any mistakes now," he rambled. "You can see they believe in each other, and the coaches all live in New York and you can get them on the phone, so I'm very proud of these fellas, which did such a splendid job, and if they keep improving like this, they can keep going to Christmas. The Mets are amazing."

We were amazing indeed. The Amazing Mets! We partied well into the night, slept little or not at all, and showed up early the next morning for a ticker-tape parade up Broadway, the third such parade in the city that year. In January, the New York Jets. In August, the Apollo 11 astronauts. In October, the New York Mets. Amazing! Simply amazing!

CHAPTER 8

We had won the World Series with a pitching staff that had an earned run average of 2.99 and included seven pitchers who were all twenty-six years old or younger. Among our starters, Jerry Koosman was twenty-six, Tom Seaver twenty-four, and Gary Gentry twenty-three. They combined for 55 wins, 14 shutouts, 748 innings, and 542 strikeouts. Tug McGraw, who won 9 games and saved 12, was twenty-five. Nolan Ryan was twenty-two. Jim McAndrew was twenty-five.

Most of our starting position players, including our right-handed half of our right-field platoon and the left-handed half of our first-base platoon, also was no older than twenty-six.

We had every reason to believe we were at the onset of a baseball dynasty. We had youth and success at a young age and we had Gil Hodges, who was not only shrewd as a manager but also a stern taskmaster whose powerful persona, we felt, was certain to guard against any complacency on our part. If we weren't a dynasty in the making, we figured we at least had the nucleus of a team that could win two or three more championships over the next five or six years.

We never thought it was just luck that enabled us to win in 1969. After all, we won 100 games, and you don't win that many games on luck. We felt that we were the National League counterpart to the Baltimore Orioles, who were a sort of an American

League dynasty through that era. We thought the winning should carry on for us, too.

The group that assembled in St. Petersburg in the spring of 1970 was pretty much the same cast that had won the 1969 World Series. What was different was the other teams' attitude toward us. Prior to 1969, teams had taken us lightly. But when we won the World Series, teams woke up. Now we were the team to beat and they were gunning for us. Right from the first day of spring training, they were looking to kick our butts. They were aggressive against us, even in spring training.

I could imagine players on the other teams saying, "Yeah, those guys are good, but we took them lightly." Nobody thought we could win in 1969. The oddsmakers didn't. Probably the only people who figured how good we were from the start were Hodges and our coaching staff. Gil was good at convincing us that we could do certain things and achieve certain goals with our abilities.

So it was naturally a letdown when we saw how everybody got up against us in the Grapefruit League. Not that we were sleeping after we won in 1969, but everybody had a different approach to us. First pitch, they might brush you back. Things like that. It had never happened to us before. Pitching had carried us to our World Series title, and pitching would let us down the next two years. In 1970 Seaver picked right up where he left off in the championship year, winning his first six decisions, including a tremendous performance in San Diego on April 22 when he struck out 19 Padres and ended the game by striking out the last 10 hitters. No pitcher had ever struck out 10 consecutive hitters, and none in the modern era had ever struck out 19 batters in a day game.

But after going 6-0, Tom lost 5 of his next 6 starts. He later went on a 9-game winning streak, but lost 6 of his last 7 decisions and finished with a record of 18-12, which was disappointing in light of his 25-7 record of the previous year.

Bothered most of the year by a sore elbow, Jerry Koosman went from 17-9 in '69 to 12-7 in '70. Gary Gentry, who had shoulder trouble, fell from 13 wins to 9, Tug McGraw from 9 wins to 4, Nolan Ryan went from a record of 6-3 to 7-11.

Among the hitters, only Donn Clendenon, with 22 homers, 97 RBI, and an average of .288, and Tommie Agee (24, 75, .286) surpassed or equaled their 1969 production. Cleon Jones slipped from .340 to .277, and Eddie Kranepool, who hit 11 homers and drove in 49 runs in the championship year, failed to hit a homer and had driven in only 3 runs in 43 games and was sent to Tidewater, our AAA International League farm team.

After winning 100 games in 1969, we fell to 83-79 in 1970 and finished in third place, 6 games behind the front-running Pittsburgh Pirates, the "We Are Family" team of Roberto Clemente, Willie Stargell, Al Oliver, and Manny Sanguillen that rose up and dominated the National League East in the early 1970s.

The 1971 season was more of the same, although Seaver rebounded to win 20. But Koosman was 6-11 and Ryan 10-14. Agee fell off from 24 homers and 75 RBI to 14 and 50, and Clendenon from 22 and 97 to 11 and 37 and was released. We finished with the exact same record as the previous year, 83-79, but fell one more rung to fourth place and finished 14 games out of first this time, again behind the Pirates.

Ironically, the 1970 and '71 seasons were two of my best. I reached a RBI high with 42 in '70 and, at .252, was two points below my high in batting average in '71. I also made the All-Star team both years, as a backup to Don Kessinger in 1970 and as the starting shortstop in 1971 when I won my only Gold Glove.

In the 1970 All-Star game in Cincinnati's Riverfront Stadium, I replaced Kessinger in the seventh inning with the AL leading, 1–0. They scored in the top of the seventh to make it 2–0 and I led off the bottom of the seventh against Gaylord Perry and singled to center in my first All-Star at bat. I came around to score to make it 2–1.

The American League scored 2 in the eighth and we came to bat in the bottom of the ninth trailing, 4–1. Dick Dietz led off the inning with a homer to make it 4–2. We had no other shortstop, so they couldn't pinch-hit for me and I lined a single to center off Catfish Hunter. Two at bats in the All-Star game and 2 hits off two guys who would eventually be elected to the Hall of Fame. I scored again and we wound up getting 3 runs to tie the game, 4–4, and force it into extra innings. We won it in the twelfth inning when Pete Rose barreled into Ray Fosse to score the winning run with a devastating pile-driving body block that knocked Fosse head over teakettle and left him writhing on the ground in pain. That sort of maneuver earned Rose his reputation as a hell-for-leather, no-holds-barred competitor, and something I would experience firsthand just three years later.

I remember Seaver and I walking into the National League clubhouse early in my first All-Star game. I looked around in awe. There's Roberto Clemente, Hank Aaron, Rico Carty, Johnny Bench, Dick Allen, Willie McCovey, and my idol, Willie Mays. Bob Gibson was there, and Tom went over to him and said, "Gibby, how are you doing?" and shook his hand.

I put my stuff down and walked over to Gibson, said, "Gibby," and extended my hand.

"Hi, how are you doing?" he said. But he wouldn't shake my hand.

Years later, Gibson was the Mets' pitching coach and I would see him once in a while and we would talk. One day I said, "I have a question to ask you," and I mentioned the incident in the 1970 All-Star game in Cincinnati. "You shook Seaver's hand but you wouldn't shake my hand."

"I never shake the hand of a hitter," he said.

Now I had him. "You considered me a hitter?"

He couldn't keep a straight face as he mumbled, "I pitched everybody the same."

I started the '71 game, batted twice, flied out to right and grounded out. That was the game in Detroit where 6 home runs were hit, including Reggie Jackson's monster shot that crashed against the clock in right field. Before the game I went out, shagged, took ground balls at shortstop, but I didn't take batting practice. With all those sluggers launching bombs, I figured nobody came to see me lay down three bunts and punch a couple of opposite-field loopers.

At the pregame introductions when they were announcing the starting lineup, I was getting ready to go out when my name was called. The public address announcer is introducing all these superstar sluggers . . . Willie Mays . . . Henry Aaron . . . Joe Torre . . . Willie Stargell . . . Willie McCovey . . . Johnny Bench . . . and behind me I hear somebody in our dugout say, "Buddy . . . you got a lot of guts going out there with those guys." I turned around, pointed to the array of stars lining up, and said, "There's nobody out there that can play shortstop." The moral of that story is there's a place for everybody. If you get good enough at something to make an All-Star team, you've earned it.

In 1972, Pirates manager Danny Murtaugh, who was the manager of the National League team in the All-Star game in Atlanta, picked me for the team as a backup to Kessinger. I declined out of pride. They said, "You made the All-Star team, do you want to go?" I said, "No. When is [Giants shortstop] Chris Speier going to go? He's having an All-Star year. He has more home runs than all of us put together. When is he going to go?"

So Speier went.

People say you should never decline no matter what. If I had been voted the starter, I would have gone, but it was a backup situation, not a starting position. What was to be gained by going? To have All-Star on my résumé? I already had All-Star on my résumé.

I had improved as a fielder largely because I wore out so many coaches hitting me ground balls, a routine I began all the way back in my high school days when I used to bug coach Don Curley to hit me ground balls by the hundreds, and continued right through my major league career. People used to tell me, "You take too many ground balls; you're going to wear yourself out." And I'd say, "Shouldn't I be the judge of that?"

I took ground balls to learn how the ball came off the dirt and the grass, which is different from one ballpark to the next and often from one day to the next. I always got a teammate—usually Seaver when he was available—to go to first base to take my throws because I didn't want to throw the ball back to the guy that hit it. That would be unnatural, something I'd rarely have to do in a game. You're trained that when the ball is hit to you, you have a timing mechanism in your head. You field the ball and you throw it to first base. That was usually what you had to do in the game, so that's what I did in practice.

Yogi Berra, when he was a coach for the Mets, was the fungo hitter that helped me the most. He had a knack for slicing them out there, and he would try to get them past me. That helped a great deal in improving my backhand. If I missed one, I was disappointed, and it didn't matter how they were hit, whether they were sliced or if they were scooters, whatever they were. I wanted all kinds of ground balls, every kind would go into my visual computer that I could draw upon when it came up in a game. I'd make a play and somebody would say, "How did you do that?" My answer was always the same: "I've seen it before." That's the benefit of taking thousands of ground balls in practice.

I played at a time when the National League had many outstanding shortstops, such as Maury Wills, Dick Groat, Dal Maxvill, Bobby Wine, Larry Bowa, Bill Russell, Dave Concepcion, Don Kessinger, Garry Templeton, Ozzie Smith, and my personal favorite, Roy McMillan.

When the Mets brought me up for 19 games in 1965, the regular shortstop was Roy David McMillan of Bonham, Texas, and I was there to be his backup because he was injured a lot. When I first saw him, I thought he was a coach. He was all banged up. He had a pull in his biceps and the muscle in his arm was all bunched up from all the injuries he'd sustained over the years. His ankles looked as if they had been broken a thousand times; they stuck out on the sides. He wore glasses. He was thirty-six, but looked older. I was twenty-one, and I'm sure I looked younger. But he treated me as an equal; like a pro.

Before coming to the Mets, McMillan had spent ten years with the Cincinnati Reds and three and a half seasons with the Braves in Milwaukee. He led National League shortstops in fielding percentage five times, three with the Reds and two with the Braves. He was the National League's starting shortstop in the 1956 and '57 All-Star Games. He won three Gold Gloves and would have won a few more but he was already in his seventh big league season in 1957 when Rawlings began awarding the Gold Glove for defense.

The first year, they gave out one award for both leagues, and McMillan won it at shortstop over Alvin Dark, Dick Groat, Luis Aparicio, Chico Carrasquel, and Harvey Kuenn. After that, they gave out an award at each position for each league. Roy won it at shortstop in the National League in 1958 and 1959.

I didn't see McMillan when he was in his prime. When I saw him, he was on the downside of his career. Because of all the injuries he had suffered, his arm was shot and he couldn't run well, but he sure could pick it at shortstop. He was still such a brilliant fielder at the age of thirty-six, I could only imagine how great he must have been at twenty-five or thirty.

Roy wasn't a big home-run threat or a big run producer, but he was a good, smart hitter; a dangerous hitter. I learned so much from him, and he was always nice to me and helpful. He wasn't the kind of guy that would impose himself on a young player, but I learned from him just by watching how he did things.

I'd skip batting practice a lot of times just to go out and take ground balls with him. I didn't want to get in his way or interrupt his routine, so I'd ask him, "Mac, can I take ground balls with you?" He would always say sure, and we'd alternate taking ground balls, Mac first and then me. He circled the ball to his right because he didn't have an arm. He'd glide to his right and get rid of the ball as soon as it hit his glove. I'd watch how he did it, and then I'd try to do it the way he did. I was a pretty good fielder to start with, but after watching Mac, I could sense that I was getting a fluidity that I didn't have before.

I'd say, "Mac, I like the way you move to your right for a ball," and he'd say, "You do it just fine." He didn't say change or do it my way. Simply, "You do it just fine."

Mac wasn't talkative. He wasn't the type to get into your head. If you do it enough, after a while you start doing things just the way he did. He had a great attitude; he always came to play. I like to think some of that rubbed off on me.

Maybe it was because he was an older player and I was so young and impressionable; maybe it was because I knew how much he had accomplished in his career; maybe it was because he was so nice to me; whatever the reason, I just idolized Mac so much. I considered him a role model and a mentor. Although he wasn't purposely going out of his way to help me—that wasn't his job, it was the coaches' job—he wasn't blowing me off either. He answered any questions I asked, showed me things I wanted to see, and always was positive and encouraging.

People would see the way I hung with McMillan like a puppy dog and they'd say to him, "You're helping this kid and he's going to take your job," and in that low-key Texas drawl of his Mac would say, "When it's time."

It was time in 1966. He reinjured his shoulder and that was it, he was done. I took over at shortstop. The Mets released Roy and made him a coach.

I liked McMillan a great deal. I liked him when he was a player and I liked him when the Mets kept him around as a coach. I owe so much to him. I wish I had let him know how much. Roy died in 1997 in Bonham, Texas, where he was born.

After McMillan retired, I got to see so many good shortstops, but I didn't see one as good as him until Ozzie Smith came along . . . and I still haven't. I admit that I didn't see Luis Aparicio, but I heard so much about him, and I know Omar Vizquel is phenomenal, but I haven't seen enough of him. To me, Ozzie Smith is number one at shortstop. He didn't have a great arm, but then the shortstop I admired most before Ozzie was Roy McMillan, and he didn't have a great arm either, but he'd still get you.

I always said to Ozzie, "I've never paid to get into a baseball game, but I'd pay to watch you play." And I meant it. He would just laugh.

Generally, I'll take the sure-handed shortstop that consistently makes the routine play over the flashy shortstop that makes the spectacular play but occasionally botches the routine play. I didn't try to be flashy when I played; I just tried to be basic. Ozzie is the one guy who is the exception. He could be both flashy and basic. He made the routine play and he made the highlight-reel plays. He was fabulous. Ozzie could do it all. He made the big plays and he did it with flair. When I look at a shortstop, I look for someone who does everything, goes in the hole between short and third, ranges far to his left for the ball over second base, gets rid of the ball quickly on the double play, is not afraid of outfielders and roams out far for pop flies.

Back in the day, the shortstop was generally a little guy in there primarily for his defense. In recent years—I guess it started with Baltimore's Cal Ripken Jr.—shortstops were bigger men and offensive forces as well as defensive specialists. Guys such as Barry Larkin, Hanley Ramirez, Troy Tulowitzki, Miguel Tejada, Alex Rodriguez, Derek Jeter, and Nomar Garciaparra.

Because I'm in New York and still involved with the Mets, I tried to keep close tabs on Jose Reyes. As I said before, I don't like flashy stuff, and Jose is flashy, but he is extremely gifted. He's got so much going for him. He's got speed, he's got an arm, he's got power; he can crank a ball. He was a catalyst on offense, the guy who makes things go. But he has to concentrate on trying to put the ball in play and not try to hit it out of the park.

I see that a lot with players who come out of the big leagues and play in the independent leagues. I tell them that if speed is their game and they want to get back to the big leagues, the most important thing for them is on-base percentage. If you're a leadoff hitter, you have to be able to bunt. You have to show bunt to bring the infielders up and then try to slap the ball past them. Sure, you can run, but you can't run if you strike out.

Reyes is a case in point. He's trying to hit the ball out of the park when he should just be trying to put the ball in play the way he can run. I can understand trying to go for the long ball on the first pitch of an at bat or even the second pitch. Go for it. After that, you have to play contact baseball; what Casey Stengel called "butcher boy." Hit down on the ball and just go; take off running like hell. You don't have to swing from your ass. You don't have to impress anybody with your power. We know you have power. A guy like Reyes will get a lot of leg hits and he'll raise his on-base percentage, and that's what he should be concentrating on doing.

Reyes is best when he hits down on the ball, line drives and ground balls. He has the speed to beat out a lot of infield hits. His focus should be to try to get on base, because with his speed he can be an asset by getting on base and stealing second or going from first to third on a hit.

On defense, Jose makes some great plays, but I'd like to see him be a little more consistent. He doesn't position himself well. I don't think he plays the count enough and studies the hitters. As an example, when I was playing and Johnny Bench came to bat, I stationed myself in the hole between third and short. Before he had any strikes on him, he'd try to pull the ball in that hole. With two strikes, he wouldn't try to pull the ball; he'd take a breaking ball away and just hit it up the middle, so I'd play him up the middle. I learned that by paying attention when Bench was hitting.

Same with Dave Winfield. He'd kill a pitcher if you threw him a breaking ball with two strikes. He didn't try to pull it. He would hang back and go up the middle with awesome power. But Roberto Clemente was different. He was always trying to hit the ball to the right side or up the middle with two strikes or no strikes. I would dare him to pull the ball, but he was more interested in hitting rockets to right. Occasionally, he'd go up the middle, so as a short-stop, where am I going to be? Up the middle. And that's where I played him. He'd hit the ball through the pitcher's legs and I'd be right there. I'd throw him out at first and he'd say, "Why you play me there?" I said, "Because that's where the ball is."

Sometimes I think the glove Reyes uses is too small. It's like a second baseman's glove. At shortstop you do a lot of diving and reaching, and for that reason I believe a shortstop needs a glove with length.

Still, the thing I worry most about with Jose Reyes is his health. For his team to succeed, he simply has to stay healthy.

CHAPTER 9

As it always does, spring training brought hope to the Mets in 1972. We still had basically the same corps that won the 1969 World Series, but we were older, wiser, more mature, and more experienced. For the most part, we were healthy. We also were reinforced with two impressive twenty-two-year-old newcomers: John Milner, a left-handed power hitter from Atlanta who would belt 17 home runs in 362 at bats, and Jon Matlack, a hard-throwing, six-foot-three-inch left-hander from West Chester, Pennsylvania, who would win 15 games, pitch to a 2.32 earned run average, throw 244 innings (no pitch-count limits back then, remember) and 4 shutouts, strike out 169 batters, and be voted National League Rookie of the Year.

Another newcomer to the 1972 Mets was the veteran Jim Fregosi, who was our big off-season acquisition in a trade with the California Angels. The Mets, for some time, had coveted Fregosi, an 11-year veteran and a 6-time American League All-Star. He made those All-Star teams as a shortstop, but the Mets didn't get him to play shortstop. They (ahem!) already had a shortstop.

What the Mets didn't have—and had never had—was a third baseman. In their first ten years, they had used forty-five third basemen. In those ten years, they also had eight different third basemen on opening day, from Z (Don Zimmer in 1962) to A (Bob Aspromonte in 1971). The Mets believed Fregosi was athletic enough to make the switch from shortstop to third base and, at twenty-nine, was young enough to hold down the position for several years.

The deal was made on December 10, 1971. To obtain Fregosi, the Mets gave up four young players, one of whom was Nolan Ryan. The Angels had refused to trade Fregosi unless they received a major league pitcher in return, and Ryan was their choice. Although still only twenty-four and the hardest-throwing pitcher in the National League, Ryan was considered the most expendable among the Mets pitchers, largely because of his wildness. Besides, Nolie was said to be unhappy in New York and had asked the Mets to trade him.

In an effort to expedite Fregosi's transition from shortstop to third base during spring training, manager Gil Hodges took on the project himself and attempted to force-feed Fregosi's conversion by hitting him hundreds of ground balls. Bad move! I consider myself something of an expert on ground-ball fungo hitters, and in all my years of taking ground balls, and the hundreds of thousands I have fielded, I never saw anybody hit harder ground balls than Hodges and big Frank "Hondo" Howard.

I warned Fregosi, "If Gil picks up a fungo bat, walk away. Get out of there, man. He'll kill you." Sure enough, one day early in spring training, Hodges was hitting fungoes to Fregosi and smashed one that jumped up and caught Jim on the thumb.

That was it! A dislocated thumb would keep Fregosi out of all but five exhibition games. Eager to get off to a good start with his new team, Fregosi rushed back into the lineup before the thumb was completely healed. As a result, he got off to a bad start and never became the player for the Mets that he had been with the Angels. He appeared in only 101 games that season, had 5 homers and 32 RBI, and a .232 batting average, his lowest since he hit .222 in 11 games for the Angels as a nineteen-year old in 1961. In 1973, Jim was batting .234 with no homers and 11 RBI in 45 games in July when the Mets sold him to the Texas Rangers. Later, Fregosi would become a respected major league manager for four teams, including the Philadelphia Phillies, whom he piloted to the National League pennant in 1993.

The Ryan-for-Fregosi trade is widely regarded as the worst the Mets ever made and one of the worst in baseball history. After leaving the Mets, Ryan would play 22 more seasons, win 295 games, strike out 5,221 batters, pitch 59 shutouts and 7 no-hitters for the Angels, Houston Astros, and Texas Rangers, and retire at the age of forty-six.

All through the spring of 1972, major league players were rumored to be preparing to strike for increased contributions to their pension and medical-benefit funds while the union and the club owners were negotiating those issues.

On Thursday, March 30, exactly one week prior to the scheduled start of the 1972 season, at a meeting in a hotel near the Dallas airport, player representatives voted to strike. On that same day, the Mets' confidence was sky-high as we defeated the Cincinnati Reds, 4–1, to give us a record of 15-8 in the Grapefruit League, the best exhibition record in Mets history.

In the next four days, however, we would endure unspeakable disappointment, torment, and tragedy that would turn our lives upside down.

We were scheduled to break camp in St. Petersburg that Friday and fly to West Palm Beach on Florida's east coast, where we would play one game with the Yankees in Fort Lauderdale and one game with the Montreal Expos in West Palm. On Monday we would head north and stop off in Kinston, North Carolina, and Norfolk, Virginia, for exhibition games against the Yankees at each stop. We would then continue to New York, settle in, work out for a few days, then go to Pittsburgh to open the season on Thursday, April 6. But with no new talks scheduled in the labor dispute, everything was in limbo. All remaining exhibition games were canceled, and the players were left pretty much on their own. Contractually, the teams' only obligation to the players was to provide them with transportation home or to New York.

The Mets and Yankees had agreed to share a charter plane to New York on Monday, April 3, carrying managers and coaches, executives, front-office workers, and their families. Players were welcome to board the flight, but to do so they would have to remain in Florida for three days at their own expense. I chose to fly home immediately after the strike was called.

Gil Hodges and his coaches, Rube Walker, Eddie Yost, Joe Pignatano, and Yogi Berra decided to spend the weekend at the Mets' hotel, the West Palm Beach Ramada Inn, resting, relaxing, and playing golf, then fly home Monday on the charter.

Sunday, April 2, was Easter. Hodges and Pignatano would attend morning mass, have breakfast, then meet up with Walker and Yost back at the Ramada for a round of golf on the hotel's course, Palm Beach Lakes. Berra was not included because he had made plans to have Easter dinner with some friends in the area.

According to Pignatano, Hodges and the coaches played eighteen holes, after which Hodges left, saying he wanted to arrange to have some fruit shipped home. He returned after fifteen minutes, and the foursome teed off and played nine more holes. When they were finished, they repaired to the clubhouse for a cold drink with the club pro, Jack Sanford, a former pitcher and rival of Hodges's, with the Philadelphia Phillies and the San Francisco Giants.

A half hour later, the group left the clubhouse and headed back to their rooms. On the walkway leading from the golf course to the inn, the group separated, Walker and Yost going one way to their rooms, Hodges and Pignatano going to their rooms in the opposite direction.

As they parted, Piggy asked, "What time should we meet for dinner?"

"Seven thirty," Hodges replied.

Those were the last words he ever said. According to Pignatano, he had turned his back to Hodges and was walking to his room when he heard Gil say, "Seven thirty." The next thing he heard, Pignatano said, was the sound of Gil's clubs hitting the walkway. When Piggy turned, he saw Hodges sprawled on the ground, blood gushing from a cut on his head. Piggy rushed over to him and cradled Gil in his arms.

Eddie Yost raced to the nearest phone and called the local police, a fire emergency unit, and an ambulance. Within minutes Hodges was being transported to nearby Good Samaritan Hospital, where he was pronounced dead. A doctor later told Piggy that Gil was dead when he hit the ground. It was two days before his forty-eighth birthday.

To this day, I still can't remember how I found out about Gil's death. I know I was back home on Long Island when I got the news. I also remember placing a call to Seaver, who was at his home in Greenwich, Connecticut, and I had the sad duty of breaking the horrible news to Tom. We spent a long time on the phone, talking about Gil, mourning his loss, and, yes, shedding a tear or two. Before the day was over, and in the next few days, I talked to many of my teammates and we all expressed the same emotions.

We were all devastated. Everybody loved him. Scared shitless of him, but respected and loved him.

After suffering his heart attack three and a half years before, Hodges made an effort to take better care of himself. He made certain to get his proper rest and he walked a lot. He came to spring training in 1969 looking fit. He was generally mild and soft-spoken to begin with, but now he was even more laid-back. Still, as a manager, he always got his message across. Sometimes he did it with merely a look.

Gil was respected by everybody. He knew how to handle the press. He knew how to handle the players. He knew how to handle the front office. He was such a physical specimen, you never thought about him dying. He was . . . Superman.

The people I talked to who were on the charter flight from

Florida to New York on Monday told me it was the most difficult flight they ever took, Gil's body, in a casket, being carried on board the plane as a reminder of man's mortality. Only the presence of children on the plane managed to lighten the mood a little.

A few days later, I attended Hodges's funeral in Brooklyn and grieved for him along with many of my teammates, Mets officials and office workers, as well as Gil's wife, Joan, and their children. It was Thursday, April 6. We were supposed to be in Pittsburgh that day, opening the 1972 baseball season against the Pirates, but the game had been canceled because of the players' strike. Instead of being in Pittsburgh playing a game, we were in Brooklyn bidding a solemn farewell to a man we'd all admired, respected, and loved.

CHAPTER 10

How fickle life is. One day we were riding high, filled with confidence, hope, and optimism for the season ahead, and only a few short days later we not only faced the possibility of no baseball for nobody knew how long—maybe the entire season—and if and when there was baseball, it would be without our leader, the one person who engendered those good feelings in us.

On April 13, seven days after Gil Hodges was buried and the 1972 season was scheduled to start, a settlement was reached in the baseball labor dispute. The season would open in two days (players had been working out on local high school and college fields across the country), and the schedule would be picked up from that date. The first general player strike in baseball history would erase 86 games from the schedule. The Mets would have 6 games shaved off their schedule.

On the night of Gil's funeral, the Mets announced (somewhat callously, insensitively, and dispassionately, many thought) that they had decided on Hodges's successor as manager. To cause as little upheaval as possible, and to continue the program implemented by Gil, they would give the job to one of his coaches. But of Hodges' four coaches—Rube Walker, Eddie Yost, Joe Pignatano, and Yogi Berra—the only one with managerial experience was Berra.

Eight years earlier, Berra had managed the Yankees to 99 victories and the American League pennant, but lost the 1964

World Series to the St. Louis Cardinals in 7 games and was fired as manager after only that one season. Now, lovable Yogi was going to be the manager of the Mets, faced with the burden of a players' strike and the challenge of replacing an icon.

The Mets players approved of the choice of Berra as Hodges's successor. We knew Yogi as a coach, and we liked and respected him. Just three months earlier, Berra had been elected to the Baseball Hall of Fame, and he would be inducted that summer along with Sandy Koufax and Early Wynn. That further elevated his stature in our eyes.

Yogi is one of God's gentlest and most likable creatures. He's the Sara Lee of baseball—"nobody doesn't like Yogi"—but he wasn't Gil Hodges, and that was a concern to some. It meant things were going to be done a little differently from what we were accustomed to, and since ballplayers are creatures of habit, that could be a problem.

For example, with Hodges, when I went to spring training and stepped on the scale and the needle stopped at 147 pounds, it was "You're the strongest 147-pound player I've ever seen."

With Yogi, when I went to spring training and I stepped on the scale and the needle stopped at 147 pounds, it was "Oh, God, Shorty, we haven't even played a game yet and you're already down to 147 pounds. You're gonna die down here."

Yogi always called me Shorty. He still does. I once asked him, "How can you call me Shorty when I'm taller than you are?"

"Oh, no, you're not."

I asked him how tall he was.

"Five-ten."

Now official records list him at five feet seven, and I think that's even giving him the benefit of the doubt.

"If you're five-ten," I said, "then I must be five-twelve."

No knock on Yogi. I love him. But he had a different style from Hodges's, not better, not worse, just *different*. With Gil, it was always positive; you'd walk away feeling that you could conquer the world. With Yogi, you'd walk away scratching your head, or chuckling, or both.

In fairness to Berra, stepping in to replace Hodges, who was beloved by all his players, and the way it came about, couldn't have been easy for him. Yogi knew how much we all admired Gil, and even though we liked and respected Yogi, inevitably there would be comparisons.

Fortunately for Yogi, we got our season off to a good start by beating the Pittsburgh Pirates, 4–0, in the delayed opener on April 15, 1972, before a sparse, and perhaps disillusioned, Shea Stadium crowd of only 15,893. Tom Seaver started, allowed 5 hits, no walks, and struck out 6 in 6 innings. Tug McGraw finished up with 3 hitless innings.

That day also marked the Mets debut of Daniel Joseph "Rusty" Staub, aka Le Grand Orange. With Donn Clendenon having been released, the Mets needed a big bat to replace him and focused on Staub, a nine-year veteran with the Astros and Expos. He was a 5-time All-Star and a prolific run producer who had hit 78 home runs, driven in 270 runs, drawn 296 walks, and twice batted over .300 in the previous three seasons with Montreal. To acquire Staub, the Mets gave up three promising young players, Ken Singleton, Mike Jorgensen, and Tim Foli, but, at the time, the team's mantra was to win now and let the future take care of itself, a program further mandated by the loss of Hodges.

The trade had actually been consummated before Hodges's death, with Gil's full knowledge and approval. However, because of the impending strike—and then Hodges's death—announcement of the deal was delayed.

Staub played right field in his Mets debut and moved seamlessly into the cleanup position in the batting order. In his first at bat, he singled leading off the second inning. Later he was intentionally walked, flied to center, and grounded to short. Rusty's season was shortened to 66 games by injury, but in the next three years he would bat .279, .258, and .282, hit 53 home runs, and drive in 259 runs. After the 1975 season, Staub was traded to the Detroit Tigers, but six years later, he became a free agent and returned to the Mets. He played the final five years of his tremendous 23-year career with the Mets and became not only one of the most popular Mets ever, but a New York favorite and one of my dearest friends. In 1986, I was honored to join Rusty as the first two players inducted into the Mets Hall of Fame.

After winning on opening day, we lost our next 2 games, then ran off 7 straight wins, 3 against the Cubs at home, 3 in San Diego, and 1 in Los Angel's. On April 28, our record was 8-2, the best start in Mets history.

Two weeks later, on May 11, the Mets announced they had traded for my baseball idol, the man I, and many others, consider the greatest player in baseball history.

As I mentioned earlier, as a kid I was a Yankees fan and Mickey Mantle was my favorite player. That was mainly because the only major league baseball I saw was the "Game of the Week" on television, and the Yankees seemed to be on all the time. When the Giants moved from New York to San Francisco, they were my hometown team, so I became a Giants fan. My dad and I would go to Candlestick Park, and that's when I discovered Willie Mays. I still admired Mantle for his awesome power and speed, but Mays did things on the baseball field that I never saw anybody else do . . . and I still haven't seen anybody else do.

First I admired Mays as a fan, and then I admired and respected him as an opponent. Now I was going to be his teammate. He was coming to the Mets in exchange for a young, right-handed pitcher named Charlie Williams, who would win 23 games in 8 major league seasons, and $50,000. I couldn't believe my great good fortune. I idolized Willie. When we got him, I was thrilled. How could we get Willie Mays? What, are they crazy? I wasn't thinking like an owner. I didn't understand the ramifications of the trade: the Giants looking to cut ties with him—he was getting to be a problem because he was Willie Mays and he was deserving of respect and adulation, but he was holding back the development of some of their young players—and the Mets wanting him to put people in the seats, and because their owner, Joan Payson, was a big New York Giants fan back in the day and Willie was her favorite player. The plan was for Mays to finish out his career where it began, in New York.

For a kid from Northern California that became a Giants fan, and a Willie Mays fan, having my idol as a teammate was a dream come true. Willie must have noticed that I went out of my way to hang near him or indulge him in baseball talk just to hear what he had to say or to watch what he did to pick up some pointers that would help me improve my game. If he did notice me hanging around, he never complained. I think he realized what I was doing, and why I was doing it.

When Mays joined us, the guys on the team, the veteran players, were calling him Buck, his nickname, and patting him on the back, and I was thinking, "You're not allowed to do that. He's an idol! What's more, he's *my* idol! You can't touch him like that."

We didn't know if Mays had anything left, but we soon found out that he still had plenty in his tank. When we got him, he had been in 19 games for the Giants, had 67 at bats, and was batting .184 without a home run and only 3 RBI. But he'd walked 17 times, proving he still commanded respect. About a week before the trade, we had played a 3-game series in San Francisco. Willie didn't start the first two games, but he pinch-hit in the first game and walked. He started the third game and had two hits and walked twice. Again, it showed that pitchers still feared him.

Mays's first game as a Met came on Sunday, May 14, eight days after his forty-first birthday, and it came at Shea Stadium, fittingly against the Giants. The happening attracted 35,505 fans, exactly the reaction the Mets hoped for. Because we had a set out-field of Cleon Jones in left, Tommie Agee in center, and Rusty Staub in right, Willie played first base and batted leadoff. I batted second. Imagine that, me batting behind my idol! In the first inning, Giants' starter, "Sudden" Sam McDowell, walked Mays, then he walked me and Agee to load the bases. Staub followed with a grand slam and we had a quick 4–0 lead.

In the second inning, Mays struck out. When he came to bat again, it was to lead off the bottom of the fifth with the score tied, 4–4, the Giants having scored 4 in the top half of the fifth against Ray Sadecki, another of their former players now with the Mets. Mays connected for the 647th home run of his fabulous career to give us a 5–4 lead. The crowd went berserk. It was just what they were hoping to see. Leave it to Willie to provide such an exciting and memorable moment in his first game in a Mets uniform. Jim McAndrew would pitch 3 shutout innings to protect the 5–4 victory over Willie's former team.

Mays's home run, and his presence, seemed to energize us. We won 11 straight games and on May 21, we had a record of 25-7 and were in first place in the National League East, 6 games ahead of the Pirates. It was beginning to feel like 1969 all over again.

Mays was used sparingly, but when he played, he contributed like the Willie of old. His second start as a Met came four days after his first. He walked to lead off the bottom of the first. Teddy Martinez followed with a shot to right, and Mays scored when he knocked the ball out of the mitt of Montreal catcher John Boccabella. We won, 2–1.

Three days later, Mays hit a 2-run homer in the eighth inning off Steve Carlton to give us a 4–3 win over the Phillies. Four days after that, in Chicago, his single in the fourteenth inning drove in what proved to be the winning run in a 3–2 victory over the Cubs.

Mays reached base at least once in each of his first 14 games as a Met. In that stretch, he batted .348, hit 2 home runs, scored 11 runs, and drove in 13.

Watching him daily in the field, on the bench, on the base paths, even at his age, was such a great joy. He did stuff on the bases that I never saw anybody else do. I remember one time against us when he was still with the Giants. He was on first base and he took off to steal second. I was covering and the throw was high. He slid in, and I jumped up for the throw, and when I came down, Mays grabbed me around the waist and started shoving me toward third base, yelling at me, "Hey, man," in that high-pitched, squeaky voice of his. The umpire had turned to watch the ball fly out to center field, and with his back to us, he couldn't see that Mays had me all entangled. When the ump turned around, Willie let go of me and the umpire said, "Interference, go to third." I got an error and Mays went to third. I got even with him another time when I got a hit to center field, rounded first base, and he threw behind me trying to pick me off. When he did, I went to second. He told me later that nobody ever did that to him. High praise from my idol!

Even when he was with us, he was still running wild on the bases. He'd round third and he'd be watching the throw home, and the next thing you knew he was kicking the catcher's mitt and knocking the ball away. Many times I saw him knock the ball away from the catcher as he scored on a hit, allowing the guy that hit the ball to go all the way to third base. He made it look like a Little League game with the ball getting away and players running all over the place.

On the bench, he was chirping all the time, shouting encouragement to his teammates. He's Willie Mays. He didn't have to do that. But he did it.

I saw him get knocked down, pitchers throwing up and in, knocking his helmet off and sending him sprawling in the dirt. Once I saw him get knocked down and watched as he got up, calmly put his helmet back on, and got back in the box without saying a word. The next pitch was six inches off the plate outside, but he reached out and hooked it into the left-field corner.

I had one not so pleasant experience with Mays when I stepped on his foot going after a pop fly. I always took pride in my ability to go back on pop flies. I'm proud that such a longtime knowledgeable observer as Ralph Kiner, who has followed baseball from as far back as the 1940s, used to say that I went into the outfield to get balls that he never saw other shortstops get. I learned that when a pop fly is hit to the outfield, it's the shortstop's (or second baseman's) ball until he's called off by the outfielder.

Apparently, Mays never learned what I learned, or he just didn't believe in it, because one day I went back into short center field for a pop fly. I listened, expecting to hear the great Willie Mays call me off the ball. When I heard no such thing, I figured he couldn't reach it and it was my play. I reached up to catch the ball, and as I did, I stepped on Willie's foot. Oh, no!

"Hey, Pee Wee, what are you doing out here?" he squealed.

"I didn't hear anything," I said.

"I don't call for the ball."

"Well, if you don't want to get stepped on again, you better start calling for it."

The next time he was in center field and there was a pop fly, he called for it.

I hadn't seen Willie in years when the Mets commemorated the final game in Shea Stadium at the end of the 2008 season by bringing in former Mets to take part in the ceremony. All the big names were there: Yogi, Tom Seaver, Mike Piazza, Darryl Strawberry, Dwight Gooden, Davey Johnson, and Willie Mays, all of them sitting in a row on the field. I was told Willie's eyesight was fading, so when I went over to him, I got real close, in his face, and said, "Willie, Bud Harrelson!"

"No shit!" he said in that familiar high-pitched voice. "I can see you."

Then he surprised me and proved he still has all his faculties and keeps up with things when he said, "You got a team here. How's it doing?"

*   *   *

Although he was no longer the great player he had once been, in 1972 Mays put up decent numbers for a part-time player of forty-one. He appeared in 69 games—at first base, in center field, and as a pinch hitter—batted .267, hit 8 home runs, drove in 19 runs, and walked 43 times.

There were brief flashes of his former brilliance, and some memorable moments, but they were all too few, and they couldn't overcome a succession of crippling injuries that struck other members of the team. At one time, Mays could carry a team, but at forty-one, he was no longer able to help us overcome such adversity as:

- On June 3, Staub, off to a flying start as a Met with a .317 average, 7 home runs, and 27 RBI in 43 games, was hit on the hand by a pitch from Atlanta's George Stone. X-rays were negative, but the pain persisted. Unable to firmly grip a bat, Staub's average dwindled and his power declined. Two weeks later, when the pain had still not subsided, Rusty was shut down for a month. He returned to the lineup on July 18 with the team in Los Angeles, had a single in 4 at bats, but complained to Berra that the hand still bothered him. The Mets sent him for more X-rays. This time doctors discovered a fractured bone. Two days later, an operation was performed, and Rusty was sidelined until September 18. In all, he missed 90 games, batted .293, hit 9 homers, and drove in 38 runs, only 2 of his homers and 11 RBI coming after he first injured his hand on June 3.
- On June 16, Cleon Jones injured his elbow in a collision with Joe Morgan. He would miss 50 games and finish with a batting average of .245, a decline of 74 points from the previous season.

- Late in June, Tommie Agee pulled a groin muscle. He missed a week, returned to the lineup, and reinjured the groin, which put him on the sidelines for three more weeks. His average would fall from .285 in 1971 to .227 in '72, and he would be traded to the Houston Astros after the season.

- Jim Fregosi, our big off-season acquisition, missed 55 games because of his fractured thumb and batted .232 with 5 home runs and 32 RBI, hardly the production the Mets had in mind when they traded for him.

- I suffered much of the season with a bad back and missed 41 games.

Little wonder that things began to fall apart after our fast start. It's no surprise that the decline began with the injury to Staub, whose bat had been a major reason we had jumped off to that good start and had such high hopes for the season. On June 5, two days after Rusty was hit on the hand by a pitch, we dropped out of first place. We managed to get back into first place a week later, and for the next two weeks we jockeyed for first place on and off with the Pirates.

On July 2, we lost to the Expos, 4–3, our 20th loss in our last 38 games. We dropped out of first place for good and began our free fall in the standings. Two weeks later, we were five games out of first, and by August 19 we had fallen 12 games behind the Pirates. We ended the season in third place, 13½ games out of first.

As difficult a position as Yogi was in taking over for Hodges, and under the circumstances in which he got the job, it would have been much tougher for him had we won the World Series, or even a pennant, under Hodges in 1970 or '71.

As it was, under Berra we won 83 games, the exact same number we had won in '70 and '71 with Hodges as our manager. In fact, because we had 6 games canceled by the strike, Yogi's record of 83-73 was better than the 83-79 records of Hodges' last two seasons.

Nevertheless, the jackals were out after Berra in full force, and Yogi's job was squarely on the line as we began the 1973 season.

CHAPTER 11

By 1973, the euphoria of the Miracle of 1969 had worn off. No doubt spoiled by the team's sudden and unexpected success, the natives were getting restless. For three years, the Mets were underachievers, wallowing in mediocrity and hovering around the .500 mark, which meant we were losing just about as many games as we were winning. In those three years we won 249 games and lost 231, a mere 18 games over .500, and a winning percentage of .519, which our fans considered less than satisfactory.

Two more important members of our 1969 world championship team were missing when we reported for spring training in 1973. Tommie Agee had been sold to the Houston Astros, and Gary Gentry was involved in our one big off-season deal. He and another pitcher, Danny Frisella, were sent to the Atlanta Braves for left-handed pitcher George Stone (the guy who threw the pitch that broke the bone in Rusty Staub's hand) and second baseman Felix Millan.

Millan, who was a seven-year veteran and a 3-time All-Star, was to be my double-play partner. He was a smooth-fielding, sure-handed glove man who was a master at turning the double play. He didn't have much power at bat, but he was a tough out, an excellent line-drive hitter who, over the 1969-70-71 seasons, accumulated 524 hits for the Braves. When he fell off to 128 hits in 1972, the Braves traded him, probably thinking he was on the decline. But he

129

was only twenty-nine years old and he bounced back to get 185 hits and bat .290 for us in 1973. He also turned out to be the best double-play partner I ever had.

Once again, hopes soared when we got off to another fast start in 1973. We won our first 4 games of the season and finished the month of April with a 1–0 victory over the Braves on Jerry Koosman's 4-hitter, his 4th win of the season. Going into May, we were 12-8 and in first place, a half game ahead of the Cubs.

We lost the next 5 games, but rebounded and hung around the .500 mark through most of May. On May 24 in Los Angeles, we beat the Dodgers, 7–3, in a 19-inning marathon to improve our record to 20-17. But the game lasted five hours and forty-two minutes, which apparently took a lot out of us, because we then lost our next 4 games and 12 of our next 15 to drop to 23-29 and fall into fifth place, 8½ games out of first.

On June 4 in Cincinnati, Bill Plummer barreled into me attempting to break up a double play, connected with my glove hand, and broke a bone. I wound up on the disabled list and didn't return to the lineup until July 9. That gave my backup, Teddy Martinez, his chance.

Martinez was a kid out of the Dominican Republic who had a world of talent; but he was slightly lacking in ambition. He would complain to me that he never got a chance to play, then when I got hurt and he had to play every day, he told me, "When you come back? Me tired."

Martinez played 9 seasons in the big leagues with four teams, but the most games he ever played in any season was 116 in 1974, and the most he ever started was 90, also in '74.

On July 31, exactly twenty-two days after I returned from the disabled list, I was injured again. It happened against the Pirates at Shea. We had Rennie Stennett in a rundown, and as I tagged him, he crashed into me. I suffered a fracture of the sternum and would be out for another three weeks. We lost the game, 4–1, which dropped our record to 44-57. We were last in the National League East, 10½ games out of first, and members of the media as well as most of our fans were calling for Yogi to be fired.

While all around him there was panic, Yogi remained calm, confident, and optimistic (some might say he was unrealistic). He insisted that we were not dead yet and frequently pointed out that every team in the NL East had had a little hot streak except the Mets. "We got ours coming," he preached, and reminded one and all that the Mets weren't out of contention until they were mathematically eliminated.

My latest injury would keep me out for 16 games, and the team would lose 9 of them and fall to a season-low 15 games under .500, yet miraculously we gained ground. We were still in last place, but instead of being 10½ games out of first, we were now only 7½ games behind.

I returned on August 18 in time to take part in a 12–1 beating of Cincinnati. We split the next two games with the Reds and beat the Dodgers in the first game of a 3-game series at Shea. On August 22, we trailed the Dodgers 3–2 when Cleon Jones opened the bottom of the ninth with a single. Tug McGraw sacrificed him to second, but Wayne Garrett flied to center and we were down to our final out.

Felix Millan singled to left to score Cleon with the tying run. Staub singled to send Felix to second and John Milner followed with a single that scored Millan to give us a dramatic, come-from-behind, 4–3 victory.

After the game, Berra addressed the press and is reported to have said something like "I told you guys it ain't over until it's over," words that would become a rallying cry for our season and would become indelibly entered into the language, in and out of baseball, and be repeated thousands of times in succeeding years, even to this day.

Despite the win, we were still in last place, but only 6 games out of first, and even after we lost 3 of our next 4 games and remained in last place, we were only 6½ games out of first and still had 34 games left.

It was just about that time that M. Donald Grant, the Mets' chairman of the board, decided to pay a rare visit to our clubhouse and try to boost our spirits with a pep talk. He said, in essence, the usual platitudes athletes hear from coaches beginning in Little League on up to the majors. He told us there was still time to turn our season around, that we shouldn't give up. He said we had to have faith and believe in ourselves and in our teammates. He went on like that, frequently uttering the word *believe*. When he was finished, Mr. Grant started walking toward the exit. He was just about out the door when Tug McGraw, always a bit of a flake, a little kooky, outspoken and irreverent, jumped up and began shouting, *"You gotta believe, you guys. You gotta believe."*

I'm sure Tug thought Grant was already out the door, but he wasn't. Hearing Tug shouting and obviously thinking he was being mocked—and he probably was—Grant came back into the clubhouse and confronted McGraw. Leave it to Tug to think quickly and turn a negative into a positive. He looked Grant right in the eye and said, "You're right, Mr. Grant. You gotta believe," and all around him players were nodding their heads in agreement.

Grant bought the whole thing, and the next thing you knew, "You gotta believe" became another rallying cry for us. Whenever we'd win a game, we'd rush into the clubhouse and Tug would be shouting at the top of his voice, *"You gotta believe! You gotta believe!"*

It didn't hurt that at the time Tug was having a career renaissance after a terrible August. In his last 19 appearances of the season, he would win 5 games and save 12 others without losing a game or blowing a save.

On August 31, McGraw got the win when we beat the Cardinals in St. Louis, 6–4, in 10 innings and climbed out of last place.

On September 7, we went to Montreal and swept a doubleheader from the Expos. In the first game, Tug replaced Jon Matlack with 2 outs and runners on first and second in the bottom of the ninth and got the final out to save the 1–0 victory. In the second game, Tug pitched 5⅓ innings in relief and got the win when we scored 3 runs in the top of the fifteenth (Tug drove in 2 runs himself with a single) for a 4–2 victory.

With the sweep, we had won 4 straight games and 7 out of 10 and had moved up to fourth place only 4 games out of first.

Two weeks later, we received an omen that maybe we were destined to win the pennant. It came on September 20 with the first-place Pirates at Shea for the middle game of a crucial 3-game series. We had won the series opener and were now tied with the Cardinals for third place, just a game and a half behind the Pirates.

On the afternoon of the second game of the series, Willie Mays announced that the 1973 season would be his last. He did, however, say he would be with us if the Mets made it to the World Series.

That night, we were tied with the Pirates 3–3 after 9 innings. We went to the thirteenth, still tied, 3–3, when Richie Zisk singled with one out. After Manny Sanguillen flied out for the second out, rookie Dave Augustine hit a drive to deep left field. When it left the bat, it looked like a home run, but it hit the top of the wall, on the point of the wooden fence, like a "pointer" in stoop ball. A fraction of an inch higher and it would have ricocheted off the wall and gone over for a home run. Instead, it bounced back onto the field and right into the glove of the left fielder, Cleon Jones, who turned quickly and fired a perfect strike to third baseman Wayne Garrett, the cutoff man. Garrett, in turn, whirled and threw a perfect strike to catcher Ron Hodges (no relation to Gil) at the plate. Zisk was out.

We had dodged a bullet, the sort of thing that happens to teams on their way to winning a pennant. In the bottom of the thirteenth, Hodges singled home the winning run for a 4–3 victory. We were now a half game behind the Pirates and beginning to feel that this was our year. *You gotta believe!*

The next afternoon, we hit 3 home runs, by Milner, Garrett, and Staub, and pounded out 13 hits to clobber the Pirates, 10–2, completing a sweep of the 3-game series and taking over first place.

It felt good being back in first place. It wasn't quite the euphoria of 1969, when it was so unexpected. This time it was vindication. Once you get a taste of winning, it's tough to let go of that feeling, and it had been four years since we won; four long years of high expectation and complete failure.

Once we got into first place, we refused to let it go. We won our next 3 games to build our winning streak to 7 and went into the final weekend of the season in a three-team race with the Pirates and Cardinals for the National League East title. We held the upper hand, a game ahead of the Pirates, 2½ games up on the Cardinals. We were scheduled to finish up with 4 games in Chicago, Friday night, Saturday afternoon, and a doubleheader on Sunday, against the Cubs, who were 4 games back.

It rained on Friday. We were now faced with doubleheaders on Saturday and Sunday. It rained again on Saturday. It meant we would have to extend the season to Monday, with doubleheaders, if needed, on both Sunday and Monday.

As we started play on Sunday, September 30, our lead was 1½ games over the Cardinals, 2 games over the Pirates. The standings looked like this:

	WON	LOST	GAMES BEHIND	GAMES REMAINING
New York	80	78	—	4
St. Louis	80	81	1½	1
Pittsburgh	79	81	2	2

We lost the first game of the Sunday doubleheader to the Cubs, 1–0. The Cardinals won their game and the Pirates lost theirs. At that point, we were only a half game ahead of the Cards, who had completed their schedule, and 2 games ahead of the Pirates, who had 1 game remaining. We had 3 games left, including the second game of the Sunday doubleheader.

We coasted to a 9–2 win over the Cubs, which eliminated the Pirates and gave us a 1-game lead on the Cardinals, whose only chance now was to finish tied with us if we lost both games of the Monday doubleheader.

Tom Seaver started the first game of the doubleheader and took a 6–2 lead into the bottom of the seventh when Rick Monday put the pressure on us with a 2-run homer that cut our lead to 6–4. Tug McGraw came in and held the Cubs to just 1 hit over the last 3 innings to protect the 6–4 win. We would not have to play the second game of the doubleheader.

After the game, while Mets players sprayed champagne in Wrigley Field's visitors' clubhouse, Tug stood in the center of the room shouting, *"You gotta believe! You gotta believe!"*

Yogi had said, "It ain't over till it's over," but now it *was* over. We had won 24 of our last 33 games, and we were champions of the National League East with a record of 82-79, a winning percentage of .509, the lowest in baseball history for a champion.

Now the fun was really going to start. We would be meeting the Cincinnati Reds, Sparky Anderson's Big Red Machine of Johnny Bench, Tony Perez, Joe Morgan, and Pete Rose, in the best-of-five National League Championship Series.

CHAPTER 12

They were the Big Red Machine, a name to strike fear in the hearts of players and fans of National League teams in St. Louis, Chicago, Pittsburgh, Los Angeles, and New York.

They were the Cincinnati Reds, managed by Sparky Anderson, a young, aggressive, swashbuckling, progressive-thinking leader who took over the reins at the age of thirty-six and immediately changed the fortunes of the National League's oldest franchise. As a rookie manager in 1970 he won 102 games, 13 more than the previous season, and led the Reds to their first pennant in nine years.

Now, he was coming off his third pennant in four seasons, with 99 wins and a four-year record of 375-265, for a winning percentage of .586, and fortified with a powerhouse lineup that included five members of that season's National League All-Star team, three of them starters.

Three Reds, Johnny Bench, Tony Perez, and Joe Morgan, had combined for 78 home runs and 287 runs batted in, with Bench third in the league with 104 RBI and Perez sixth with 101.

Pete Rose was the league's batting champion with a .338 average. He was the consummate leadoff man with 230 hits, tops in the league, 65 walks, an on-base percentage of .401, 115 runs, to go along with 5 homers and 64 RBI.

Pete was an all-out, hell-for-leather, hard-nosed player whose recklessness earned him the name Charlie Hustle, a reputation that was solidified in the 1970 All-Star game in Cincinnati when he rammed into catcher Ray Fosse of the Cleveland Indians in the bottom of the twelfth inning to score the winning run. I was on the bench at the time and I could see the collision clearly. The force of the blow and seeing Fosse sprawled on the ground in pain almost made me nauseous.

The National League won the game and Pete was the hero of the victory, but at the same time he cost Fosse his career. Fosse had been a promising twenty-three-year-old catcher who made the All-Star team in his first full season. He was batting .312 with 16 homers and 46 RBI. The collision left him with a separated and fractured shoulder. When he returned to the active roster, he would have missed 34 games, and he would hit only 2 more home runs and drive in 15 runs the remainder of the season. Two years later, the Indians traded him to Oakland. Fosse would play 12 seasons with four teams, but he would never be the same player after the collision.

Rose never apologized to Fosse or showed any remorse for the collision. His only comment when he was asked about it was the sort of justification you might expect from as fierce a competitor as Rose was: "I was trying to get to home plate and he [Fosse] had it blocked."

The 1973 Reds didn't have a great pitching staff, but they were efficient. Jack Billingham won 19 games and pitched 7 shutouts. Don Gullett won 18 games with 4 shutouts. The bullpen was led by Pedro Borbon, with 11 wins and 14 saves, and Clay Carroll, with 8 wins and 14 saves.

In Anderson's first three seasons, the Reds had won two pennants, but lost both World Series. In 1970, they were done in by the brilliant defense of Brooks Robinson and lost to the Baltimore Orioles in 5 games. In 1972, they lost in 7 games to the Oakland A's and the pitching of a couple of Hall of Famers, Jim (Catfish) Hunter, who won 2 games, and Rollie Fingers, who appeared in 6 of the 7 games, won 1 game and saved 2 others. The Reds were still seething over losing to Oakland, so they remained unfulfilled and hungry coming into the National League Championship Series. Having beaten us 8 out of 12 games in the regular season, they were extremely confident and were overwhelming favorites. That didn't bother us. The Baltimore Orioles also were heavily favored against us in the 1969 World Series.

Tom Seaver had had another outstanding season with 19 wins (one win short of a third consecutive 20-win season), a league leading 2.08 earned run average, 18 complete games, and 251 strikeouts. But he had been having some shoulder discomfort, probably because of fatigue caused by his heavy workload. Still, he was chosen by Yogi Berra to pitch Game 1 against the Reds and figured to benefit from four days off before the start of the series.

We opened the NLCS in Cincinnati on Saturday, October 6, and Seaver was brilliant. Through the first 7 innings, he held the Reds to 3 hits, a double by Bench in the second, a double by Dan Driessen in the fourth, and a single by Cesar Geronimo in the fifth. Not only was he leading 1–0, Tom had driven in the only run himself with a double that scored me after I had been walked by Billingham with two outs in the second.

Seaver would set a league play-off record by striking out 13 Reds, but in the bottom of the eighth, Rose hit a home run to tie the score, and with one out in the bottom of the ninth, Bench homered and we were beaten, 2–1. While it was a heartbreaking loss, we consoled ourselves with the thought that we had seen this before. We also lost the first game of the '69 World Series on the road, and Seaver was also the losing pitcher then. We all know what happened after that. Now, for Game 2 against the Reds, we were putting our faith in 14-game-winner Jon Matlack, hoping he could stifle the Big Red Machine just as another Mets left-hander, Jerry Koosman, had done to the Baltimore Orioles in Game 2 of the '69 World Series.

Matlack did even better. Rusty Staub's home run off Gullett in the fourth gave us a 1–0 lead, and Jon protected it all the way into the ninth, when we scored 4 more runs. Matlack was superb. He shut the Reds down on 2 singles, both by Andy Kosco, and struck out 9 for a 5–0 win that made the Big Red Machine look like a Tinkertoy. And that's how all the fuss got started.

My misfortune was that Matlack's locker in Riverfront Stadium was next to mine. The game was over and the writers came in and were huddled around Matlack's locker, but Jon wasn't there; he was being interviewed on national TV. So there I was, fair game, just sitting there in front of my locker. The writers must have been bored or impatient waiting for Jon because they decided to talk to me. (I did have an RBI single in the ninth that knocked in our fifth run, but I doubt that was why they were talking to me; in fact, my single and RBI never came up in the conversation.)

"What did you think about the Reds against Matlack?" someone asked.

"They looked like me hitting," I replied.

I didn't single out Pete Rose, or anybody else. I meant the whole team, but I think it got twisted because somebody came back to me later and said, "So-and-so in the other clubhouse said this and that," and I said, "What?" I couldn't understand why anybody would be upset. What I said was typical of my weird sense of humor. My statement was more of a put-down of me than it was of any of the Reds, saying that they all looked like me hitting against Matlack. And they did. They couldn't hit. Not that day. This great team: the Big Red Machine. Matlack just dominated them. They were defensive, like me with two strikes.

I didn't think anything of it until a day later when we were taking batting practice before Game 3 in Shea Stadium. I was at the cage with Rusty Staub, and Joe Morgan came over and he was mad. He grabbed me by the shirt and said, "If you ever say that about me again, I'll punch you."

I knew Morgan. He's about a year older than me and we grew up in the same area in Northern California.

Rusty jumped in and said to Joe, "I don't know what's going

on, but Bud didn't say anything about you or about anybody in particular."

I don't know what was actually said by a writer or how it got twisted, but the Reds had been built up as this juggernaut and Matlack shut them down, and then some writer goes in their clubhouse and repeats my remark to them, so you can see why they'd get all ticked off about it.

Staub seemed to calm Morgan down because Joe said to me, "Okay, I'm fine with it, but Pete's not and he's going to use it. Pete's going to get you. He'll do anything to win."

And that's how things stood when we started Game 3 on October 8.

We jumped all over left-hander Ross Grimsley from the start. Staub hit a solo home run in the first inning and a 3-run homer in the second, when we scored 5 runs for a 6–0 lead.

The Reds scored 2 in the third on a home run by Denis Menke and 3 straight singles by pinch hitter Larry Stahl, Rose, and Morgan. With only one out and Tony Perez and Johnny Bench due up, this was the Reds' chance to get back in the game. But Jerry Koosman got Perez on a fly to center and Bench on a force-out, and you could see the air come out of the Reds' balloon.

By the fifth inning, we had increased our lead to 9–2, which only added to the Reds' mounting frustration. With one out, Rose singled and I thought this would be the perfect time for the Reds to start something. They were behind by 7 runs, Koosman was pitching well, the game was as good as lost; they could have been looking for something to motivate them for the remaining two games, and Rose was just the guy to motivate them. As Morgan told me, Pete "will do anything to win." I found out later that Pete had said he was going to do something to get me at second base to fire up the team.

Sure enough, Morgan smashed a ball to first baseman John Milner, who fielded it and fired to me at second to start the double play. That's when all hell broke loose.

Somehow I managed to get the throw off to first for the double play, and as I did, Rose came barreling into me. I had no problem with his intention. I had a huge problem with his execution. I knew what he was doing, trying to motivate his team, but I thought the way he went about it was unnecessary and over-the-top.

Let me say that I've always liked Pete. I never had a problem with him before that incident. I got along with him fine. In fact, he and another Red, Tommy Helms, were kind of mentors to me. When I first came up, they told me they liked my enthusiasm and the way I played the game. When I struggled, they encouraged me. They told me to relax, and they gave me some pointers. I never forgot that. I had a lot of respect for Pete, but here, in Game 3 of the NLCS, I didn't like what he did. He hit me after the play was over.

I was really mad, but I wasn't worried about being beat up or anything. To me it was a cheap shot and I let him know that. I wanted to make my point, that I thought it was unnecessary. I'd already made the double play. I was watching the ball going to first base and he slid in there and *pow!* I was pissed. I said something to him, cursed him, and he said I didn't know him well enough to talk to him like that. I really wanted to hit him, but I was afraid to hit him. I figured it would be better not to hit him. After all, he was one of my idols. But if my brother had done that, I would have been in his face, too. I never was afraid to stand up for myself against anybody.

When he took me down, I thought, "This is serious stuff."

We were rolling around on the ground, in the dirt, and guys were pouring out of the dugouts and out of the bullpens, and little scuffles erupted all over the field. Buzz Capra, one of our pitchers, came running out of our bullpen. At the same time Pedro Borbon came running out of their bullpen, and he blindsided Capra, threw a punch when Buzz was looking the other way and hit him in the ear. Then the two of them started pummeling each other.

Willie Mays grabbed Capra to protect him, and when the Reds saw Willie holding Buzz, they backed off because nobody wanted to mess with Willie. In the melee, Capra's cap flew off and was lying on the ground. When things quieted down, Borbon picked up Capra's hat thinking it was his and put it on his head. One of Borbon's teammates pointed at the cap, so Pedro took it off, looked at it, and when he saw it was a Mets cap, he took a big bite out of it. Ripped it into three pieces! Funny thing—both Pete Rose Jr. and Pedro Borbon Jr. played for me with the Long Island Ducks.

I thought I was going to get thrown out of the game, but I wasn't. Neither was Pete. We would probably have both been thrown out if it were a regular-season game, but I guess they let us stay because it was the play-offs. Too bad! If we were both thrown out, that's a bad trade for Cincinnati, losing a .338 hitter while we lost a .258 hitter.

Eventually, peace was restored, but when the Reds took the field for the bottom of the fifth, the fans acted disgracefully. They threw things at the players, fruit and vegetables, eggs, programs, cups filled with liquid, beer cans and bottles. When a whiskey bottle whizzed past the ear of Rose, standing invitingly and unprotected in left field, Pete headed for the dugout and Sparky Anderson waved his entire team off the field. I didn't blame Sparky. I'd have done the same thing in his place. A manager has to protect his players and not subject them to injury.

National League president Chub Feeney called Yogi Berra to his box and asked him to plead with the fans to stop throwing stuff at the Reds. A public address announcement warned that if such behavior continued, the Mets would forfeit the game. Berra then led a contingent of Mets—Mays, Seaver, Staub, and Cleon Jones—to left field to plead with the fans, and the game continued without further incident.

Koosman finished up, allowing 2 more hits but no runs. He completed the game with 9 strikeouts and no walks in the 9–2 victory, which gave us a 2–1 series lead.

I was naturally a center of attention from the media after the game. I tried to answer questions without making any more remarks that might be misinterpreted. I didn't want to cause any more problems or give the Reds, Rose especially, any more bulletin-board material.

I wanted to low-key things after that. I didn't want to talk to anybody, but Tom Seaver said, "Just make light of it." And that's what I did. The next day I pulled out this old Superman shirt that I liked to wear under my uniform shirt. I took two strips of white adhesive tape and taped them across Superman and wrote *Ha! Ha!* on the tape.

I was sorry that the whole thing happened, but I wasn't sorry that I stood up to Rose.

CHAPTER 13

I tried as best I could to put the ugly incident of Game 3 of the National League Championship Series behind me. We all did. Although we were in a commanding position—up 2–1 in a best-of-five series and with the final two games in our own ballpark—we still had some work ahead of us. We knew the Reds, Pete Rose especially, were going to be all fired up and determined for the next two games, and we were right.

The fourth game was a classic, a 12-inning nail-biter. The pressure on both teams was stifling, not quite as intense on us as it was on the Reds because we had our hometown fans to cheer us on and we had a safety net: if we lost this game, there was always tomorrow. The Reds, however, were fighting for their lives and doing it on the road, in front of a wildly hostile crowd. To their credit, the Reds players held up under the heat.

The game turned into a tremendous pitchers' duel of veteran left-handers—George Stone for us, Fred Norman for them—who were relatively new to their respective teams. We had acquired Stone from the Braves in the Felix Millan deal during the off-season, and George had been a major contributor to our division championship with a record of 12-3. The Reds got Norman from the San Diego Padres just three days before the June 15 trading deadline, and Norman won 12 games for Cincinnati.

We scored the first run of the game in the bottom of the third on two walks and a single by Millan. Through five innings, that was our only hit off Norman, who was gone when we came to bat in the bottom of the sixth. With time running out on him, Sparky Anderson had no choice but to pinch-hit for his pitcher in the top of the sixth and in the bottom half, Sparky brought in his Game 2 starter, the hard-throwing lefty Don Gullett.

Stone, meanwhile, was being just as stingy as Norman. He retired the Reds in order in each of the first 3 innings.

In the fourth, Rose led off with a single, and I have to admit, I was a little antsy watching Pete lead off first. When Tony Perez hit a bouncer to second baseman Millan, I couldn't help thinking, "Oh, oh, here we go again."

I said to myself, "Let him come." I wasn't going to back off. I was prepared for anything.

As he always did, Rose came in hard to second base, attempting to break up the double play. He slid underneath me and I jumped over him and threw to first to complete the double play. I had no problem with his slide this time. It was hard, but it was clean. The day before his slide was *not* clean, it was unnecessary.

In the fifth, Johnny Bench also led off with a single, and he, too, was erased on a double play. And in the sixth, Stone got the Reds out in order.

Morgan led off the top of the seventh and Stone got him on a comebacker to the mound. The next hitter was Tony Perez, who had been held hitless by the Mets in 14 at bats. This time he connected, sending one into the left-field seats to tie the score, 1–1. Stone got Bench to pop to Millan, but when he walked Andy Kosco, Yogi went to the bullpen and brought in Tug McGraw.

At that point, the left-handers, Gullett and McGraw, took control of the game. Gullett pitched 4 shutout innings through the ninth, allowed only 2 singles and struck out 3. He left for a pinch hitter in the tenth. Clay Carroll replaced Gullett and pitched 2 hit-less innings.

McGraw pitched 4⅓ shutout innings, allowed 4 hits and 3

Back in Sunset High School, I went by my maiden name, not Darrell, not Derrell, not Darryl, but Derrel, with one "L." That's D-E-R-R-E-L. (*Author's Collection*)

I dazzled them in New York when I showed up at Shea Stadium in this nifty getup. I still have that jacket and it still gets stares of envy. At least I think the stares are envy. (*Author's Collection*)

I'm erased at second base in the start of a double play by the Baltimore Orioles in the first inning of Game 4 of the 1969 World Series. What irony that Davey Johnson, the Orioles' second baseman on this play, would later become the manager of the Mets and I would be one of his coaches. (*Author's Collection*)

With three of my favorite people, Rusty Staub, my roommate Tom Seaver, and my baseball father, Gil Hodges. Little did I know that, sadly, Hodges would die of a heart attack a short time later; Seaver would be traded to Cincinnati; and, happily, Staub would become my teammate. *(Author's Collection)*

Batting against the Red Sox in a spring training game. *(Author's Collection)*

The momentous "Duel in the Sun" at Shea Stadium; the fifth inning of Game 3 of the 1973 National League Championship Series against the Cincinnati Reds on October 8. Here I am hitting Pete Rose on the fist with my jaw. *(Author's Collection)*

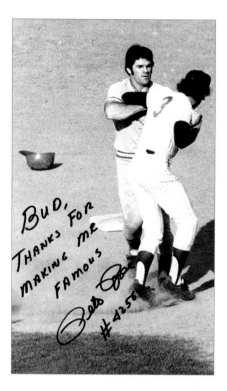

Me make Pete Rose famous? Is he kidding? I always got along well with Pete before our showdown and this photo shows that we buried the hatchet. See that number under his signature, 4,256? That's how many hits he got in the majors. I'd have to have four careers to pass him. (*Author's Collection*)

The day after the "Duel in the Sun," I tried to make light of the situation by putting adhesive tape over the Superman logo on my T-shirt. (*Author's Collection*)

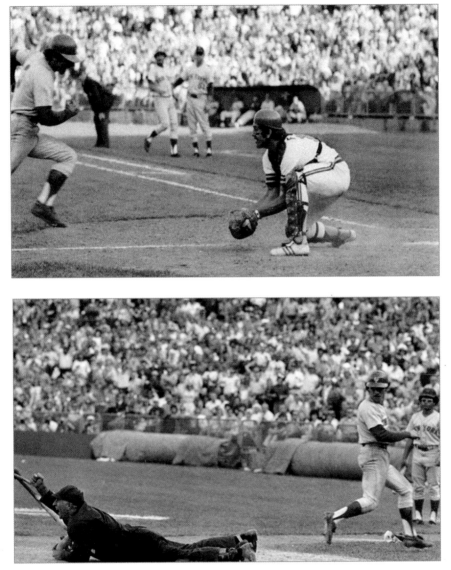

With the score tied at 6-6 in the top of the 10th inning of Game 2 of the 1973 World Series against the Oakland A's, I was certain I had scored the go-ahead run past Oakland A's catcher Ray Fosse, who never tagged me. But umpire Augie Donatelli, who'd fallen down on the play, thought otherwise and called me out. *(Author's Collection)*

After fifteen years in the Mets' organization and three more with the Phillies, I signed on as a free agent with Texas in 1980 and played in 87 games. I found out what it felt like to be the Lone Ranger. (*Author's Collection*)

I was honored to be inducted in the Mets Hall of Fame in 1986, especially because I went in with my dear friend, Rusty Staub. (*Author's Collection*)

You can tell by the faces of Mets players and fans that this home run by Darryl Strawberry was the clincher in the 1986 World Series. It came off Al Nipper in the eighth inning of Game 7 on an 0-2 pitch and gave us a 7-5 lead. We ended up winning the game, 8-5, and the Series. (*Getty*)

If it looks like a Duck and quacks like a Duck, it must be a Duck. And it is. Come out to see the Long Island Ducks of the Independent Atlantic League, of which I am a part owner, and I'll quack for you from my perch in the first base coach's box. (*Author's Collection*)

Tom Seaver, second from left, poses with three sluggers, me, Darryl Strawberry, and Mike Piazza, who among us accounted for 769 home runs, all but 762 of them by me. (*Author's Collection*)

That old gang of mine, players and coaches from the 1969 World Series championship team, get together to celebrate the fortieth anniversary of the team. That's me third from the right, in the front row between Jerry Koosman (No. 36) and Rod Gaspar (No. 17). (*Author's Collection*)

walks, pitched out of bases-loaded jams in the ninth and tenth, and left the more than 50,000 fans in Shea Stadium limp. Tug was removed for a pinch-hitter in the eleventh, and Harry Parker, a twenty-five-year-old right-hander who had won 8 games for us as a spot starter and reliever, came in to pitch the twelfth.

Parker got Ken Griffey Sr., pinch-hitting for Carroll, on a fly ball to left to lead off the inning. That brought up Rose. And wouldn't you know it? Pete drove one into the seats in right field to put the Reds ahead, 2–1. Here's a guy who hit only 5 home runs in 752 plate appearances during the regular season, but in 4 play-off games he had hit one home run to tie the score in the eighth inning and a second home run to put his team ahead in the twelfth inning. Love him or hate him, you had to admire Pete for his ability to come through in the clutch.

Pedro Borbon, another of our Game 3 antagonists, rubbed it in on us with a perfect twelfth and the series was tied. We lost, but we weren't beaten. We felt good about our chances in a winner-take-all Game 5, playing at home, in front of our fans, and with our ace, Tom Seaver, on the mound. But we were going to have to do it without our most dangerous hitter, Rusty Staub, who had hit 3 home runs and driven in 5 runs in the first four games of the series. Rusty had saved Game 4 when he crashed into the wall and caught Driessen's bid for an extrabase hit with 2 runners on base and 2 out. In so doing, Rusty banged up his right shoulder, and now he could not lift his right arm or swing a bat.

In Game 5, Seaver would be opposed by Reds' ace, Jack Billingham, a rematch of Game 1. In that game, Billingham held the Mets to 1 run and 3 hits in 8 innings and the Reds came from behind to win, 2–1, on home runs by Rose in the eighth and Bench in the ninth.

This time, we struck early against Billingham, scoring 2 in the first on a bases-loaded single by Ed Kranepool. Seaver gave up an unearned run in the third and an earned run in the fifth on a double by Rose, of course, and a single by Perez to tie the score,

2–2. But in the bottom of the inning, we took much of the tension out of the crowd by scoring 4 runs and knocking Billingham out of the game. Cleon doubled home one run. Mays pinch-hit for Kranepool and singled home one run. A third run scored on two infield outs. And I drove Mays home with the fourth run of the inning with a single.

We tacked on another run in the sixth and, while Seaver wasn't as good as he was in the first game when he struck out 13, he was good enough. He allowed 7 hits and 5 walks, struck out 4, and pitched into the ninth inning, when the Reds made one last-ditch attempt to get back in the game. Naturally, Rose was right in the middle of that rally, too. His walk loaded the bases with one out and drove Seaver out of the game.

McGraw came in to get Morgan on a pop to me and Driessen on a bouncer back to the mound. Tug fielded it, threw to John Milner, and the celebration was on. We were National League champions.

Tug had told us since August that "You gotta believe," and now we believed. For the second time in five years, we were going to the World Series.

From the time we scored 4 runs in the fifth inning, many in the Shea Stadium crowd began getting unruly. They jumped from the upper stands to the lower and pushed toward the railings, getting ready to jump onto the field when the final out was made.

By the ninth inning, the mob of young fans was uncontrollable, pushing and shoving in the aisles near the box seats where Reds executives and players' wives were seated. As a precaution, the umpires halted the game to allow the Reds' wives and officials to leave the stands and head for safety through the visitors' dugout.

When the final out was recorded, the mob stormed onto the field and overran it. I'm sorry to say many of our fans were vandals, tearing up the field and grabbing whatever they could get their hands on for souvenirs—the bases, home plate, the pitching rubber, clumps of sod and turf, parts of the outfield fence—just as in 1969.

The one consolation was that the World Series was scheduled to open in the American League city, and the Mets had a week to repair the field.

If the Cincinnati Reds were the powerhouse of the National League, a dynasty in the making under Sparky Anderson, the Oakland Athletics, our World Series opponents, were their American League counterpart under manager Dick Williams.

Like Anderson, Williams had come through the Dodgers farm system. They were teammates on Dodgers farm teams in Fort Worth and Montreal. Williams, who had won a pennant with the Boston Red Sox in 1967, took over as manager of the A's in 1971 and succeeded immediately. He improved the team by 12 games and finished first in the American League West with a record of 101-60.

The next year, Williams hit the lottery, winning the Athletics' first World Series since 1930, when the team played in Philadelphia and was managed by Connie Mack. Now the A's were going after their second straight World Series victory with a team that was similar to the one we had just defeated.

Like the Reds, the Athletics had a potent offense led by three players, Reggie Jackson, Sal Bando, and Gene Tenace, who combined for 85 homers and 299 RBI. Jackson led the league in homers with 32 and in runs batted in with 117. He also led in runs scored and slugging percentage. Bando was tied for first in doubles and total bases and tied for fourth in home runs and RBI. Centerfielder Billy North was second in the American League in stolen bases, and shortstop Bert Campaneris was fourth.

Oakland's offense was every bit the equal of Cincinnati's, and their pitching was much better with three 20-game winners, Jim "Catfish" Hunter, 21-5, Ken Holtzman, 21-13, and Vida Blue, 20-9, and a lockdown closer in Rollie Fingers, who won 7 games and was third in the league with 22 saves.

Six A's had been selected to the '73 American League All-

Star team: Jackson, Campaneris, and Hunter as starters, plus Holtzman, Blue, and Bando. Oakland was going to be no walk in the park. Beating them would be a tall order, but we had come through other challenges in the past and were ready for this one.

As if the A's weren't tough enough, we were faced with a couple of other obstacles in this World Series: we were going to have to play four of the seven games in Oakland, and at least for Game 1, we would be without Rusty Staub, our most productive hitter.

The Series opened in Oakland on October 13 with Jon Matlack opposing Ken Holtzman. That was the year the American League adopted the designated-hitter rule, so no Oakland pitcher batted more than once all season. Four of them hadn't batted at all, including Holtzman, so when he strolled to the plate in the third inning with two outs and nobody on, it was his first at bat of the season. Damned if he didn't stroke a double down the left-field line.

Holtzman scored the first run of the Series when Campaneris's ground ball to second squirted through Felix Millan's legs. Campaneris then stole second and scored on Rudi's single to right. Those 2 unearned runs would be all Holtzman and two relievers needed. We got one run back in the fourth on a double by Cleon and a single by Milner, and that was it. From that point on, we were shut down by Holtzman, Fingers, and Darold Knowles, who got the last two outs to nail down the 2–1 victory.

We were in a familiar position. We had lost the first game of the 1969 World Series and the '73 NLCS and come back to win both series. There was no reason we couldn't do likewise in the 1973 World Series.

At the time, Game 2 in Oakland was the longest World Series game in history, a 12-inning, four-hour-and-thirteen-minute roller-coaster marathon. Both starters, Vida Blue for Oakland and Jerry Koosman for us, a pair of quality left-handers, were knocked out early, Koos in the third inning, Blue in the sixth when, down 3–2, we rallied for 4 runs. Don Hahn and I singled in the first 2 runs and the next 2 scored on an error by relief pitcher Darold Knowles.

Berra brought Tug McGraw in to protect the lead in the sixth inning, but Tug gave up a run in the seventh, and the A's tied the score with two outs in the bottom of the ninth on RBI singles by Reggie Jackson and Gene Tenace. Tug, who had pitched 2 innings in Game 1 the previous day, was pitching his fourth inning in Game 2, something that never would happen in today's game.

We thought at the time that we scored the go-ahead run in the top of the tenth, and we still think so to this day, but we didn't get the call. I opened the inning with a single, and McGraw, who was still in the game, sacrificed me to second. Wayne Garrett hit a tapper in front of the plate that Tenace grabbed, but his throw to Rollie Fingers covering first was wide. Garrett was safe and I raced to third. Millan lifted a fly ball to left, not deep, but the one thing I could always do was run, and third-base coach Eddie Yost and I figured it was deep enough for me to score. We probably wouldn't have tried it with none out, but with one out, it was worth the gamble.

The ball was hit along the left-field line so I tried to stay up as long as I could to block catcher Ray Fosse's view of the throw. Willie Mays, who had gone into the game as a pinch runner for Rusty Staub in the ninth inning, was the on-deck hitter and on his knees signaling me to slide, but I saw Fosse reaching down for the ball and I figured my best bet was to go in standing up. Which I did! Fosse never touched me. I was safe, only plate umpire Augie Donatelli didn't agree. Of course, he was wrong, but his opinion was the only one that mattered.

Donatelli had fallen trying to get in position and never saw that Fosse didn't tag me. He just assumed Fosse tagged me, but he didn't. There's a famous picture of Mays on his knees looking up with his arms spread apart in an appeal to Donatelli, but to no avail, and Berra on his way from the dugout to the plate to join in the debate.

Naturally, we lost the argument, and the game went into the twelfth inning when I led off with my third hit of the game, a double to right-center off Fingers. Two outs later, I was on third base when Mays singled to center and I scored the go-ahead run. After we loaded the bases, errors by second baseman Mike Andrews on two consecutive plays, which produced dire consequences, brought in 3 more runs.

In the bottom of the twelfth, Jackson tripled and Tenace walked to knock out McGraw. George Stone relieved him, and after giving up an RBI single to Jesus Alou, retired Fosse, Vic Davalillo, and Campaneris to nail down the 10–7 win and send us home for the next three games tied in the Series at one game apiece.

The next time I saw Augie Donatelli, he made a point of telling me, "See, you won the game anyway." Yeah, right!

The next day was a travel day, and a day of controversy. It was reported that Charles O. Finley, the A's meddlesome and rather kooky owner, was fed up with Mike Andrews and wanted to replace him with Manny Trillo. Finley persuaded Andrews to sign a statement that he was injured, a tactic that brought the Major League Baseball Players Association down on Finley and so angered his manager that Williams called a meeting of his players and told them he was resigning after the Series.

With that controversy as a backdrop, Game 3 featured a matchup of future Hall of Fame pitchers Hunter and Seaver. Both pitched well but neither figured in the decision. Hunter left for a pinch hitter in the seventh, trailing 2–1. Seaver left for a pinch hitter in the bottom of the eighth after giving up the tying run in the top of the inning on a single by Campaneris, a stolen base, and Rudi's single. For the second straight game, we went to extra innings.

McGraw, who had pitched 8 innings in the first two games,

pitched 2 more scoreless innings in Game 3. Harry Parker took over in the eleventh and with one out walked Ted Kubiak. He then struck out Angel Mangual, but the third strike got past Grote for a passed ball. Kubiak went to second and scored what would be the winning run on Campaneris's single and we were down two games to one.

Staub had returned to the lineup in Game 2. His right shoulder still bothered him. He couldn't throw, but he sure could hit. He had a single in Game 2, a single and a double in Game 3, and he practically won Game 4 one-handed (or one-armed) when he banged out 4 hits—3 singles and a home run—and drove in 5 runs in our 6–1 win. Matlack was brilliant once again. He pitched 8 innings, allowed 3 hits and 1 unearned run. In three play-off and World Series games against the powerhouse Reds and Athletics, Jon had now pitched 23 innings, allowed 8 hits, no earned runs, and struck out 17.

As great as Matlack was in Game 4, Koosman was even better in Game 5. We had scored a run in the second and another in the sixth while Koos held the A's scoreless, allowing just 2 hits. In the seventh, he walked Gene Tenace leading off the inning, then gave up a one-out double to Ray Fosse, putting runners on second and third with one out. Tug McGraw came in and walked Deron Johnson to load the bases, but pitched out of that jam with a pop out and a strikeout.

In the eighth, Tug walked Jackson and Tenace with two out, but got Jesus Alou on a line drive to third. In the ninth, he retired the side in order. We were now up in the Series, 3–2, and in great shape going to Oakland for Game 6 and, if necessary, Game 7.

For the last two games, Yogi had a decision to make that some thought was difficult and others thought was a no-brainer. He could start his ace, Seaver, in Game 6 on three days' rest and have the red-hot Matlack available, also on three days' rest, if there was a Game 7. Or he could hold Seaver out for Game 7, when he would be pitching with normal rest, and for Game 6 slot in George Stone, who was 12-3 during the season and had held the Reds to 1 run and 3 hits in 6⅔ innings in Game 4 of the NLCS.

Yogi opted for the former. He thought it was a no-brainer to have his two best pitchers working the last two games, even on short rest. What it came down to for him was Matlack or Stone, and he chose Matlack. His critics argued that by pitching Stone in the sixth game, he would still have his ace, Seaver, for Game 7, and Tom would be pitching at his best, with full rest.

One thing was certain: whichever decision he made, Yogi was certain to be criticized if it didn't work out.

Seaver and I talked about it, and Tom was firm in his opinion. He thought he should pitch Game 6. He wanted to get the Series over with. He had no qualms about it. He just got beat. By holding Berra accountable for his decision because we lost Game 6 does not give the Oakland Athletics the credit they deserve. They were a great team. Who's to say they wouldn't have won the Series no matter what decision Yogi made on his starting pitchers for the last two games?

Seaver was up to the task in Game 6 as he held the A's to 2 runs over 7 innings, Jackson driving in both runs with doubles in the first and third innings. Unfortunately for Tom, he was matched up for the second time in four days with Catfish Hunter. Their first matchup in Game 3 had been a standoff—both pitchers allowed 2 runs—but this one went to Hunter. Through 7 innings he had shut us out on 3 hits. In the eighth, with one out, Ken Boswell batted for Seaver and singled, knocking Hunter out. Knowles replaced him and gave up singles to Wayne Garrett and Felix Millan. We had a run in and trailed 2–1 with runners on first and third and one out. Knowles, a left-hander, was left in to face Staub and struck him out.

With Jones due up, Fingers replaced Knowles and got Cleon on a fly to center. The A's scored an insurance run off McGraw in the eighth, and Fingers pitched a perfect ninth and we were beat, 3–1. The Series was tied, three games each. There would be a sudden-death seventh game, but we were confident because we had Matlack going for us and he had been all-world in the postseason.

This time, however, Jon couldn't get out of the third inning when the A's ambushed him for 4 runs. Just as he had in Game 1, Ken Holtzman started the rally with a double down the left-field line (Matlack had faced Holtzman twice, and both times the A's pitcher had doubled). Campaneris followed with a home run over the right-field fence. In tribute to Mets pitching, it was the first home run of the Series for the A's, a team with a potent offense that had blasted 147 homers during the regular season, tied for third most in the American League. (By contrast, the Mets, who had hit 85 homers during the season, second lowest in the National League, belted 4 homers in the World Series). Rudi singled and Jackson, who had not yet been dubbed Mr. October, nonetheless followed with a home run into the seats in right-center field. That knocked Matlack out of the game. Berra's decision had been wrong and it would eventually cost him his job.

Was it pitching with only three days' rest that did Matlack in? Was it that the A's batters had seen so much of him across nine days that they were ready for what he threw? Or was it simply the law of averages catching up to him, and us?

The Athletics tacked on a run in the fifth for a 5–0 lead, and Holtzman set us down meekly until the sixth, when we picked up a run on back-to-back doubles by Millan and Staub that sent Holtzman to the showers. Fingers relieved for the sixth time in seven games and pitched into the ninth, when we staged one last gasp of a rally. A walk, a single, and an error by first baseman Tenace brought in one run and left runners on first and third with two out. That brought up Wayne Garrett, a left-handed hitter, as the tying run. And that, in turn, brought in left-hander Darold Knowles, who pitched in all seven games.

Yogi still had catcher Duffy Dyer and Willie Mays on the bench, but he chose to stay with Garrett. He popped to short and that was that.

There would be no Miracle II for the Mets in 1973. Nevertheless, it was a memorable season. We won only the Mets' second pennant, took the powerful Oakland Athletics (they had three future Hall of Famers, Reggie Jackson, Catfish Hunter, and Rollie Fingers, and were in the midst of three straight World Series titles) to 7 games, and entered Yogi's famous "It ain't over till it's over" into baseball lore.

CHAPTER 14

This was spring training 1975. We were scheduled for a rare night game in the Grapefruit League, and a friend of my wife's had come to Florida for a visit. One day my wife said, "Let's get a boat and go for a ride." We were renting a place on the Intracoastal Waterway, so we simply went down the street, rented a boat, and were going to spend the afternoon sailing along the Intracoastal.

We were tooling around on the boat and all of a sudden it just died. I'm not very mechanical. I don't know the first thing about boats. I don't know a tiller from a tailor or the hull from a hole in the wall. I know even less about motors; still I said, "I'm going to pull the cover off the engine and turn it over." I wanted to see if I could spot anything that would give me a clue to why the engine just died.

I took the cover off the engine and turned it over, and stuff started flying out of the engine—smoke, pieces of metal—all these parts going in the water. We weren't far from land, so I went into the water thinking I could pull the boat to shore. Mind you, there are stingrays in those waters and probably alligators and crocodiles, too, and sharks for all I knew, so I was taking a chance and I was nervous.

Luckily I got the boat onto the shore and I called the rental place and reported the problem. They said they would send someone out to get us, which they did. We were gone several hours and it was getting close to the time I had to be at the ballpark for the game. We rushed back to our rented apartment, and as soon as we got there, the telephone rang. It was Joe Torre, who had come to the Mets from the Cardinals in a trade just after the 1974 season.

"PeeWee"—Joe always called me PeeWee—"where were you?"

"I broke down in a boat, and I had to get a ride back to the dock."

"Well, get here as soon as you can. Yogi's pissed that you're not here."

I'm thinking, "I'm never late, give me the benefit of the doubt." Punctuality is an obsession of mine, which was probably why they were concerned about me. I had a reputation of usually being the first one in the clubhouse. The funny thing is, the one guy I could never beat there was Yogi. As hard as I tried, I could never arrive before him.

I changed clothes as fast as I could, jumped in my car, and dashed over to the ballpark in plenty of time for the start of the game. All I missed was batting practice. What's the big deal?

I was at my locker getting dressed when Yogi came into the clubhouse and walked right by me and into his office without saying a word. A moment later, he came out of his office, walked over to me, and said, "Next time get a boat that works."

Lawrence Peter "Yogi" Berra is among a handful of the greatest catchers in baseball history, and one of the game's most popular, beloved, and easily recognized characters. Under ordinary conditions, he's also one of the most likable people you'd ever want to meet. But in the spring of 1975, Yogi was irritable. He was under extreme pressure. His job was squarely on the line.

Yogi had almost been fired in June of 1973 when we plummeted to last place, but he survived and rallied the team by refusing to press the panic button and maintaining a positive attitude. Berra got his reward in the form of a two-year extension on his contract.

Now he was in trouble and his job was in jeopardy again.

The 1974 season had been a disaster for us and a huge disappointment for our fans. We were expected to at least challenge for a second straight pennant, but we were never even in the conversation.

Perhaps we were guilty of complacency by both the players and the front office. We players seemed to lose some of our fire. The front office chose to stand pat and failed to make any significant additions to our roster. Consequently, when we were hit with a rash of injuries, we didn't have the backup players to pick up the slack.

The tone for the season was set on day one, April 6, in Philadelphia. Tom Seaver, coming off 19 wins and a second Cy Young Award, was our opening-day starting pitcher for the seventh straight year. He was opposed by the Phillies' ace, Steve Carlton. Twice in the first 6 innings we gave Tom a lead, and both times the Phillies came back and tied the score. We went ahead again, 4–3, in the seventh, and in the eighth Seaver left for a pinch hitter.

Tug McGraw came in to pitch the eighth. He had been a sure thing in these similar situations in the pennant year with 25 saves, and it looked like more of the same when he breezed through the eighth inning by getting Del Unser on a fly ball to left field and striking out the dangerous Greg Luzinski and Willie Montanez.

In the bottom of the ninth, a leadoff single and a sacrifice put a Phillies runner on second with one out and brought up Mike Schmidt. No problem. At the time, Schmidt was not the Hall of Fame third baseman and home-run king he would become. He was a work in progress, a twenty-four-year-old kid who had hit .196 the previous season and struck out 136 times in 367 at bats and was such a question mark the Phillies batted him eighth. But he teed off on McGraw and drove one into the left-field seats for a 2-run homer and a shocking, sudden-death, 5–4 Phillies victory. Schmidt would hit 35 more home runs that season.

Five days later, we lost a doubleheader to the Cardinals and fell below .500 at 2-3. We would never again reach the .500 mark all season. We went on a 7-game losing streak, and on April 18, we had a record of 2-8 and were in fifth place, 5½ games out of first.

We kept hoping for another comeback as in 1973, another miracle, but it never came.

On June 12, I was hit by a pitch and broke a bone in my right hand, the fifth time I had sustained a broken bone since I joined the Mets. I had my share of injuries as a player, but my injuries were never self-inflicted. They were broken bones as the result of a throw or a collision. Throughout my career I never had a sore arm and I never had a pulled muscle. I like to say that the reason I never had a pulled muscle is because I had no muscles to pull, but I did have a few "pulled" bones.

I wound up playing in only 106 games in 1974, having my worst season since I became a Met a decade earlier. I batted .227, hit 1 home run, and drove in only 13 runs. I was just a small part of what was a feeble offense. Our leading hitter, Cleon Jones, batted .282. Our top home-run hitter, John Milner, hit 20. And our big RBI guy, Rusty Staub, drove in 78.

As bad as the hitting was, the real culprit in our demise was our pitching, which had been our strength in winning the pennant the previous year. Largely because of a strained sciatic nerve in his left buttock, Seaver went from 19-10 to 11-11, the lowest win total in his eight-year career. He also had an eight-year high in earned run average at 3.20, his strikeout total of 201 was his lowest since his rookie season, and he failed to make the All-Star team for the first time.

Seaver was not alone. George Stone, who was 12-3 with a 2.80 ERA in '73, fell to 2-7 with a 5.03 ERA in '74. But perhaps the biggest drop-off was in our bullpen. Our saves leader was Harry Parker with 4. We were fourth in the league in saves in 1973 with 40. In 1974, we were 12th (last) with 14. Tug McGraw, who saved 25 games in '73, saved only 3 in '74.

None of this was Yogi's fault, yet he was the one walking the tightrope, and his job was on the line.

•   •   •

Changes were needed, and changes were made prior to the 1975 season. The biggest need was to beef up our offense, and toward that end, the team made three significant acquisitions.

On Sunday, October 13, 1974, in Los Angeles, as the Oakland A's and LA Dodgers were preparing for Game 2 of the World Series, the Mets announced that they had acquired Joe Torre from the St. Louis Cardinals ending the pursuit of a player they had coveted for some six years. A 14-year veteran and 9-time All-Star, Torre had been named National League Most Valuable Player just three years earlier when he led the league in batting with a .363 average, in RBIs with 137, and struck 24 home runs.

Now thirty-four years old, Torre was expected to provide us with veteran leadership and a productive bat. He would play third base and a little first base, and while he still was a threat at bat, he had slowed considerably. He hit into 22 double plays, including 4 in one memorable game against the Houston Astros in Shea Stadium on the afternoon of July 21. He facetiously blamed the 4 DPs on teammate Felix Millan, batting ahead of him in the order.

"If Felix hadn't hit four singles," Torre reasoned, "I wouldn't have hit into four double plays."

On December 3, 1974, the Mets came to a sorrowful parting of the ways with fan and team favorite Tug McGraw by sending him to the Phillies with centerfielder Don Hahn in exchange for Del Unser and John Stearns.

Unser was thirty years old, a seven-year veteran with Washington, Cleveland, and Philadelphia. He would step into Hahn's spot as our center fielder and was considered an upgrade over Hahn both offensively and defensively. For us, though, the key man in the deal was Stearns, hard-nosed, tough-as-nails, and an outstanding catching prospect.

Only twenty three, John was taken by the Phillies as the No. 2 pick in the nation, behind David Clyde and ahead of Robin Yount and Dave Winfield, in the 1973 free agent draft. An all-America defensive back at the University of Colorado, Stearns also was drafted by the NFL Buffalo Bills.

On February 28, 1975, the Mets, still looking for another big bat, seized on an opportunity to acquire the player that would become the team's single-season home-run leader. Reacting to rumors that Horace Stoneham, owner of the San Francisco Giants, was having trouble meeting spring training expenses, the Mets moved quickly and offered the Giants $150,000 for Dave Kingman, a six-foot-six-inch, twenty-six-year-old slugger who had blasted 77 home runs and driven in 217 runs to go with 422 strikeouts, in three and a half seasons with the Giants.

As advertised, in his first year as a Met, Kingman belted 36 home runs, breaking the team record of 34 set by Frank Thomas in 1962, the Mets' first year. Kingman also drove in 88 runs and struck out 153 times, second in the league to Philadelphia's Mike Schmidt. In 1976, Kingman hit 37 homers to raise his record, which has since been exceeded several times.

While the plan to beef up the offense was a success (we scored 74 more runs in 1975 than in 1974), and Seaver bounced back to win 22 games, pitch 5 shutouts, lead the league with 243 strikeouts, and win his third Cy Young Award, and we won 11 more games than the previous year, we still had a disappointing season.

Our best hitter, Cleon Jones, who batted .282 in '74, underwent off-season knee surgery and would play in only 21 games and bat .240. I was also having problems with my right knee, but I tried to play through it by having the knee periodically drained. Finally, when it was no longer possible to drain the knee, I had no choice but to have an operation, which caused me to miss 128 games.

For the second straight year, Seaver and Carlton hooked up on opening day, this time in Shea Stadium, and this time with a different result. We won the game, 2–1, and two of our new bats produced the victory. Kingman tied the score with a home run in the fourth, and Torre singled in the winning run with one out in the ninth.

We followed that up by losing our next 5 games and fell into last place in the National League East, 4 games out of first already. We were a team of streaks in the early weeks of the season—a 7-game winning streak from April 20 to 29 that moved us into second place only a half game out of first; a 6-game losing streak from May 3 to 10 that dropped us back into the cellar, 7 games out of first; a 5-game winning streak from May 11 to 17 that pushed us back over the .500 mark and into fourth place, 3½ games out; a 7-game losing streak from June 18 to 23 that left us back at .500 and 7 games out of first.

On August 2, when Matlack shut out the Pirates, 6–0, we were on a roll. We had won 12 of 17, moved a season-high 8 games over .500, and were in third place, only 6 games out and ready to challenge the leaders. But we lost our next 5 games, fell 9½ games out of first, and on August 5, ownership dropped the other shoe, fired Berra, and named my old mentor Roy McMillan to replace him on an interim basis with a chance to audition for the job full-time.

Some people compared Roy to Gil Hodges, the strong, silent type and a quiet leader. At least the quiet part was right. McMillan never was cut out to be a manager, and the hope that he would rally the team for a run at first place, never materialized. We did have a little spurt that got us as close as 4 games out of first on September 1, but we soon dropped back. Our record under McMillan was 26-27 and we finished in third place, 10½ games out of first.

CHAPTER 15

The 1976 season began for the Mets with a new manager in place, a surprise choice to most of us. By naming Joe Frazier as manager, were the Mets brass continuing the policy of hiring a recognizable name, a successor to Casey Stengel, Gil Hodges, and Yogi Berra, and someone with a knockout punch?

No, it wasn't *that* Joe Frazier! This Joe Frazier was a baseball lifer and a career minor leaguer. An outfielder, Frazier spent 14 seasons in the minors, played in 1,776 games, had 6,135 at bats, and hit 144 home runs. He had a few big league cups of coffee, 217 games and 282 at bats with the Cardinals, Indians, Reds, and Orioles. When his playing career was over, he spent seven years managing teams in the Mets farm system in Pompano Beach, Visalia, Memphis, Victoria, and Tidewater, where he managed future Mets John Milner, Danny Frisella, Buzz Capra, Bob Apodaca, Ron Hodges, Craig Swan, Mike Vail, Hank Webb, and George "Stork" Theodore, and had only one losing season. He had paid his dues and now he was getting his big chance.

I was healthy again and I got off to a good start under Frazier, and so did the team. On April 27 we moved into first place and remained there for a couple of weeks as we won 12 out of 14 games. On May 12, I was batting .259, getting on base (25 walks in 30 games), and scoring runs. M. Donald Grant, the chairman of the board of the Mets, was thrilled with the way we were playing. He had taken to coming into the clubhouse after a win to pat us on the back and congratulate us for the way things were going.

One day Grant came walking through the clubhouse, praising everybody for our good start. When he got to Seaver, Tom—always brash, always outspoken, never afraid to speak his mind, rock the boat, and stir things up—said, "Mr. Grant, you know why we're doing so well? See that little guy in the corner over there"—Seaver was pointing right at me—"that guy whose salary you cut? He's the reason we're winning. He's on base all the time."

The year before, when I was hurt and played in only 34 games, the Mets had cut my salary by 20 percent, the maximum cut under terms of the Basic Agreement between the owners and the Major League Baseball Players Association.

When I first came up with the Mets, I was told, "You're one of the few players in our entire minor league system that never sent a contract back unsigned."

I said, "Well, that's going to change now."

It didn't really change that much. I rarely was a problem when it came to what I wanted and what I was offered. But some things did bother me. I kept noticing that the team was giving raises to guys simply because they lived out of town. But because I lived in the New York area, they knew I'd do promotional events for the Mets during the winter. I thought they were taking advantage of me, and I said something about it. Why should I be penalized because I lived in New York?

One winter I estimated I attended eighty banquets for the Mets. Okay, I got paid for the appearances, but I'd get $50 for a banquet and I would be spending five and a half hours, using my own car, and paying for gas all for a lousy fifty bucks. What's that, less than $10 an hour? Practically the minimum wage! Obviously I wasn't doing those banquets for the money. And I certainly wasn't doing it for a free meal. I never cared about the money. I did care about how I was perceived by the fans. I was making those appearances because I thought it was good public relations for me and for the team, and it bothered me that the Mets didn't appreciate my efforts.

I realized there were budget considerations, but I never liked the game you had to play during negotiations. My approach was to go in to talk to the general manager and tell him, "Here's what I think I deserve," instead of throwing out an unrealistic number and then going through the usual give-and-take of negotiations. Even though money wasn't my main priority, I wanted to be appreciated for what I did on the field, and I didn't want them to take advantage of me.

One year I gave the general manager a number and was told, "If you had hit higher, we'd give you a better raise."

"Like who?" I said.

"Well, like Felix Millan."

Millan was a terrific hitter, but he never got a lot of walks. The year was 1974 and Millan outhit me .268 to .227, but I had an on-base percentage of .366 and Felix had an on-base percentage of .317.

I said, "Who got on base more, me or Felix?"

"You did."

"Who would you rather have on base, me or Felix?"

"You!"

"So what are we talking about here?"

"Okay, how much do you want?"

After the Mets cut my pay, Seaver was pissed. He thought it was unfair for them to cut my salary when I had a bad season because I missed so many games because of an injury. He thought I should not have to pay the price for something that was out of my control, so when he saw an opportunity to make a statement to Grant in support of me, he took advantage of it.

The next day I got a message that Grant wanted to see me in his office. I went upstairs and Grant told me he was tearing up my contract and not only restoring the cut, but giving me a new two-year deal for $90,000 a year, the most I ever made as a player.

• • •

After our fast start, we cooled off and came back to the field. In Frazier's first shot at managing a major league team, he led us to 86 wins, an improvement of 4 games over the previous season, and we finished third in the six-team National League East; our fifth third-place finish in the last seven years. We were drowning in a sea of mediocrity.

Mediocrity didn't seem so terrible when we lost 19 of our first 29 games in 1977. On Monday, May 30, Memorial Day, we played the Montreal Expos in a doubleheader at Shea Stadium in front of a holiday crowd of more than 41,000. We lost the first game, 5–1, and we lost the second game, 3–2, for our sixth straight loss. That dropped our record to 15-30. We were in last place, 14 games out of first. But it was still early, plenty of time to make a run at the leaders. What we needed, the brass decided, was a new manager to inject some life into us.

On the afternoon of May 31, as we were preparing to face the Expos in the final game of a 3-game series, the Mets announced that Joe Frazier was out as manager and was being replaced by Joe Torre, who would be a player-manager. Torre was only thirty-six. He had never managed before, he had never been in the ring with Muhammad Ali, but he was a big name in baseball and a native New Yorker, born and raised in Brooklyn. Maybe the Mets had finally found the new Gil Hodges.

Even before Torre took over as manager, the makeup of our roster had undergone some changes. They were breaking up that old gang of mine. A youth movement of sorts was under way. Gone were many of the important contributors to our 1969 and 1973 pennant winning teams—Wayne Garrett, Rusty Staub, Cleon Jones, Tommie Agee, Duffy Dyer, Ken Boswell, Tug McGraw, Ron Swoboda, and Art Shamsky—and a new wave of Mets had taken their place: Craig Swan, age twenty-six, John Stearns, twenty-five, Mike

Vail, twenty-five, Bruce Boisclair, twenty-four, and a Brooklyn-born, twenty-two-year-old rookie named Lee Mazzilli.

Soon, there would be even more changes, cataclysmic ones.

For some time, bad blood had been brewing between the Mets' executive leadership and their greatest player, Tom Seaver or "Tom Terrific" or "The Franchise." The Mets were miffed over Seaver's outspoken and proactive involvement in the union, the Major League Baseball Players Association, and they called Tom greedy when he asked for a long-term contract with the payment and security that went along with it. At one point, the Mets were rumored to be in talks with the Dodgers about a one-for-one trade that would send Seaver to Los Angeles in exchange for Don Sutton. The deal of star pitchers never came off.

Eventually, Seaver and the Mets resolved their differences. Tom didn't get his long-term deal, but he signed the most lucrative contract in Mets history, which, of course, he deserved.

The rift between Seaver and the Mets would resurface when free agency came to baseball in 1977 and Seaver campaigned for the Mets to sign a free agent hitter to bolster their attack. He also pouted that based on what free agency had created, he was now underpaid, which he was. Tom pled his case to the team's ownership and got a promise of a contract extension.

Relieved, Seaver figured he would be a Met for the rest of his baseball life. Everything changed on June 15, the major league trading deadline, while we were in Atlanta scheduled to play the Braves in the final game of a 3-game series. Tom learned of a report in a New York newspaper charging that Tom's wife, Nancy, was jealous of Ruth Ryan, whose husband, Nolan, had signed a contract with the California Angels that was richer than Seaver's.

For Seaver, that slur was the last straw. He decided then and there that he no longer wanted to be a Met, not for life, not even for another day. What came next would be called in the New York newspapers and known in the annals of the Mets as "the Midnight Massacre."

As we arrived at the stadium for the game that night, we started hearing the rumors that Seaver was going to be traded. Every inning, I'd come back to the dugout and I'd ask Tom, "Have you heard anything?" The answer was always the same: "Nothing yet." The Mets had until midnight to move Seaver under the trading deadline, and as time passed, I was getting increasingly optimistic that there would be no trade. Then, along about the sixth inning, I went back to the dugout and Tom wasn't there. I was told he had gone back to the clubhouse to change into his street clothes. In Atlanta, the clubhouses were not close to the dugout, but I raced up to the clubhouse and caught up with Tom before he left.

Seaver was somber. "I can't believe it," he kept saying. "I can't believe they really did it."

I was crying. I was hurt. My best friend was leaving. They didn't want him talking to the press, so they contacted him on the bench during the game and told him about the trade. They just got rid of him. He left the dugout and went to the clubhouse, got dressed, and left before the game ended. He took a cab to the airport.

Seaver was on his way to Cincinnati, to join the Big Red Machine of Bench and Morgan and Perez and, yes, Pete Rose. We got four players in return, Doug Flynn, a terrific second baseman who would give the Mets five years of superlative defense; Steve Henderson, a twenty-four-year-old outfielder who would bat .287, hit 35 home runs, and drive in 227 runs in four years with the Mets; Dan Norman, a twenty-two-year-old outfielder who never lived up to his potential and hit only 9 homers in 4 seasons as a Met; and Pat Zachary, a serviceable pitcher for the Mets who won 41 games in 6 years (in the same period, Seaver won 75 games for the Reds).

We beat the Braves, 6–5, that night and I had 4 hits, but there was nothing to feel good about. On the charter flight home we learned that we had also traded Dave Kingman to the San Diego Padres for two players, pitcher Paul Siebert, who would win 2 games and save 1 in two seasons with the Mets, and a onetime outstanding prospect from Connecticut, now twenty-seven years old, whose career was impaired by a serious leg injury. His name was Bobby Valentine.

The two trades were something of a wake-up call to how the game was changing. Today, with free agency and long-term contracts in vogue, trades of superstars like Seaver and Kingman are expected. Back then, such superstars often stayed with one team for their entire career. These days that's rare. We had been a new organization with all these kids that came up together, the Seavers and Koosmans, the McGraws and Swobodas, and to see it being dismantled was a shock to our system. Clearly the Mets leadership was making a statement. Before long, we were all gone.

The trade of Seaver and Kingman put us in a deep funk, which was reflected in our less-than-spirited play on the field. From June 17 through July 8, we lost 17 of 21 games and fell an impossible-from-which-to-recover 21½ games behind the first-place Cubs. Clearly, there was to be no 1969 or 1973 miracle this year. We were, however, to have one "light" moment of significance.

It came at Shea Stadium on Wednesday, July 13, and it was a night to remember. Did I say it was a "light" moment? It actually was a dark moment, New York's Blackout of '77, but we were able to make "light" of it.

We were playing the first-place Cubs with Jerry Koosman and Ray Burris locked in a pitchers' duel. I didn't start the game, but I would have a key role nonetheless. As we came to bat in the bottom of the sixth, we trailed, 2–1. Steve Ontiveros had hit a 2-run home run off Koosman in the second, and Mike Vail hit a solo homer for us in the fifth.

Koosman led off the bottom of the sixth by grounding out to second baseman Manny Trillo. Just as Lenny Randle was coming to bat, the place went dark, eerily, frighteningly, ghoulishly pitch-black, officially at 9:34 p.m. We later found out that several lightning strikes in the northern suburbs knocked out power lines that threw most of the city into darkness, which led to wholesale looting and vandalism. At Shea Stadium, we were in the "dark," no pun intended. Everything went black except the auxiliary lights, the scoreboard, the lights in the press box, the floodlights that illuminated the field. We had no idea at the time what had happened or how long the blackout was going to last, if it was going to be an hour or two weeks.

I have always had a weird sense of humor, and to fill the void I had a plan. First, Craig Swan and I and two or three others went to the players' parking lot, got into our cars, drove them onto the field, and kept our lights on. The fans were a little nervous and the players were bored, so I figured a way to keep the fans amused and to pass the time. "Let's take a phantom infield," I said. "No ball; just a fungo hitter and infielders taking infield practice in pantomime." And that's what we did. We had a phantom infield in the light from the cars. It was pretty funny. We pantomimed making the double play and throwing the ball around the horn. The crowd loved it. It was kind of like what you see when there's a rain delay and the field is covered with a tarpaulin and guys come out and slide on the tarp. It's entertainment.

We wound up waiting seventy-five minutes, and when the lights didn't come back on, the umpires called the game. The next day there still was no power, and even though we were scheduled for an afternoon game, and it turned out to be a beautiful, sunny day, that game was also called off because of a health issue. The toilets in the stadium operated on an electric ejector system. With no power, the toilets would not be working.

Power was restored the night of July 14. The game that had been suspended was completed on September 16.

Nine weeks after the Midnight Massacre, on August 19, Seaver came to Shea Stadium for the first time as a member of the Cincinnati Reds. The 4-game series included a twi-night doubleheader on

Friday, and day games on Saturday and Sunday. We lost both games of the Friday doubleheader, and since it was a late night, Tom and I agreed to get together after the game on Saturday.

We also lost the Saturday game, and after the game Tom and I went to Lum's Chinese Restaurant near Shea Stadium. Tom was pitching the next day, so over dinner I asked him, "Roomie, how are you going to pitch to me tomorrow?"

He said, "I just don't want to hit you."

The game on Sunday, August 21, was a happening. A crowd of 46,265 came out in tribute to Seaver (it was some 10,000 more fans than we drew for the Friday-night doubleheader and 20,000 more than for the Saturday game). They came to praise Seaver, not to bury him.

It was strange to see Tom in a Reds uniform pitching against us, and just as strange that he was being opposed by his longtime friend and pitching partner, Jerry Koosman. Rose doubled to lead off the game and scored on George Foster's single. I couldn't help thinking, "There's your run, Tom, make it stand up."

I was the second batter Seaver faced in the bottom of the first. I deliberately stood right on top of the plate to take away the outside corner from him. His first pitch was outside . . . or so I thought.

"Strike one," said plate umpire Jim Quick.

The next pitch was farther outside.

"Strike two!"

The next pitch was even farther outside than the previous two.

"Strike three!"

"He's good," I told Quick, "but not *that* good. You can't give him those strikes."

Later, when I talked to Tom, I said, "There's no way those were strikes."

He said, "Hey, he gave me the first one. I just wanted to find out how much I could get."

I came to bat in the fourth inning and Tom struck me out again, swinging this time. Two at bats, 2 strikeouts! In my next at bat, in the sixth inning, I really bore down. Tom threw me a curveball and hung it, and I hit it right through the middle, into center field for a single.

When it was my turn to bat in the eighth, we were down by 4 runs, so Torre had John Stearns pinch-hit for me.

We lost the game, 5–1. Tom went the distance, allowed 6 hits, and struck out 11. It was his 14th win of the season. Talk about consistency. In 69 days with us, he was 7-3. In 67 days with the Reds, he was 7-2. He would finish the season 21-6 with a 2.58 earned run average and a league-leading 7 shutouts. We wouldn't see Seaver again that season, and I wouldn't hit against him until two years later when I was with the Phillies. I didn't play much with the Phillies. I was mostly a backup second baseman behind Ted Sizemore, so I figured I wasn't likely to be hitting against Seaver. If he was pitching, I wasn't going to be playing. But late in May 1979 we had a rash of injuries to infielders and I wound up starting 15 straight games, most of them at second.

While I was on my run of consecutive starts, the Reds came in for a 3-game series on June 15, and Seaver was scheduled to pitch the first game. That meant I would be batting against my old roomie.

A few weeks earlier, I was talking with my manager, Danny Ozark, and I asked him, "Danny, have you ever put on the squeeze play with a count of three-and-two?"

"I would never squeeze three-and-two," he said. "I wouldn't do it with Larry Bowa."

"You can squeeze with me on three-and-two," I boasted, and let it go at that.

I had forgotten all about that conversation until June 15, when I came to bat against Seaver in the second inning. Greg Luzinski and Mike Schmidt had opened the inning with walks, and Bake McBride drove them both in with a triple. McBride held third as Bob Boone grounded out, so here I was hitting with a runner on third and one out, the perfect time for a squeeze bunt. The count went to 3-2.

I looked down at third-base coach Bobby Wine, and he was giving me the bunt sign. A squeeze play on 3-2; just what I had discussed with Ozark.

But Seaver?

I didn't mean against *him,* Danny.

Tom threw me a slider, believe it or not; this dinky little slider down and in on 3-2. He knew I wasn't going to take anything close in that situation, and he was going to give me a ball I couldn't lift in the air. I bunted it just fair, the ball hugging the first-base line. Seaver was off the mound, chasing after the bunt, and all the while as he was going for the ball, he was cursing me. He told me later that he never anticipated the bunt. Not because he didn't think I would bunt in that situation, but because he didn't think Ozark would call for it. He picked up the ball, yelling at me, "You so-and-so, blankety-blank, @#$%$#@," and just to emphasize what he thought about my bunting, he tagged me extrahard.

I was out, but I got the last laugh. McBride scored.

I came up against Seaver in the fourth, and once again McBride, who had hit another triple, was on third. But this time there were two outs and no bunt sign. I swung away and hit a ground ball to first.

That was the last time I batted against Seaver. My career log against him: 5 plate appearances, 1 single, 1 sacrifice, 2 strikeouts, 1 ground ball and 1 RBI, and one black-and-blue mark from where my buddy tagged me hard and in anger after I bunted on him with a runner on third and a 3-2 count.

Tom Seaver would pitch for the Reds through the 1982 season. After the '82 season, the Reds traded Seaver back to the Mets. He spent the 1983 season with the Mets, then was left unprotected and selected by the Chicago White Sox as a free agent compensation pick. In 1984–85 with the White Sox, Tom won 31 games, including his 300th major league win. On June 29, 1986, the White Sox traded Seaver to the Boston Red Sox, who wanted him to help them in their race for the American League East championship.

The 1986 season was Seaver's twentieth, and last, in the major leagues. He retired after the season having pitched in 656 games with 647 starts and 4,763 innings. He won 311 games, pitched 231 complete games and 61 shutouts, with an earned run average of 2.86, 3,640 strikeouts, and three Cy Young Awards.

I'm proud to say that in 1992, my friend and my roomie was elected to the Hall of Fame, when he was named on 425 of the 430 votes cast, a percentage of 98.84, which, as of 2011, is still the highest ever recorded.

After he retired from baseball, Seaver tried his hand at a variety of pursuits, such as broadcasting for both the Mets and the Yankees, but he was restless. For years, he had thought about returning to Northern California to grow grapes. About ten years ago, with his children grown and on their own, he purchased 116 acres in Calistoga in the Napa Valley, sold his home in Greenwich, Connecticut, and returned to California.

Now he is a vintner, a winemaker, that is. He's also a member of the board of directors of the Baseball Hall of Fame. I visited him recently and I have never seen Tom so content. He's got three new dogs, Labrador retrievers, and he wakes up at dawn every morning and goes to his vineyard and checks on his grapes.

My old roomie is happy and I'm happy that he's happy.

CHAPTER 16

I should probably have realized after what happened during the Midnight Massacre that my days with the New York Mets were numbered. It should have been obvious to me that the Mets were rebuilding and attempting to get younger.

A month after Tom Seaver was traded, I broke my right hand diving back into first base. I wound up missing 55 games and experienced the worst season of my career. I batted a pathetic .178, hit 1 home run, and drove in only 12 runs, leading the Mets' brain trust to the logical conclusion that I was coming to the end of the line. As the season was winding down, I kept hearing rumors that the Mets were in the market for a shortstop.

On December 7, during the winter meetings, I was at home playing backgammon with my wife, Kim. The radio was on, tuned to the sports, and I heard an announcement that the Mets had purchased the contract of shortstop Tim Foli from the Giants. Foli had been chosen by the Mets as the first pick in the free agent draft all the way back in 1968. He played for them for only a couple of seasons and was part of the trade in 1972 that brought Rusty Staub to the Mets from Montreal.

After 6 seasons with the Expos, Tim was traded to the Giants for Chris Speier. Now he was coming back to the Mets, no doubt to replace me and take over as their shortstop.

By spring training, 1978, the only remaining members of the

1969 world championship team were Ed Kranepool, Jerry Koosman, and me, and I was just a few months shy of my thirty-fourth birthday, which made me vulnerable. I was miserable. I was hardly playing during the exhibition schedule. Instead, the Mets were using me mostly as a player/coach. They had me working with Bobby Valentine and some of the other infielders, which to me was a clear sign that their mind was made up. Foli was going to be their shortstop, and I wasn't going to have a legitimate chance to compete for my old job.

I might have been able to stay as Foli's backup, insurance against an injury to one of the regulars, but that didn't appeal to me. It's difficult to be a backup for a team with which you have been a starter for eleven consecutive years, so I asked to be traded. Piggy (coach Joe Pignatano) wanted me to stay. He begged me to reconsider, but my mind was made up. It was a tough decision, but I didn't appreciate the way I was being shoved aside in spring training and I wanted out.

On March 24, the deal was announced. I was going to the Philadelphia Phillies, our most heated and hated rival, in exchange for a young infielder named Fred Andrews, who had played in only 16 games for the Phillies. The Mets sent Andrews to their AAA farm team at Tidewater, and he actually had a pretty good year there, a .273 average with 12 homers and 75 RBI. But he didn't get the call to the big leagues and was not heard from after that season.

The move from the Mets' training camp in St. Petersburg to the Phillies' training camp about twenty miles to the north in Clearwater was easy, less than a half-hour drive if you didn't run into one of the many drawbridges on the Intracoastal. The toughest part of the trip was packing all my stuff in my car and leaving so many of my longtime teammates and friends.

I joined the Phillies for the last two weeks of spring training and went north with them to open the season against the Cardinals. When I was introduced on opening day, I was booed by 47,000 fans, partly because I had been a New York Met, but mostly because

I was replacing Terry Harmon. He was popular with the Philly fans and I knew that, but to make room for me on the roster, the Phillies had to release Harmon.

My job with the Phillies was to be a backup to both shortstop Larry Bowa and second baseman Ted Sizemore. It wasn't so hard to take a subordinate role with a new team as it would have been if I had stayed with the Mets as a backup. The irony of it all is that Bowa and I had so much in common. Like me, Bowa came from Northern California (Sacramento) and was a switch-hitter. We're about the same height and weight and about the same age (I'm a year and a half older than Larry).

Despite the similarities between us, there also were differences, particularly in our style of play. Bowa was a one-handed, throw-on-the-run guy who specialized in the spectacular play. I was a more conventional shortstop, not flashy. I put a higher priority on making the routine play than on the spectacular one.

Bowa and I were rivals for most of our careers and competed for spots on the All-Star team. Despite that rivalry, there was no ill will between us. I had tremendous respect for Bowa as a shortstop and not a bit of resentment at being his caddy. After all, the Phillies were Larry's team, and he was popular and successful. Up to that point, Bowa had made the All-Star team three times, twice as a starter, and had won one Gold Glove.

I wound up playing in more games at second (43) for the Phillies than at shortstop (15). I batted .214 in 103 at bats and drove in 9 runs. We won the National League East, but lost to the Dodgers in the NLCS. When the season ended, I retired.

I thought my career as a baseball player was over, and I was content to limit my ballplaying to slow-pitch softball in a men's league on Long Island in the spring of 1979. I also hooked on with SportsChannel for a gig as a television baseball analyst. One day in May, I was in Baltimore for a game when I got a call from the Phillies. Bowa had broken his thumb and the Phillies were in need of a veteran player to fill in while he was out. They asked me what I had been doing and I exaggerated slightly and said I was playing soft-ball (I didn't say it was a slow-pitch league and they didn't ask). That seemed to satisfy the Phillies. They offered me a contract and I accepted. I rented a car, packed my bags, and drove from Baltimore to Philadelphia.

I signed with the Phillies on May 25. The next day I was playing second base for the Phillies against the Cubs, entering the game in the eighth inning and fielding ground balls off the bat of the first two hitters, my former teammate Dave Kingman and Bobby Murcer.

A week later we went to Cincinnati for a 4-game series. The first game was on a Friday night, June 1. I got the start at shortstop. Our starting pitcher was Steve Carlton. The starting lineup was posted and here's how it read:

> Rose,1b
> McCarver, c
> Schmidt, 3b
> Luzinski, lf
> Unser, rf
> Maddox, cf
> Aviles, 2b
> Carlton, p
> Harrelson, ss

Batting ninth, behind the pitcher, didn't bother me. At the time, I had had only 5 at bats and I still wasn't in game shape having missed all of spring training. And Carlton was a pretty good hitter. Besides, I never had that kind of ego. I was just happy to be in the lineup.

While batting ninth didn't bother me, it apparently bothered Pete Rose, my old buddy and sparring partner who had signed as a free agent with the Phillies that winter. He checked the starting lineup and said, "That's ridiculous," as he ripped the lineup card off the wall and tore it up. Someone simply put another lineup card back on the wall with the same lineup.

Batting eighth, Carlton was hitless in 3 at bats. Batting ninth, I singled in the third inning, struck out in the fifth, flied to center in the seventh, and was lifted for pinch hitter Doug Rader in the ninth.

The next day I batted eighth and had 2 hits, a walk, and stole a base. The day after that, I batted second in both games of a doubleheader and had 2 more hits in each game, giving me 7 hits in 14 at bats for the series. At one point when it was my turn to hit in the second game of the Sunday doubleheader, my batting average was posted on the scoreboard. It was something like .350. I walked to the plate and Johnny Bench looked up and said, "So much for spring training, huh!"

When we left Cincinnati, I was batting a cool .368. Although that didn't last, I wound up with a .282 average, the highest of my career, in 71 at bats. I played in 25 games at second base, 17 at shortstop, 9 at third base, and I even got into one game as a left fielder, the only time in my professional career I played anything but the infield. On August 26 against Houston I was in left field for the ninth inning. I regret I got no chances, so I was unable to display my latent talent as an outfielder, which would probably have had baseball people comparing me with Willie Mays and Joe DiMaggio.

The Phillies must have been satisfied with the job I did because they brought me back in 1980, but on April 4, one week from the start of the season, I was released. I would have quit right then, but I had already gone through spring training. I figured, why waste it? The Texas Rangers were looking for a veteran infielder as a backup and offered me a contract. I jumped at it.

I wound up playing in 87 games at shortstop for the Rangers, 77 of them as a starter. I batted .272 with a homer and 9 RBI. When the season ended, I was once again a free agent, but this time there were no offers. Funny thing, in my last two seasons, I had the two highest batting averages of my career, .282 and .272, but I couldn't get another job. Just when I was getting the hang of it, I was finished. Now it was time to think about what I was going to do with the rest of my life.

I filled a variety of roles for the Mets, including a roving instructor and analyst on cable television alongside Ralph Kiner and Tim McCarver. By 1982, Joe Torre had been fired as manager of the Mets and replaced by George Bamberger, a New York native who had been a journeyman pitcher for the New York Giants and Baltimore Orioles, and later a highly respected pitching coach for Earl Weaver with the Orioles (he was the O's pitching coach against us in the 1969 World Series) and still later the manager of the Milwaukee Brewers for two seasons.

With Bamberger came new coaches, and I was invited to be Bambi's first-base coach. I eagerly accepted and dived passionately into my new role. I wanted to do my best to help Bamberger succeed as the manager of the Mets. He had a reputation as a pitching guru, but unfortunately his success as a pitching coach did not carry over to his managerial career.

We finished last in 1982, and by the first week of June in 1983, we again were last. After 46 games, we had a record of 16-30 and Bamberger had had enough. He never wanted to manage the Mets in the first place. He had suffered a heart attack in 1980 and was retired from baseball when he got a call from Mets general manager Frank Cashen. The two men, Cashen and Bamberger, had formed a bond when they were together in Baltimore, Bambi as pitching coach, Cashen as GM. Cashen begged Bamberger to come to the Mets as their manager, and Bambi found it difficult to say no to his friend. He took the job against his better judgment.

Now Bamberger was calling it quits, and the Mets were in the market for a new manager. In the meantime, for the remainder of the season they turned the team over to one of their coaches, the gentle giant, Frank Howard, affectionately known as Hondo.

Who doesn't like Hondo? He's one of the most lovable creatures that ever walked the earth. It has often been said that it's a sign of God's compassion that Hondo was created with such a pleasant and amiable disposition. Listed in the record books as six feet seven inches tall and 255 pounds (a gross underestimate), Frank Howard could have wreaked unspeakable havoc on mankind had he been created with a mean streak. If somebody crossed him and he ever got angry, he'd have wound up in jail. He'd have killed somebody. Maybe several somebodies.

Howard had been a college basketball star, an all-America at Ohio State University who could have had a successful career in the National Basketball Association. Instead, he opted for baseball and was signed by the Dodgers as a free agent in 1958. Two years later he was voted National League Rookie of the Year.

In 16 seasons with the Dodgers, Washington Senators, Texas Rangers, and Detroit Tigers, Howard put up career numbers of 382 home runs and 1,119 runs batted in and was a 4-time All-Star. He led the American League in home runs twice with Washington, in 1968 and 1970, each time belting 44 homers. In 1969, he hit 48 home runs but finished one behind Harmon Killebrew for the league lead. In 1970, he also led the league in RBIs with 126. Four times he drove in more than 100 runs in a season.

People who saw him in his prime say Hondo hit some of the hardest balls and longest home runs in baseball history. Three seats in the upper reaches of Washington's RFK Stadium are painted white to commemorate where mammoth home runs hit by Howard landed. I can believe all the stories I've heard about his power and strength as a hitter because he hit the hardest fungoes I have ever seen.

As a coach, Hondo was as loyal as he could be no matter who the manager was. He worked his tail off and tried everything in his power to help that ball club win because he was part of the manager's team and the record of the team was a reflection of him as a coach.

When I became a coach for the Mets, Hondo was already there, and he kind of took me under his wing. I can still hear him in that big, booming voice:

"All right, you're the new coach. You're the rookie coach. You're in charge of the balls."

Hondo wanted to grab all the scuffed baseballs from the batting cage and take them on the road because we would be playing on turf and the balls would get cleaned up. Hondo, like Yogi Berra before him, was always the first one at the ballpark. No matter how hard I tried, I couldn't beat either of them to the park, home or away. The first thing Hondo did when he arrived at the park and got into his uniform was put his street clothes in the washer and then hang them up to dry. After the game, he'd have freshly washed clothes to wear. We never saw him with a suitcase. I'm convinced he owned one shirt, one pair of slacks, and one jacket. After all, how many size 62 jackets can you buy?

One day in Houston, he and I were out on the field. The players weren't out yet, so I said, "Hondo, grab a bat. I'll throw to you."

First pitch, he hit it off the fence. Second pitch, he hit one into the seats. He was in his fifties by then and he kept popping balls out of sight as if it were nothing.

One of the deals when Gil Hodges became our manager was that we were to play the Washington Senators every year in spring training, the first time in the spring of 1968. I was at shortstop when Hondo came up and Gil waved to me to play deeper. I moved back onto the outfield grass, and Gil waved at me to get even deeper. I ended up practically in left field, as if I were the short fielder in softball, and Hondo hit a wicked line drive right at me. I was about to jump for it, but the ball had topspin and it sank, and I caught it at my knees.

I don't know where Hondo is now, but wherever he is, I know

he's somewhere hitting fungoes, even if it's to his grandkids. He's probably killing his grandkids. When I was a scout for the Mets, Hondo was with the Tampa Bay Rays, and I was over at the old Payson complex saying hello to some guys. Hondo was there and was with a minor leaguer, just the two of them, and the whole time I was there, maybe more than an hour, Hondo was hitting fungoes to this kid.

After Bamberger left and Howard took over as manager, we played a little better, a record of 52-64, but we still finished last. I think Hondo was hoping the team would do well enough that the Mets would keep him on as manager, but Frank Cashen had other ideas. His choice to manage the Mets was Davey Johnson, another with a Baltimore connection. Johnson had hit the fly ball that Cleon Jones caught for the final out of the 1969 World Series.

Johnson had never managed in the major leagues, but in the previous two seasons he had piloted Mets farm teams to championships in the Texas League with Jackson and in the International League with Tidewater, where he managed top Mets prospects Ron Darling, Jose Oquendo, Wally Backman, and Darryl Strawberry.

Johnson would take over as manager of the Mets in 1984, and he would be bringing his own coaches with him. That left me on the outside, looking in, but the Mets wanted to keep me in the organization and gave me my choice of several jobs. One of them—manager of their farm team in the short-season, entry-level, Class A New York–Penn League, the Little Falls Mets—appealed to me. I had often thought about trying my hand at managing, and this was my chance to get my managerial feet wet. I went to Little Falls, which is in upstate New York, near Utica. We finished second in the regular season with a 44-31 record, made the play-offs and won the championship.

The following year, I was assigned to manage the Columbia

Mets of the Class A Sally League. At Columbia, we won 22 of our first 35 games with a team that had only one player who would have an impact with the Mets, Gregg Jefferies. We were in first place when I was asked to join Davey Johnson's coaching staff.

So I packed my bags and headed home, to Long Island and Shea Stadium and to another piece of New York Mets history.

CHAPTER 17

Davey Johnson's positive impact as manager of the Mets was immediate. He started his major league managerial career by winning 6 of his first 7 games in 1984, and he took a team that was last in the National League East with a record of 68-94, 22 games out of first, and improved them by 22 games.

The Mets' record of 90-72, a winning percentage of .556, was their best since 1969, the second-best record in franchise history, and it lifted them to second place, just 6½ games behind the Cubs, all impressive for a rookie manager. He had guided the Mets out of a seven-year abyss in which they never had a winning season, had an aggregate record of 434-641, a winning percentage of .404, and finished sixth in a six-team division five times and fifth twice.

Only forty-one years old himself, Johnson appeared to be the perfect leader and role model for a team that relied heavily on its young players. With a bevy of young talent, the future was promising for the Mets. Wally Backman was twenty-four, Ron Darling twenty-three, Kevin Mitchell twenty-two, Sid Fernandez twenty-one. Darryl Strawberry, twenty-two, had been voted National League Rookie of the Year in 1983. Dwight Gooden, nineteen, was NL Rookie of the Year in 1984.

Added to that collection of young talent was a mix of proven veterans such as Keith Hernandez, obtained in a trade with the Cardinals midway through the 1983 season, George Foster, acquired from Cincinnati before the 1982 season, Ray Knight, who came from Houston in August of '84, Jesse Orosco, acquired from the Minnesota Twins for Jerry Koosman back in the winter of 1979, and Mookie Wilson, drafted by the Mets in 1977.

Expectations were high in 1985, especially after General Manager Frank Cashen continued to tinker with the roster. Roger McDowell, drafted in 1982, came up and teamed with Jesse Orosco to form an effective lefty-righty bullpen tandem. Rick Aguilera, a 1983 draftee, arrived and moved into the five-man starting rotation. Rafael Santana, a veteran presence and a slick fielder who was signed as a free agent the previous January, replaced the inexperienced Jose Oquendo at shortstop. Cashen traded pitcher Walt Terrell to the Tigers and in return got Howard Johnson, "HoJo," a switch-hitting third baseman with a world of still-untapped power.

But the big blockbuster trade came on December 10, 1984, and it would be a difference-maker. In time it would come to be known as the trade that delivered the final piece of the puzzle to the Mets. In exchange for four players (the only one of note being Hubie Brooks), the Mets obtained from Montreal Gary Carter, the premier catcher in the National League. Only thirty-one, Carter, known as the Kid, was a 7-time All-Star and a 3-time Gold Glove winner. In 10 seasons with the Expos, he had hit 215 home runs and driven in 794 runs. He was the perfect guy to handle the Mets' young pitching staff and to fit in the middle of an already potent batting order.

Cashen's deals made the Mets a strong contender for the 1985 National League pennant, and they broke quickly from the gate, winning their first 5 games and 8 of their first 9.

Like the big club, my Columbia Mets were off to a flying start in the South Atlantic League. On May 17, we were in first place when I got a call from New York. The Texas Rangers had fired their manager, Doug Rader, and hired Davey Johnson's third-base coach, Bobby Valentine, to replace him. That left the Mets without a third-base coach, and I was being asked to report to New York immediately to fill the position. My burgeoning managerial career would have to be put on hold.

I arrived home to find the Mets already in first place by a game and a half over the Cubs. Through the months of May and June, we played hopscotch with the Cubs and Expos for the lead, but in July, the Cardinals came on and forged into the lead. We spent much of the summer chasing the Cards, but never fell more than 4 games behind them.

By August, the National League East had become a two-horse race, us and the Cardinals, with the Cards of Ozzie Smith, Vince Coleman, Willie McGee, Jack Clark, and Terry Pendleton maintaining a slim lead. We stayed close to them and then overtook them and grabbed a 1-game lead on September 12. But the Cards ran off 7 straight wins and 14 in their next 15 games, and on the morning of September 28, we found ourselves 4½ games behind with only 8 games left.

We could have folded our tents right then and there and tried to regroup for 1986 and nobody would have accused us of quitting. But we didn't, and that was a credit to Davey Johnson's leadership and to the character of the players on that team. We won that day and the Cardinals split a doubleheader. We won the next day and the Cards lost. That left us 3 games out as we went into St. Louis for a showdown 3-game series on October 1, 2, 3. It meant our fate was in our hands. A 3-game sweep and we'd be tied for first place with momentum on our side. No team can ask for more than that.

We won the first game, a brilliant and tense pitchers' duel between Ron Darling, who gave us 9 scoreless innings, and John Tudor, who pitched 10 scoreless innings. With two outs in the top of the eleventh, Darryl Strawberry put us ahead when he blasted his 28th home run off left-hander Ken Dayley. Jesse Orosco set the Cards down in the bottom of the eleventh, and we were only 2 games behind.

The next night, Doc Gooden pitched a complete game, striking out 10 and beating the Cardinals, 5–2, for his 24th win (at age twenty, Gooden would finish with a 24-4 record, lead the National League in wins, ERA at 1.53, complete games with 16, innings pitched with 276⅔, and strikeouts with 268, and he would pitch 8 shutouts and win the Cy Young Award).

Two down and one to go! We had won the first 2 games of the 3-game series, beaten the Cardinals twice in their own ballpark in front of their rabid fans, and now we were only 1 game behind. But the next night, Danny Cox outpitched Rick Aguilera, the Cardinals beat us, 4–3, and we fell 2 games behind with 3 games to play.

We weren't officially eliminated until the next-to-last game of the season when we were beaten by Montreal. The Cardinals won the division and then beat the Dodgers in the National League Championship Series to capture the pennant, but then lost the World Series in seven games to the Kansas City Royals.

Of course we were disappointed to have come so close and not won the pennant, but we had no reason to be dejected. We had won 98 games, the second-most wins in team history, we had drawn 2, 761, 601 fans to Shea Stadium, the most by any New York team, Giants, Dodgers, Yankees, or Mets, and our young players had gained some valuable experience that was certain to help us down the road.

Everybody—most experts included—believed we were ready to win the pennant in 1986. Even with the nucleus of our team already in place, Frank Cashen figured we needed a bit of fine-tuning, and he pulled off two trades in the off-season that would help us immeasurably. From the Minnesota Twins, he acquired Tim Teufel, who would prove to be a valuable right-handed bat off the bench and a capable extra infielder at three positions, first base, second, and third. From the Boston Red Sox, he obtained pitcher Bob Ojeda, a five-year veteran who had won 33 games in the previous three seasons. Ojeda was experienced, he was tough, he was smart, and he was left-handed.

We won the first 2 games of the season, lost the next 3, then ran off 11 straight wins with Doc Gooden winning 3 of the 11 and allowing just 3 runs. On April 30, after only 16 games, we were in first place in the NL East by 5 games over the Montreal Expos. The Braves stopped our winning streak, but the next day we started a new streak and ran off 7 straight wins to raise our record to 20-4.

On July 4, we were 12½ games ahead of the pack, and we kept the pedal on the metal. On August 1 our lead was 16½ games, and on September 1, it was 19 games. There was simply no stopping us. This was a team with a mission. It also was a team with a reputation . . . for playing hard and partying hard.

The 1986 Mets were gifted, they were cocky, and they were rowdy, a rollicking, rip-roaring collection of hooligans that battled each other and the opposition. The media dubbed them the Wild Bunch, a bunch of guys with chips on their shoulders, and they took out their hostility on one another and on the rest of the National League.

They had their differences, but every player on that team would be in the foxhole with you. You didn't want to fight that team. You didn't want to start anything with that ball club because they'd fight you and kick your butt. They wouldn't take anything from anybody. You'd throw at them and they'd let you know they wouldn't stand for it. They had a swagger. They came to beat you. Other teams thought the Mets were arrogant . . . and they were. They had talent, a unique chemistry, and a manager that would look the other way and let boys be boys.

Davey Johnson was the right manager for that team with all of its diverse personalities and their wild lifestyle. He did everything right. He was a players' manager and not much of a disciplinarian. If you didn't want to take infield practice, you didn't have to take infield practice on Davey's team. And he handled the press great. But at times he annoyed Cashen. Cashen didn't like that Davey would tell it like it was. He'd say, "We need a left-hander, we're struggling here," or, "We need a right-handed bat off the bench. We need this. We need that." Davey would say it and the writers would write it and people would read it and the next thing you knew, the fans were getting on the talk shows criticizing the front office for not getting the players the manager wanted. Davey thought like a general manager, and he usually got what he wanted. And he had guts.

In 1982, before Davey took over, the Mets had made a big splash by obtaining George Foster in a trade with Cincinnati, then signing him to a five-year contract for $10 million, a king's ransom at the time. Foster had set the baseball world on its ear when he hit 52 homers and drove in 149 runs in 1977, and now, five years later, the Mets were looking for more of the same.

But in his first four years, Foster never hit more than 28 homers, never drove in 100 runs, never batted higher than .269, and never impressed Johnson. Davey didn't want Foster on his team. Midway through the 1986 season he said he wanted the Mets to bite the bullet, pay off Foster, and release him. He said he wanted to get rid of Foster and keep rookie Kevin Mitchell. It was a big thing for the organization when Foster came to the Mets, and now the manager wanted to get rid of him. It took courage on Davey's part to defy the front office and suggest such a move, but Davey never lacked courage.

And it turned out to be the right move. Foster hooked on with the White Sox, batted .216 in 15 games, hit 1 home run, and drove in 4 runs for them the remainder of the year, and never played another season in the majors, while Mitchell was a key contributor in 1986 in both the regular season and the postseason. Getting rid of Foster and promoting Mitchell was another example of Johnson's ability to evaluate players and understand their character. As difficult as that 1986 team was to manage, Davey handled them and he did it his way. Sometimes it was simply "go ahead and let them tear up the plane." Almost nothing was off-limits as long as the team performed, and they performed better than most. We won 108 games, which at the time made us only the ninth team in baseball history to win that many, clinched the division title on September 17, with 17 games still to play, and finished 21½ games ahead of the Phillies.

Once we clinched the division, Davey turned to me and said,

"It's all yours, go get 'em. I'm done." He had done his job, clinched the division, and now he was turning the team over to me to manage the rest of the regular season.

In the National League West, the Houston Astros had been almost as dominant as the Mets. They won 10 of their first 14 games and were in first place through most of June before dropping out of first. The Astros regained first place to stay on July 21. By August 25, they were 8 games in front. They would win 96 games and finish the season 10 games ahead of Cincinnati's Big Red Machine.

Houston and the Mets had joined the National League as expansion teams together in 1962. While their division title in 1986 was the Mets' third, and they had won pennants in 1969 and 1973 and the World Series in '69, the Astros had won only one other division title, in 1980, and they had never won a National League pennant.

The 1986 Astros were powered by first baseman Glenn Davis, tied for second in the league in home runs with 31, and fourth in the league in RBI with 101, and by outfielder Kevin Bass, fourth in the league in batting at .311 to go along with 20 homers and 79 RBI.

The strength of the Astros, however, was their pitching, led by Mike Scott, left-hander Bob Knepper, reliever Dave Smith, and an ageless Nolan Ryan, my old teammate. At thirty-nine, Ryan was still overpowering. He won 12 games, lost 8, and was second in the league in strikeouts with 194 in 178 innings. Knepper was 17-12 and Smith was third in the league in saves with 33. But Scott was the ace of the Astros' staff.

Like Ryan, Scott also started his career with the Mets. He was taken by them out of Pepperdine University in the second round of the 1976 draft and reached the big club in 1979. In four years with the Mets, Mike won 14 games and lost 27, so he was shipped to Houston for outfielder Danny Heep, who was an important contributor to our success in 1986. Used as a fourth outfielder and pinch hitter, Heep batted .282 with 5 home runs and 33 RBI in 195 at bats.

In Houston, Scott turned his career around with the help of another former Met, Roger Craig, who taught Mike the split-finger fastball. The splitter was Scott's bread-and-butter pitch (although rumors throughout baseball said the real reason for his success was that he was putting a little more than "butter" on the baseball). Whatever he was doing (the consensus said it was sandpaper), Mike threw a pitch that would suddenly drop out of sight as it reached home plate and was practically unhittable.

For the second straight year, Scott had won 18 games for the Astros in 1986. He was tied for third in the National League with those 18 wins, first in earned run average at 2.22, first in strikeouts with 306 in 275⅓ innings, and tied for first with 5 shutouts.

Scott had won his 18th game of the season against the Giants on September 25 as the Astros clinched the National League West championship, and he embellished it by pitching a no-hitter and striking out 13. He was obviously coming into the National League Championship Series at the top of his game.

We had faced the Astros 12 times during the regular season, 12 skirmishes in a six-month war. We held a 7–5 edge over them, 6 of the 12 games decided by 1 run and 2 of them in extra innings. The Astros were a tough foe. Knepper beat us 3 times, but we beat Ryan 3 times. Still, we hadn't seen the Astros since the middle of July when we went to Houston for a 4-game series.

In the first game of the series, on July 17, we ripped Ryan and scalded the Astros, 13–2. Backman knocked in 5 runs and Strawberry 3. The next night, Knepper pitched a 3-hitter, struck out 9, and beat Darling, 3–0. No big deal. We were still 60-26 and 12 games in front in the NL East.

After the game, a few of our virile, young athletes decided to blow off steam and drown their sorrows in a Houston watering hole called Cooter's. There, things got a little rambunctious and Ron Darling, Tim Teufel, Bobby Ojeda, and Rick Aguilera, four of our upstanding examples of young athletic prowess, ended up spending the night in one of that fair city's finest holding establishments.

The following night, Scott would make his only start against us during the regular season. He hooked up with Doc Gooden in a marquee matchup of aces. After 3 scoreless innings, the Astros pushed across a run in the fourth and 2 in the fifth. When the Astros loaded the bases with nobody out in the sixth, Gooden was removed.

Meanwhile, Scott took a 4–0 shutout into the top of the ninth. To that point, he had allowed just 2 hits—a double in the fourth by Wally Backman, and a single in the eighth by Mookie Wilson—and struck out 7. In the ninth, Scott either tired or his "splitter" stopped splitting and we rallied. Lenny Dykstra led off with a home run. After Backman tried bunting for a base hit and popped it up, Keith Hernandez singled, and Gary Carter doubled him home to make it 4–2.

Dave Smith was brought in to try to get the final out and nail down the win for Scott. However, Darryl Strawberry greeted Smith with a tremendous home run into the right-field seats to tie the score. We got two more base runners in the inning, but Kevin Mitchell grounded out to end the rally, and in the bottom of the ninth, after the first two Astros batters were retired, Reynolds belted a home run off Roger McDowell to give Houston a 5–4 victory.

The final meeting between us and the Astros in the regular season on July 20 turned out to be a preview of things to come, a shoot-out with five lead changes and two ties that went 15 innings and took five hours and twenty-nine minutes. We trailed 4–2 in the top of the eighth when we scored 3 times to take a 5–4 lead. In the bottom of the eighth, the Astros scored 4 times and grabbed an 8-5 lead, but we scored three in the top of the ninth on Dykstra's lead-off home run and Strawberry's 2-run shot to tie at 8–8. And that's how it stayed until the Astros pushed across the winning run in the bottom of the fifteenth.

Now we were about to meet again in a best-of-seven National League Championship Series to determine the 1986 National League champion. Two evenly matched teams with the Astros having the slight advantage of playing Games 1 and 2 and, if necessary, Games 6 and 7 at home, and a greater advantage in Mike Scott, new and improved since July 19 and ominously looming ahead of us with a chance that he would start Games 1, 4, and 7, if needed.

The 1986 National League Championship Series had all the makings of a barn burner.

Game 1 of the National League Championship Series took place in the Houston Astrodome on the night of October 8 and featured a marquee matchup of the two teams' respective aces, Mike Scott for Houston, Doc Gooden for the Mets. Often when there is a much anticipated matchup of star pitchers, it falls flat and doesn't live up to the hype. Not this time. Both pitchers were on their game and would wind up in a classic pitchers' duel.

Scott established his dominance right from the outset when, after Wally Backman reached on an error with one out in the first inning, he struck out our 3 and 4 hitters, Keith Hernandez and Gary Carter.

While Gooden was not as efficient as Scott, he was tough in the clutch. Glenn Davis had led off the bottom of the second with a home run, after which the Astros loaded the bases with one out but failed to score as Gooden struck out Scott and got Billy Hatcher to bounce to third.

Hernandez got our first hit in the fourth, a single with one out, and the Astros threatened again in the bottom of the fourth, once more loading the bases with one out on 3 straight singles. But Gooden dodged another bullet by inducing Scott to hit into an inning-ending double play. The game was becoming a cliché—the big bopper hitting a home run and the ace pitchers frustrating the hitters, albeit with different formulas, Scott striking out everybody in sight and Gooden pitching out of jam after jam.

In the fifth, Rafael Santana got our second hit, a two-out single, but Gooden grounded out, and in the bottom of the fifth, Billy

Hatcher walked, stole second, and went to third on an infield out, but was thrown out attempting to score on a ground ball to short, and Gooden retired Davis on a fly ball to left to end the inning.

It was still 1–0 when Gooden was due to hit with one out in the eighth, so Davey had no choice but to lift Doc for a pinch hitter, Danny Heep, who stroked a single to center. Lenny Dykstra followed with a single, giving us runners on first and second with one out and the middle of our batting order coming up. This was our chance. But Scott would hear none of it. He struck out Backman and Hernandez.

Carter opened the ninth with a ground ball to third. Darryl Strawberry gave us hope when he singled, stole second, and moved to third on an infield out. Runner on third, two outs and down by a run with Ray Knight coming to bat. It was all up to him. But Ray was no match for Scott, who finished his gem with a flourish, ending the game with his 14th strikeout.

Scott was brilliant, every bit as dominant as we feared he might be. We were down one game to none and faced the prospect of having to hit against Scott twice more over the next seven days.

We had to put that thought out of our minds and concentrate on winning Game 2, which would be no easy task. We were going against Nolan Ryan, of all people, and he was certainly capable of doing to us what Scott had done.

Against Nolie in Game 2, we went 3 up, 3 down, in each of the first 3 innings, including 5 by strikeout. Oh, no, not again!

Fortunately, Bobby Ojeda was also on his game in the early innings after facing a threat in the second when the Astros put runners on first and third with one out. But Kevin Bass was thrown out at home on a fielder's choice for the second out, and Ojeda ended the threat by making Dickie Thon his third strikeout victim.

We finally broke through in the fourth with 2 runs off Ryan on singles by Backman and Hernandez, a double by Carter, and Strawberry's sacrifice fly, then added 3 more in the fifth, when Hernandez struck a 2-run triple.

Ryan was lifted for a pinch hitter in the bottom of the fifth, and Ojeda went the distance for the win. He allowed 10 hits, but pitched out of trouble several times and held the Astros to only 1 run. We were going back to New York, tied at one game each, so we had achieved our goal of taking at least one game on the road. Now we had to capitalize on the home-field advantage we would have over the next 3 games.

It was left-hander Bob Knepper, a 17-game winner, for the Astros against 15-game winner Ron Darling in Game 3 on a Saturday afternoon in Shea Stadium. Before we knew what hit us, we found ourselves in a 4–0 hole as the Astros scored 2 in the first inning and 2 more in the second. After 5 innings, we had only 4 hits off Knepper and no runs, and Darling was out of the game, having been lifted for a pinch hitter in the bottom of the fifth.

We awoke in the sixth. A couple of singles and an error by shortstop Craig Reynolds for 1 run, and a 3-run homer by Strawberry that tied the score, sent the crowd of more than 55,000 into a frenzy.

The Astros regained the lead with an unearned run in the top of the seventh, and that's how it stood as we came to bat in the bottom of the ninth. We were three outs away from going down two games to one, a deficit that we would have a difficult time overcoming, and we were facing a tough customer in the Astros' closer, Dave Smith.

Backman led off by bunting for a hit and moved up a base on a passed ball. Heep, batting for Santana, flied to center, and that brought up Dykstra, who had batted for Rick Aguilera in the seventh and stayed in the game. It proved to be a fortunate switch as Lenny, who had hit only 8 homers during the season, drilled one over the right-field scoreboard to pull out a 6–5 victory and put us up in the series, 2–1.

How critical was Dykstra's home run? The next day Scott, pitching with only three days' rest, dominated us again. He allowed just 3 hits, struck out 5, and went the distance for a 3–1 win, our only run coming in the eighth on a sacrifice fly by Danny Heep, batting for Santana. Our starter, Sid Fernandez, also only gave up 3 hits, but 2 of them were home runs, a 2-run shot in the second by their No. 7 hitter, Alan Ashby, and a solo shot in the fifth by their No. 8 hitter, Dickie Thon.

Now we were tied two games each with 3 games left, Game 5 at Shea, and Game 6 and, if necessary, Game 7 back in Houston. What's more, we knew that unless we could win the next two games, we would have to face Mike Scott one more time, in a sudden-death Game 7.

For the fifth game, Davey Johnson again gave the ball to Gooden, and Doc was outstanding. He allowed a run in the fifth when Ashby doubled and Reynolds singled him to third. Reynolds was forced at second in an attempted sacrifice and Bill Doran followed with a grounder to second. Backman threw to Santana for the force but Raffy's turn to first to complete the double play was too late as Doran just beat the throw and Ashby scored to give the Astros a 1–0 lead.

That was all Houston would get against Gooden, but we were up against Nolan Ryan, who was throwing as if he was twenty-nine years old, not thirty-nine. Nolie was perfect for the first 4 innings, 12 up, 12 down, 8 of them on strikeouts. After the Astros scored their run in the top of the fifth, we tied it in the bottom half on Strawberry's homer. That's how it stood, 1–1, after 9 innings when Ryan left, having allowed just 2 hits and striking out 12.

Charlie Kerfeld replaced Ryan in the tenth, and Jesse Orosco picked up after Gooden and set the Astros down in order in the eleventh and the twelfth.

In the bottom of the twelfth, Backman singled with one out and was nearly picked off by Kerfeld, who instead threw wildly to first. Backman scampered to second. Astros manager Hal Lanier walked the left-handed-hitting Hernandez to pitch to the right-handed-hitting Carter, hoping to get out of the inning with a double play. Instead, Carter lined a single to center to score Backman with the winning run. The Astros outhit us, 9–4, but we won the game, 2–1, and took a 3–2 lead in the series.

All we needed to do was win one out of two in Houston, but we knew it wasn't going to be easy. We got a break because there was no day off between Games 5 and 6, and that meant Mike Scott would not be able to start the sixth game (he would have been pitching on only two days' rest). However, he would be able to pitch Game 7 on three days' rest, which made it imperative that we win Game 6 so we could avoid facing Scott.

Game 6 of the 1986 National League Championship Series was a nail-biter that went 16 innings, took four hours and forty-two minutes to complete, involved 36 players, had more twists, turns, stops, and starts than San Francisco's Lombard Street, and left 45,718 fans, 50 players, and a dozen coaches and managers limp. Many have called it the greatest baseball game ever played, and I'm not about to dispute that claim.

Game 6 was do-or-die for the Astros, not for us, but even though it wasn't a seventh game of a series, it had the feel of a seventh game for us. We knew that if we didn't win this game, our pitching opponent in a Game 7 would be Mike Scott, and he had already tied us in knots in two previous play-off games with two complete games, one of them on three days' rest. In those two games, Scott had dominated us, allowing 1 run and 8 hits, walking 1 and striking out 19.

What chance did we have, realistically, if it came down to a seventh game in the Astrodome? Our guys were saying all the right things about having to face Scott a third time—that he'd been beaten 10 times and we had won 108 games that season, that after losing twice to him the law of averages were in our favor. But did they really believe what they were saying?

Things looked bleak when the Astros jumped all over Bobby Ojeda in the first inning of Game 6, scoring 3 runs on 4 hits and a walk. Even when Kevin Bass was thrown out at home on a botched squeeze play by Alan Ashby, it didn't appear to be too severe a blow to the Astros' chances. We had no idea at the time how important their failure to score that add-on run was going to be.

After his terrible start, Ojeda settled in and allowed just 1 more hit over the next 4 innings. The problem was that over the first 5 innings, we had just 1 hit off Houston's starter, left-hander Bob Knepper. I could begin to sense the anxiety in our dugout as the innings went by. Guys were saying, "We better win this one because we have that other guy tomorrow." That "other guy," of course, was Mike Scott.

As the game went on, things kept getting worse for us. Ojeda was removed for a pinch hitter in the sixth and relieved by Rick Aguilera, who held the Astros to just 1 hit over the next 3 innings. But Knepper went to the ninth inning still leading 3–0. He was dealing. He had allowed just 2 singles, walked 1, and struck out 6. Knepper was practically unhittable. And Mike Scott was looming.

Down by 3 runs, which seemed insurmountable the way Knepper was pitching, we faced our last chance with Lenny Dykstra leading off the top of the ninth. As he had done so often all season, Lenny gave us life and got us started with a triple. You could see our dugout visibly energized by Lenny's shot. Mookie Wilson followed with a single to score Dykstra, moved to second on Kevin Mitchell's infield out, and scored on a double by Hernandez. That made it a 3–2 game and got rid of Knepper. Dave Smith came in to relieve him.

Pitching carefully, Smith walked Gary Carter and Darryl Strawberry to load the bases. Ray Knight then hit a drive to right, deep enough to score Hernandez after the catch, and whaddaya know, we were tied. Strap in your seat belts, it was going to be a long and bumpy ride.

The Astros went down in order in the bottom of the ninth.

We went down in order in the top of the tenth.

The Astros went down in order in the bottom of the tenth.

In the top of the eleventh, Hernandez grounded out, Carter walked, Strawberry popped to third, Knight struck out.

The Astros went down in order in the bottom of the eleventh.

We went down in order in the top of the twelfth.

In the bottom of the twelfth, Davis struck out and Bass singled. Bass, who had stolen 22 bases during the regular season but had been caught stealing 13 times, was thrown out again attempting to steal, this time on a straight steal of second. Jose Cruz grounded out to end the inning.

We went down in order in the top of the thirteenth.

Houston went down in order in the bottom of the thirteenth.

Roger McDowell pitched five innings for us, from the ninth through the thirteenth, allowed 1 single, and faced the minimum 15 batters.

Larry Andersen pitched 3 innings for Houston, from the eleventh through the thirteenth, allowed one base runner, a walk to Carter.

Aurelio Lopez, "Senor Smoke," replaced Andersen in the fourteenth and gave up a single to Carter and a walk to Strawberry. Knight, attempting to bunt the runners along, forced Carter at third. But Backman singled to score Strawberry and break the tie. Knight went to third and Backman to second when the ball was bobbled by Bass. With runners on second and third, Howard Johnson popped to the catcher. Dykstra was intentionally walked to load the bases, but Wilson struck out.

Jesse Orosco came in to pitch the bottom of the fourteenth, needing three outs to get the save and clinch the pennant. He struck out Doran. With the Astros down to their last two outs, Hatcher crushed a 3-2 pitch down the left-field line, the ball landing in the seats just inside the foul pole, sending the crowd of 47,718 into hysterics. Once again the score was tied. Would this game never end?

In the top of the fifteenth, our first two batters went down and Carter singled, but was out trying to stretch it into a double.

The Astros went down in order in the bottom of the fifteenth.

Strawberry opened the top of the sixteenth with a double and scored on a single by Knight, who raced to second on the throw home. Left-hander Jeff Calhoun replaced Lopez and promptly threw a wild pitch that sent Knight to third and then walked Backman. Another wild pitch scored Knight and sent Backman to second. Orosco sacrificed Backman to third, and Wally scored on a single by Dykstra. After scoring only 1 run in the previous 6 innings, we had put a 3 on the board and with Orosco on the mound, we figured we were home free. Or were we?

Orosco struck out Craig Reynolds to start the inning, but Davey Lopes, winding down his fabulous career, batted for Calhoun and Orosco walked him. *With a 3-run lead!* Doran singled Lopes to second and Hatcher followed with a single that scored Lopes and sent Doran to second. Denny Walling forced Hatcher. The Astros were down to their final out, but they were not dead yet. Davis singled to score Doran, sending Walling to second with the tying run and bringing Kevin Bass, the Astros' leading hitter, to the plate.

A single would probably tie the score. A double could win it. The specter of Mike Scott was looming larger, and Doug Sisk was warming up in our bullpen. But this was going to be Orosco's game, win or lose. Hernandez went to the mound and told Orosco that if he threw anything but a slider, "I'll kill you."

Orosco threw nothing but sliders. Six of them. The count reached 3-2. Walling danced off second, Davis off first, Cruz waited in the on-deck circle. Another slider! A swing! A miss!

It was over. There was jubilation and relief in our clubhouse, jubilation because we were going to the World Series; relief because we didn't have to face "that other guy," Mike Scott. He could have changed history.

CHAPTER 18

We were going to the World Series for the first time in thirteen years, trying to win it for the first time in seventeen years, but if you think our fans were deprived, consider our opponents. The Boston Red Sox were going to the World Series for the first time in eleven years, and trying to win it for the first time in sixty-eight years.

The last time the Red Sox stood at the top of the heap in baseball was in 1918, when they beat the Cubs in 6 games and a young, left-handed pitcher named Babe Ruth won Games 1 and 4. Since then, they had made it to the World Series in 1946, 1967, and 1975 and, of course, had lost all three times.

And if you think we dodged a bullet with our nail-biting 16-inning victory over the Houston Astros, consider how the Red Sox squeaked into the World Series. They had won the American League East title with 95 victories and a 5½ game lead over the Yankees, then took on the California Angels in the American League Championship Series.

The Red Sox and Angels split the first two games in Boston, then the Angels went home and won the next two games, giving them a commanding 3–1 lead in the best-of-seven series. In Game 5, the Angels rallied from behind and took a 5–2 lead going into the top of the ninth. The Angels were three outs away from making it to the World Series for the first time in their twenty-six-year history.

Bill Buckner led off the top of the ninth with a single, but Jim Rice struck out. Don Baylor then blasted a home run to make it a 5–4 game, but Dwight Evans popped to third and the Angels were one out away from the World Series. They would not get that out as Rich Gedman was hit by a pitch and Dave Henderson broke the Angels' hearts with a 2-run home that put the Red Sox up, 6–5.

California bounced back to tie it with a run in the bottom of the ninth, and the teams went into extra innings. In the top of the eleventh, it was Henderson again, driving in the go-ahead run with a sacrifice fly. Calvin Schiraldi, a former Met, retired the Angels in order in the bottom of the eleventh and the Red Sox were alive. The Angels were still in pretty good shape, needing to win one of the last two games, but they were going to have to do it in Fenway Park, in front of those wild and crazy Red Sox fans.

With new life, and playing in cozy Fenway, the Red Sox were a different team. With 2 runs in the first and 5 in the third, they pounded out 16 hits in Game 6 and tied the Series with a 10–4 win. In Game 7, Boston got 2 home runs from Rice and 1 from Evans and beat the Angels, 8–1. The Red Sox were going to the World Series and the Angels were joining the Astros and going to wherever it is teams go to lick their wounds after they have come so close to reaching baseball's Promised Land.

We knew the Red Sox were not going to be an easy opponent for us, especially when the games were played in Fenway Park, with its cozy left-field wall, called the Green Monster. They had a potent offense with Wade Boggs, the American League batting champion at .357, two hitters with more than 100 RBI, Jim Rice with 110, fourth in the league, and Bill Buckner with 102, and two others close to 100 RBI, Dwight Evans with 97 and Don Baylor with 94. Baylor was tied for sixth in the league with 31 homers, Evans had 26, Rice 20, and Buckner 18.

Roger Clemens led the American League in wins with 24 and in earned run average with 2.48 and was second in strikeouts with 238.

Because of the hard-fought League Championship Series, neither team was able to start its ace pitcher in the opening game of the World Series, on Saturday, October 18, in Shea Stadium. In their stead, the Mets started 15-game winner Ron Darling, the Red Sox started 13-game winner Bruce Hurst, and they both pitched like aces.

The game was scoreless through 6 innings, and in the seventh the Sox pushed over an unearned run on a walk to Rice, a wild pitch, an infield out, and an error by second baseman Tim Teufel. Darling left after 7 innings, having allowed just 3 hits. He struck out 8. Hurst left after 8 innings having allowed 4 hits. He also struck out 8.

In the ninth, Red Sox manager John McNamara called on Calvin Schiraldi, who had been traded by the Mets to the Red Sox the previous November in the deal that brought Bob Ojeda to New York. Calvin, who had been used mostly as a starter with the Mets, seemed to find his niche as a reliever in Boston and had lately taken over as the Red Sox closer. He had 4 wins, 9 saves, and an earned run average of 1.41.

Schiraldi walked Strawberry to begin the bottom of the ninth and then retired Knight, Backman, and pinch hitter Heep to nail down the 1–0 victory. In one fell swoop, the Red Sox had taken Game 1 and the home-field advantage away from us.

We weren't too concerned because we had Gooden rested and ready for Game 2, while the Sox were going with their ace, Clemens, on three days' rest. Neither pitcher had it. Gooden was tagged for 6 runs and 8 hits in 5 innings, and Clemens was having trouble even with a 6–2 lead and was knocked out in the fifth. But we managed only 3 hits off Steve Crawford and Bob Stanley over the last 4⅔ innings and were hammered, 9–3.

Now we were in big trouble, down two games to none with the next three games in Boston. Hardly anybody gave us a chance to come back and win the Series. Few even thought we could bring the Series back to New York, which meant we had to win two games in Fenway Park. Our only reasons for optimism were (1) we had played an exhibition game in Fenway Park during the season, so our players would not be getting their first look at the Green Monster in the World Series; and (2) our starting pitcher for the third game was to be Bob Ojeda, who had been a Red Sox up until this season and had plenty of experience pitching in Fenway.

Monday, October 20, was a day off, and Davey Johnson took advantage of it and made a calculated decision. Normally, the visiting team schedules a workout on a day off in the World Series, using it primarily to familiarize itself with strange surroundings. Figuring his players were fatigued after the rigorous series against the Astros and that they needed to get away from the pressure and scrutiny of the World Series for a day, Davey gave the players the day off. He expected them to come back fresh and relaxed in Game 3, and his gamble paid off.

The first four batters against Dennis "Oil Can" Boyd hit safely and scored. Dykstra set the tone by leading off the game with a home run. Backman and Hernandez singled, Carter drove in Backman with a double, and later in the inning Heep's single scored Hernandez and Carter.

Ojeda pitched 7 innings, allowed 1 run and 5 hits and held Boston's right-handed power hitters Rice, Baylor, Evans, and Henderson to a combined 2 for 10. Roger McDowell pitched the eighth and ninth, 6 up, 6 down, and we had a 7–1 victory and new life.

The next day in Game 4, Darling pitched another gem, 7 innings, no runs, 4 hits. This time our hitters gave him some support— Carter 2 home runs, a 2-run shot in the fourth that broke a scoreless deadlock and a solo shot in the eighth, Dykstra a solo shot in the seventh—and we coasted to a 6–2 victory that tied the Series at 2–2. We were assured of taking the Series back to New York, but we would once again be going there with our backs against the wall.

For the second time in six days, we found left-hander Bruce Hurst difficult to solve in Game 5. And for the second time in five days, Gooden was a losing pitcher as the Red Sox jumped on Doc for single runs in the second and third and 2 more in the fifth.

We didn't score off Hurst until the eighth inning (he had held us scoreless for 15 consecutive innings), and he held on for a 4–2 victory that gave the Red Sox a 3–2 lead in the Series. In 17 innings of clutch, pressure-packed pitching, Hurst had held us to 2 runs and 14 hits and struck out 14.

Considering that we had lost the first two games of the Series at home, coming back to Shea Stadium down 3–2 felt as if we had gotten an eleventh-hour reprieve from the governor. We may have been on borrowed time, but at least we would be playing in front of our wild and raucous fans.

Game 6 of the 1986 World Series on Saturday night, October 25, is one of the most memorable games not only in Mets history, but in the history of baseball. Future baseball historians will be talking about this game for however long baseball is played and for as long as the Mets exist.

The Red Sox had their ace, Clemens, rested and ready. That didn't faze us because we had handled Clemens in Game 2. Besides, we had Ojeda pitching for us and he had done such a wonderful job in Game 3.

This time, however, the Sox jumped on Ojeda for a run in the first on a single by Boggs, a walk to Rice, and a double by Evans, and a run in the second on singles by Spike Owen, Boggs, and Marty Barrett. Meanwhile, Clemens was overpowering. In 4 innings, he had allowed only 1 base runner, a 2-out walk to Strawberry in the second, and had struck out 6.

Ojeda found his rhythm and was unscored on in the third, fourth, and fifth, and we broke through in the bottom of the fifth with 2 runs to tie the score, 2–2. Strawberry started it by drawing his second straight walk. He stole second and scored on Knight's single. Wilson singled and Knight raced to third when the ball was booted in right field by the usually sure-handed Evans, another of those little things that go unnoticed but are keys to winning. Knight scored when Heep, batting for Santana, hit into a double play (had Evans not bobbled Wilson's single, Knight would have been on second and could not have scored on Heep's DP).

Knight's run had tied the score, but 2 innings later, the Red Sox regained the lead with an unearned run of their own. Then in the eighth, Red Sox manager John McNamara made a curious move. With a 1-run lead, a runner on second with one out, and Clemens due up, he went for the kill and removed Clemens for a pinch hitter, Mike Greenwell. The strategy failed. Greenwell struck out, the Sox did not score, and McNamara put the game in the hands of his bullpen.

McNamara had chosen to replace the ace of his pitching staff, his horse, and Clemens was none too happy about it. We, on the other hand, were ecstatic. Clemens had been so dominant, we were glad to see him out of the game. This was before pitch counts were in vogue, so I doubt that was the reason McNamara yanked Clemens. But it was at the start of baseball's new pitching philosophy that put more emphasis on use of one's bullpen. For all his success, the 24 wins, the 2.48 ERA, the 238 strikeouts, Clemens had completed only 10 of 33 starts that season (the major leagues had ten pitchers with more), indicating McNamara's faith in his bullpen of Bob Stanley, Joe Sambito, and Calvin Schiraldi. Now McNamara was asking his bullpen to bail him out again and protect a 1-run lead for 2 innings.

Schiraldi started the eighth, and with time running out on us, we scratched out a run on Carter's sacrifice fly to tie the score at 3–3. Neither side scored in the ninth, so we were headed for yet another extra-inning nail-biter.

Both of our stud relievers, Roger McDowell and Jesse Orosco, had been in the game and removed for pinch hitters, so we were relying on Rick Aguilera, a twenty-four-year-old second-year man and our fifth starter who had won 10 games that season. Aggie got through the ninth, and now the first batter in the top of the tenth, Dave Henderson, drilled one over the fence in left to put the Red Sox up, 4–3. It was like a knife in our heart, but Aguilera shook that off and struck out the next two batters. After all we'd been through, one run didn't seem too much to overcome. Two runs? That's another story, and when Boggs doubled and Barrett singled him home, we were down, 5–3, coming to bat in the bottom of the tenth, three outs away from extinction.

Starting his third inning, Schiraldi retired Backman on a fly ball to left and Hernandez on a drive to left center, caught at the wall by Henderson. Now we were one out away from elimination. I could hear Red Sox players whooping it up in celebration in their dugout, on the third-base side, just a few feet behind me. I turned and spotted my old roomie, Seaver. The Red Sox had acquired Tom in June in a trade with the White Sox to help them in the stretch run. Seaver won 5 games and the Red Sox won the American League East by 5½ games.

Toward the end of the season, Tom's back was bothering him. He lost his last 2 starts, on September 13 and September 19, and never pitched again. He was not eligible for the postseason, but because of his Hall of Fame career and his stature, he was allowed to dress for the games and sit in the dugout. Now, when I turned to look into the Sox dugout, Seaver was standing near the box where the photographers were, only a few feet from me. He looked at me and mouthed, "I'll call you."

There were two outs. The Red Sox needed just one more out and they would win the World Series. They never got it. I would later learn that after Hernandez made the second out of the inning, Keith, as fierce a competitor as there is, was so disgusted, he refused to sit in the dugout and watch the Red Sox celebrate their victory on our turf. He angrily stormed off the field and into the clubhouse, where he flung his glove into his locker, grabbed a beer, lit a cigarette, and watched the rest of the game on television in the manager's office.

What happened over the next few minutes is mostly a blur in my mind. Oh, sure, I was there, but I was in the third-base coach's box concentrating on the job at hand, doing my best to block out the extraneous things going on around me. Much of what was going on I discovered after the fact, from television replays and film clips and from people telling me about them.

What I do remember is that Carter kept us alive with a solid single to left, and that the moment Carter's ball landed safely, a message flashed briefly on Shea Stadium's huge message board in right-center field. Either it was inadvertently illuminated by the scoreboard operator pressing the wrong button or the operator mistakenly thought Carter's ball was caught, ending the game and the World Series. In any case, the message congratulated the Red Sox for winning their first World Series since 1918.

The message was quickly extinguished so that most in the crowd of 55,078 either didn't see it or hadn't had time to read it. But it was up there nonetheless.

In the press box, an announcement was made that Bruce Hurst had been voted Most Valuable Player of the Series. That was not a mistake and the announcement would not be rescinded.

With two outs and a runner on first Kevin Mitchell was sent up to pinch-hit for Aguilera and lined a single to center. Now the crowd was getting excited, sensing (hoping for?) another miracle comeback.

Next up was Ray Knight. He hit a soft, looping, humpbacked line drive over second base, into short center field for a hit. Carter took off from second with the crack of the bat. I waved him home, then turned my attention to Mitchell, chugging around second and heading for third. I motioned for Mitch to slide, which he did. The score was now 5–4 and we had runners on first and third with Mookie Wilson due up.

McNamara went to the mound and signaled to the bullpen for a right-hander. Schiraldi was out and Bob Stanley was called in to relieve him. Stanley was primarily a sinker-ball pitcher. He also threw a palm ball and was intent on keeping the ball down. As a result, he was known to throw the ball in the dirt on occasion, so as Stanley took his warm-ups, I leaned over to Mitchell and reminded him to be alert and be ready to take off if Stanley threw one in the dirt.

Wilson, a slasher, fouled off the first pitch, took two balls, then fouled off another, running the count to 2-2. Mookie fouled off two more pitches in what was becoming an interminable at bat made even longer by the tension. The next pitch was in the dirt, and it shot past catcher Rich Gedman and went to the backstop. Alertly, Mitchell took off and scored the tying run. The crowd was going crazy. The Red Sox, in their dugout, were stunned into a deathly silence. And Mitchell was thinking I'm a genius. To this day, he still tells people, "Harrelson told me it was going to happen."

Duh, Mitch! I must have said the same thing five hundred times that season. Anytime a runner got to third, I reminded him to be alert for a wild pitch or a passed ball. Every third-base coach does.

The wild pitch made the count 3-2 and sent Knight to second base with the winning run. Mookie fouled off two more pitches— was this at bat destined to go on forever?—and then hit an easy four-hopper to first base, the simplest ground ball for any major leaguer, or minor leaguer, or Little Leaguer, only this one trickled under the glove of first baseman Bill Buckner and rolled into short right field.

Knight came racing to third base and I not only waved him home, I accompanied him on his journey. If you look at the highlights of Knight scoring the winning run, you can see me running right along with him. I was bringing him down the line anyway, and when the ball went through Buckner's legs, I jumped up and started running. I had to slow down because I had Ray beat and I couldn't touch home plate or get there before he did.

Buckner had been playing with a bad ankle that left him hobbling and unsteady. McNamara would be severely criticized for not replacing Buckner at first base on defense with Dave Stapleton, something he had done in three of the first five games of the World Series and throughout the final weeks of the regular season. McNamara's explanation was that he wanted Buckner to be on the field when the Red Sox clinched the World Series because Bill had been such a vital part of their success with his 18 homers and 102 RBI. McNamara let sentiment get in the way of his better judgment and it cost him.

I think Buckner might have taken his eye off the ball for a moment trying to decide if he needed to go to the bag or flip it to Stanley. And I think Buckner got caught in between because Stanley was not a guy that got off the mound quickly and Mookie was flying to first base. In fact, from my view in the third-base coach's box, I was convinced that neither Buckner, hobbling on a bad ankle, nor Stanley was going to beat the speedy Mookie to the bag. Mookie was going to beat the throw to first, but even if he was safe, the Red Sox would still be in it. The game would only be tied. The Red Sox could still have won it and clinched the World Series. Once the ball got under Buckner's glove and trickled out to short right field, that was it. The Sox were done.

People have asked me if I felt sorry for Buckner. Not at the time I didn't. He wouldn't have felt sorry for me in a similar situation. I was only thinking about winning the game. All these years later I can look back and realize how unfair it is that Buckner should be remembered for that one play that marred a tremendous career in which he played 22 seasons and 2,517 major league games, batted .289, had 2,715 hits, 174 home runs, and drove in 1,208 runs. Also, he faced up to that one negative incident with dignity and class.

Not often is the seventh game of the World Series anticlimactic, but that's exactly what Game 7 of the 1986 World Series was. Not only could it not possibly measure up to the excitement and intensity of the sixth game, but some of the urgency was removed when it rained on Sunday and the game had to be pushed back to Monday.

The rain was a break for the Red Sox. They had already announced they were starting Bruce Hurst, who had been so dominant in Games 1 and 5. He would have started the seventh game on just two days' rest, but the rainout meant he would get another day of rest and would be pitching on three days' rest. We had Ron Darling ready to start on a full four days' rest.

Because of what we had done in Game 6, nobody panicked when the Red Sox scored 3 runs off Darling in the second inning, or when Hurst retired us in order in 4 of the first 5 innings, and put down 16 of our first 17 batters. We felt it was only a matter of time before we would get to Hurst. Johnson kept exhorting his players, reminding them of the way they came back in Game 6 and so many other times during the season. He'd be walking up and down in the front of the dugout saying, "We're a great seventh-, eighth- and ninth-inning ball club."

In the sixth inning, Hurst obviously tired because after allowing only one base runner through the first 5 innings, we put four men on in a row. Lee Mazzilli got us started with a pinch-hit single. Mookie Wilson followed with a single, and Tim Teufel walked to load the bases with one out. Keith Hernandez singled in 2 runs and Gary Carter knocked in the third run with a fielder's choice, and we had tied the score, 3–3.

Momentum had shifted to our side. Hurst was lifted for a pinch hitter in the top of the seventh, and we scored 3 runs off three Boston relievers in the bottom of the seventh.

The Red Sox fought back to score 2 in the eighth until Orosco came in to stop them dead in their tracks, stranding the tying run on second by getting Gedman, Henderson, and Baylor in succession. When we scored 2 in the bottom of the eighth for an 8–5 lead, we could sense all of the fight coming out of the Sox.

In the ninth, Orosco got Ed Romero on a foul pop to Hernandez and Boggs on a bouncer to Backman, and that left Barrett as the last man standing for the Red Sox. The crowd was on its feet, chanting and cheering as Barrett ran the count to 2-2.

Carter called for a fastball. Orosco wound up and fired. Barrett swung. The ball landed in Carter's mitt with a thud.

We've all seen the picture hundreds of times. Jesse Orosco, having tossed his glove high into the air, is on both knees, his arms raised heavenward, his fists closed, his mouth open as he apparently let out a mighty roar. The National League Championship Series ended with Jesse Orosco on the mound having struck out Kevin Bass, and now the World Series had ended with Orosco on the mound having struck out Marty Barrett, and the field was being engulfed by players and fans running amok.

Me? I came shooting out of the dugout and headed straight for Jesse's glove in the center of the diamond. I remembered the way people went wild in 1969, when the fans were all over the place. They had policemen on horseback this time, but I figured the fans were still going to come onto the field anyway. I grabbed the glove before some fan swiped it. I gave it to Jesse later in the clubhouse.

It's not fair to ask me which team was better, the 1969 Mets or the 1986 Mets. I played on the '69 team, so naturally I'm going to choose them even though the '86 team won 8 more games. To me, the edge the '69 team had over the '86 team was pitching, guys like Seaver and Koosman, Gary Gentry, Nolan Ryan, Jim McAndrew, and Don Cardwell. We could beat you 2–1 or 3–2 all day, and with complete games. The pitchers on that staff didn't come out of the game at 100 pitches.

CHAPTER 19

After we won the World Series in 1969, we didn't expect it to end there. We figured we'd win a few more pennants, another World Series or two. It never happened.

Same thing after we won the World Series in 1986. We didn't expect it to end there, either. We figured we'd win a few more pennants, another World Series or two. That never happened either.

When we reported to spring training in 1987, two key members of our championship team were missing. Ray Knight, who got a huge hit and scored the winning run in Game 6 of the World Series, had become a free agent after the season. He wanted to re-sign with the Mets, but they wanted to make room for Howard Johnson as their full-time third baseman, so they played hard-ball with Knight, refused to meet his contract demands, and Ray walked and signed with the Baltimore Orioles. While HoJo made the most of his opportunity and became a big run producer (he would play 157 games that season, hit 36 home runs, and drive in 99 runs), we still missed Knight's veteran experience, leadership, and wisdom.

Also missing in spring training was Kevin Mitchell, who was Mr. Everything in our championship run (he had played all three outfield positions, first base, shortstop, and third base, hit 12 home runs and drove in 43 runs in 108 games; and he was only twenty-five years old). Mitch was traded to San Diego in an eight-player deal that brought Kevin McReynolds to the Mets. A year later,

Mitchell was traded again, to the Giants, and in 1989, he hit 47 homers, drove in 125 runs, led the Giants to the pennant, and was voted National League Most Valuable Player.

To make matters worse, on April 1, General Manager Frank Cashen called a clubhouse meeting in St. Petersburg and announced to the team that Dwight Gooden had tested positive for cocaine, was being suspended by Major League Baseball, and had entered a drug rehabilitation program.

Gooden would miss the first two months of the season. He returned to us on June 5 and started against the Pirates at Shea Stadium, welcomed by 51,402 fans. Doc pitched 6⅔ innings, allowed 1 run and 4 hits, struck out 5, and was the winner in a 5–1 victory. Although he pitched like the Doc of old that season and had a record of 15-7, he had averaged 19 wins a year in his first three seasons and was being counted on for at least that many in 1987. The difference between the 19 games he was expected to win and the 15 he did win would be the difference between our finishing in first place and second.

We managed to stay close to the first-place Cardinals for most of the season. On August 15 we were 5½ games behind when we got hot and ran off 15 wins in 22 games, including a 6-game winning streak. We had trimmed the lead to a game and a half with the Cardinals coming into Shea for three critical games on September 11, 12, and 13.

The game on Friday night, September 11, turned out to be the turning point of our season. We jumped on John Tudor for 3 runs in the first on a single by Tim Teufel, an RBI double by Keith Hernandez, and a tremendous 2-run homer by Darryl Strawberry, who had so many big hits for us all year (he finished the season with 39 homers and 104 RBI), that sent the capacity crowd of 51,795 into a frenzy.

The Cards scored a run in the second without getting a hit— two walks and two ground outs—but Mookie Wilson got that run back with a solo homer in the bottom of the second. Meanwhile,

Ron Darling was brilliant for 6 innings, allowing just 1 hit. But when he walked Dan Driessen to start the seventh, Davey decided Darling was through and went to his bullpen, first Randy Myers and then Roger McDowell, with Jesse Orosco in reserve, a winning formula all season.

We went to the top of the ninth with a 3-run lead when McDowell walked the leadoff batter, a cardinal (capital *C* or small *c*) sin. But Roger got the next two outs and we were one out away from moving a half game out, on our way to overtaking the Cardinals and taking over first place. Willie McGee kept the Cards' hopes alive with a single to center, and Terry Pendleton followed with a dagger to our heart, a home run that tied the score. You could hear a pin drop in Shea. More than 51,000 people were shocked into stunned silence.

We still had a chance to win the game in the bottom of the ninth when we put two runners on base. But Hernandez grounded out to end the inning. In the top of the tenth, the Cards got three consecutive singles and an infield out to score 2 runs off Orosco and we were beat, 6–4.

The next afternoon, the Cardinals were all over Gooden for 5 runs in the first inning while we played as if we were hungover from the previous night's disappointment and lost, 8–1. That dropped us back to 3½ games out of first.

We salvaged the final game of the series and even got back to a game and a half out of first on September 16, but that was as close as we came. We ended up winning 92 games, the fourth-highest total in Mets history to that point, but finished 3 games behind the Cardinals in the National League East. There was no wild card in those days, so we were left out of the play-offs and unable to defend our World Series championship.

We rebounded in 1988 to win 100 games and finish a whopping 15 games ahead of the Pirates. Darryl Strawberry led the league in homers with 39 and was second in RBIs with 101. McReynolds had 27 homers and 99 runs batted in. David Cone, who had come to us in a trade with the Kansas City Royals in the spring of '87, won 20 games and was second in the league in ERA with 2.22 and second in strikeouts with 213. Gooden won 18 games, and Ron Darling won 17.

The trade for Cone was one of the best ever made by the Mets. Unfortunately, the trade of Cone to Toronto in August of '92 was one of the worst. After he left us, Cone won a Cy Young with the Blue Jays in 1994. In 1998, to make matters worse, he won 20 games for our crosstown neighbors, and rivals, the Yankees.

With Cone, Gooden, and Darling at the top of our rotation, Hernandez, Strawberry, and Carter in the middle of the lineup, and Lenny Dykstra and Wally Backman as catalysts at the top of the batting order, we had a team we thought capable of winning another World Series and were supremely confident that we would get to the World Series when our opponent in the National League Championship Series turned out to be the Los Angeles Dodgers, whom we had beaten 10 times in 11 meetings during the season.

As high as our expectations were, that's how low we had fallen when the Dodgers beat us in the NLCS four games to three and knocked us out of World Series contention. The turning point in the series came in Game 4 at Shea Stadium. We had won 2 of the first 3 games and were ready to apply the hammer, leading 4–2 in the ninth inning with Gooden on the mound. But Mike Scioscia, who had hit only 3 home runs in 408 at bats all season, drove one into the right-field seats with a runner on base to tie the score. The Dodgers won the game in the twelfth inning to even the series. They won Games 5 and 7 and went on to beat the Oakland A's in the World Series, four games to one.

The "Scioscia" game might have been the low point in Mets history. We were convinced we had the best team in the National League, maybe in all of baseball. We thought we could go on to win the World Series, maybe even win a couple of World Series. Instead, we went home. That seemed to be the start of the Mets' spiraling downward. Not only didn't we get to the 1988 World Series, the Mets wouldn't even get to play in one for a dozen years.

Losing the 1988 NLCS was a tough blow to swallow and seemed to take a lot of the fight out of us. The next year, we were 87-75, our worst record under Davey Johnson, and finished in second place, 6 games behind the Cubs.

We got off to an inconsistent start in 1990. I had been hearing rumors that Johnson's job was on the line, and on May 27 the Padres handed Gooden his fourth defeat in seven decisions, 8–4, and we fell to fourth place, 5½ games out of first with a record of 20-22.

The following day, Monday, May 28, was a day off. We flew to Cincinnati for a series against the Reds, managed by Pete Rose, that was to begin on Tuesday, May 29. Soon after we arrived at the hotel, I got a phone call in my room at the Terrace Hilton. It was Frank Cashen.

"Come down to my suite," Cashen said. "I want to talk to you."

I went to Cashen's suite and he said, "We let Davey go. We want you to be the manager, and here's the deal. We'll give you a two-year contract with an option for a third year, which will be our option. We're going to double your salary from $70,000 to $140,000, retroactive to the beginning of this season. Next year you're going to make $200,000. None of this is negotiable."

Unfortunately, Davey had made the trip with the team, so they probably hadn't made up their minds to let him go until they got to Cincinnati and told him. It was a day off so Davey didn't have to go to the ballpark and didn't have to face the players or his coaches. He got to Cincinnati, they told him, and he was gone. I never saw him that day and I don't know anybody who did.

Since I was moving up from third-base coach to manager, an opening was created for one coach, but Cashen cautioned me about whom I could hire. "You can't have all your friends as coaches," he warned.

"In that case," I said, "I guess I better line up a few enemies."

I couldn't believe that after all he had done, they would fire Davey. I thought it was a big mistake. I still felt he was the right guy to manage all the characters on that team. They were a tough bunch to handle, but Davey handled them.

I didn't campaign for the job and I didn't prepare for it, but when your bosses ask you to take over the team, out of loyalty you can't refuse and I didn't. I never wanted to manage in the major leagues. I don't have that kind of ego, but I do consider myself a competitor, and I have to admit the job intrigued me. I was curious to find out how I would do running a big league club.

That first year, 1990, was a good experience and a lot of fun. It's always fun when you win, and we won. The players responded and we made a run at the pennant. In June, we went on an 11-game winning streak and took over first place by percentage points ahead of the Pirates.

Some things about managing I didn't particularly care for, such as the radio show on the station that carried our games. One of the "perks" of being the manager of the Mets is that you appear on the radio show and you get paid for it. Davey thrived on it, but I didn't like it. I thought the format was all wrong.

Now, the manager of the Mets is interviewed by one of the talk show hosts once a week, but back then the format was different. I had to be on every day, and instead of being interviewed by a host, I took calls from listeners. It would be Bernie from Brooklyn or Stu from Staten Island, and when we started losing in 1991, most of it was negative, fueled by the station's talk shows. Most of the fans that called wanted to second-guess you or impress you with their knowledge of baseball. You have to be gracious, you have to be respectful, and you have to be diplomatic even though most of the callers didn't know what they were talking about; they couldn't possibly have as much information about the team as the manager. But that didn't stop them from voicing their opinions. Even Jeff Torborg, who followed me as manager, said that was the part of the job he didn't like.

Everything changes when you go from being a coach to being a manager. As a coach, you can buddy-up with a player, joke with him, tease him, be his father confessor, a shoulder for the player to cry on. You can be a cheerleader. As a manager, you have to become somewhat detached. You have to be a disciplinarian, a watchdog, an enforcer.

Take, for instance, my relationship with Gregg Jefferies, a talented but immature and self-important player who came to the Mets in 1987 when he was nineteen years old and played for them through 1991. So I had Jefferies as a coach and as a manager.

Gregg was a perfectionist. He was tough on himself and had a habit of throwing stuff when things didn't go his way. He'd make an out and he's throw his helmet and gloves on the field in disgust. As a coach, I had to be his valet and pick up his equipment after one of his tantrums. I didn't like it, but as a coach I couldn't fine him.

When I became the manager, my relationship with players changed. One time in Houston, I took Gregg out of the game on a double switch, and he slammed his equipment down and went into the clubhouse. After the game, I called him into my office and said, "Don't you ever do that again. Taking you out of the game at the time was a good move. I did it because you made the last out of the inning, and now I have a better second baseman than you out there for defense."

I told him, "That coach is not your valet, so I'm charging you $100 for your gloves and $100 for your helmet, and I want the check in my office before you leave here." He gave me the check for $200 and I put it in my desk. After that, he still got mad, but he wasn't throwing things anymore. About a month, month and a half later, we made a trip to California, where Jefferies is from, and I called him into my office and handed him his check. I said, "Take your folks out to dinner. I don't want your money."

I made some changes when I took over for Davey that a lot of players didn't like. I was a little more concerned with dress code and image than Davey was. That was the Gil Hodges influence on me. My rule was no jeans on the plane. I told them that when we got to the hotel, they could wear whatever they wanted, but when we were traveling as a team, I wasn't going to insist that they wear a jacket, but I wanted them to wear a shirt and tie. And no jeans! The argument from some players was "My jeans cost more than your slacks," which was probably true. My response to that was that I was not going to be the fashion police and put myself in the position of grading jeans—"Yours are okay, but his are not okay"—so to avoid that, no jeans while we're traveling, period.

For a while that was an issue. Then the guys began to dress to the nines and try to outdo one another. Darryl Strawberry, for example, showed up for one trip in a beautiful green suit that probably cost more than I made in a month. That was okay. In the end, the players that objected to the dress code learned to deal with it, and we played well that first year and finished second.

Strawberry had another big year in '90 with 37 homers and 108 RBI. HoJo hit 23 homers and drove in 90. McReynolds was 24 and 82. Frank Viola, who was born on Long Island, went to St. John's, and came to the Mets in a trade with Minnesota in July of 1989, won 20 games. Gooden won 19, David Cone 14. John Franco, who was born in Brooklyn and, like Viola, went to St. John's, came over in a trade with Cincinnati the previous December and led the league with 33 saves.

On September 27, Strawberry had to leave the game with a bad back. He would not play again for the Mets. At the time that Straw's back acted up we were in second place, 3 games behind the Pirates with 6 games to play. With Strawberry out, we never got any closer to the Pirates and finished in second place. My record was 71-49, a winning percentage of .592. The Pirates finished first with a winning percentage of .586.

After the 1990 season, Strawberry decided to get in on the gravy train in baseball by becoming a free agent and signed a lucrative five-year deal with the Dodgers for $22.5 million. It was the end of an era for the Mets. Even with his off-the-field problems, Darryl was the golden boy of the Mets. Now he was gone and he was going to be difficult to replace.

Without Strawberry in 1991, things did not go quite so well. Viola went from 20-12 to 13-15, Gooden from 19-7 to 13-7, Cone from 14-10 to 14-14.

On Saturday, September 28, we lost at home to the Phillies, 6–2, and our record dropped to 74-80. We were in third place, 18½ games out of first. After the game, I was told that Cashen wanted to see me upstairs in his office. I had an idea what he wanted.

I walked into the office and Frank said, "I hate doing this because I hired you, but I'm going to make some changes and we're going to let you go. Maybe I shouldn't have hired you in the first place."

I was being replaced by my third-base coach, Mike Cubbage. That's how it is with being a manager. You take somebody's job, somebody takes your job. I understood that. No hard feelings. It's been going on for more than a century and it will never stop.

Actually, the Mets didn't have to fire me. They held the option on me for the next year. Only 7 games remained (one rained-out game was not made up). All they had to do was let me finish out the season and then say they were not picking up my option. Instead, there was all this hoopla when I was fired. They could have avoided the hoopla by waiting until the season was over and then announcing they weren't picking up my option. On the other hand, maybe they just didn't want the media asking them every day about my future.

Additionally, Cashen was stepping down as general manager after the season and was going to be replaced by his assistant Al Harazin, who, I was told, said to Cashen, "You have to fire Bud before you leave, I won't do it." Evidently Harazin didn't want to start his administration by firing someone the fans liked. He also didn't want to start out with a reputation as a "hit man" for the Mets. I truly believe Cashen liked me and hated firing me, but under the circumstances he felt he didn't have much choice.

I never wanted the job of managing the Mets, and I kind of wish I had never done it. Once you're a manager and you get fired, you can't go back (unless you're Billy Martin and you work for George Steinbrenner). I love coaching, and if I had never managed, I might have become this generation's Frank Crosetti (who coached for the Yankees for 21 years after playing for them for 17 years). I might still be there as a coach.

CHAPTER 20

I had the great good fortune and extreme pleasure of seeing Dwight Gooden and Darryl Strawberry early in their careers when they were carefree and uncomplicated, and managing them later in their careers when they were established veterans with impressive résumés.

When I returned to the Mets in May of 1985 as Davey Johnson's third-base coach, Doc was in his second major league season and Darryl was in his third. At the time they were both young (Gooden twenty, Strawberry twenty-three), happy-go-lucky, free of controversy, exuberant, exciting, and blessed with enormous talent and unlimited potential. They had been voted National League Rookie of the Year in consecutive seasons, Strawberry in 1983, Gooden in '84, which bode well for the Mets. The future for the team as well as for both of these young guys, it seemed, was boundless, their place in the Baseball Hall of Fame being held in reserve.

Off the field, Gooden was this naïve man-child with a perpetual smile that would light up the clubhouse. On the mound, he was Dr. K, a baby-faced assassin who had broken into the big leagues the previous year with a flourish, a record of 17-9 and 276 strikeouts. In 1985, Doc would produce one of the greatest seasons ever for a pitcher, a record of 24-4, 8 shutouts and a league-leading 1.53 earned run average, 16 complete games, 276.2 innings pitched, and 268 strikeouts, for which he would unanimously be voted the National League Cy Young Award.

Strawberry was being hailed as "the black Ted Williams," a muscular, athletic, and charismatic six-foot-six-inch 190-pounder with a quick and deadly left-handed batting stroke that generated frightening power. His prodigious home runs and awesome displays in batting practice were the stuff of legend. He had the look of a baseball superstar to go along with an engaging personality and an innate intelligence. And he had that catchy name . . . Darryl Strawberry. When Darryl seemed to regularly do a good deal of damage on a Sunday, somebody predictably referred to those as "Strawberry Sundays."

After his first two seasons, Straw had already belted 52 home runs and driven in 171 runs. He would hit 29 home runs and drive in 79 runs in 1985. In 1987, Darryl would set a team record, since broken, by hitting 39 home runs and matching that number the following season. His 252 home runs and 733 RBI as a Met are still career franchise records.

In 1985, the off-field problems of Gooden and Strawberry—getting afoul of the law, the DWI arrests, the substance abuse and subsequent rehab confinement, the domestic disputes, Straw's physical problems (he was diagnosed with cancer of the colon in 1998)—were all still in the future.

On April 1, 1987, at the Mets' St. Petersburg training base, General Manager Frank Cashen called the team together and announced that Gooden had tested positive for cocaine and had entered a rehabilitation center. He returned two months later and made his first start of the season on June 5 and didn't miss a beat, leading the team with 15 victories.

By the time I replaced Davey Johnson as manager of the Mets on May 29, 1990, Gooden's drug problems seemed to be behind him. Doc and Darryl were never a problem for me as a manager. They were two huge reasons we won 91 games and finished second in 1990. Gooden won 19 games, the second-highest total of his career, lost only 7, and struck out 223 batters. Strawberry hit 37 home runs, the second-highest total of his career, and had a career high 108 RBI.

If anything, it was *not* having Strawberry that hurt us more than *having* him. Our chances of catching the Pirates in 1990 were hurt when Strawberry suffered a bad back in the stretch run and he had to miss the last 6 games of the season. The next year, he was gone, and we fell from 91 wins to 77 and from second place in the National League East to fifth.

After the 1990 season, Strawberry was a free agent and the Mets let him walk rather than try to match the contract Darryl signed with the Los Angeles Dodgers. With the Dodgers, Darryl hit 28 home runs and drove in 99 runs in 1991.

To replace Strawberry, we had reacquired Hubie Brooks in a trade with the Dodgers. Brooks had been the Mets' third baseman in the early eighties and was the key man in the deal with the Montreal Expos that brought Gary Carter to New York. Now a veteran nearing the end of his career, Brooks was no longer a third baseman and had switched to the outfield. He was our primary replacement for Strawberry.

No knock on Hubie, who was a good player, a good guy in the clubhouse, and an easy player to manage, but he was no Darryl Strawberry. While Darryl was hitting 28 homers and driving in 99 runs for the Dodgers, playing in his place, Brooks hit 16 home runs and drove in 50 runs. I can't say for certain, but I couldn't help thinking that if we still had Strawberry in 1991, I might not have been fired as manager.

People tend to link Doc and Darryl because they were contemporaries, because of their great talent, because their careers, begun at a young age, started out like meteors and then fizzled out, and because they both had their share of off-the-field problems. But I found little about them to be similar. Strawberry was self-assured, even cocky, whereas although Gooden was a star, I don't think he had a great deal of confidence. Strawberry was outgoing and gregarious; Gooden was suspicious, shy, and reticent. I always felt that Darryl had more guidance and direction growing up than Doc did.

After I became manager of the Mets, one of my first meetings was a one-on-one with Strawberry. I wanted him to know I thought he had the potential to be a leader. He certainly had the talent. I talked to him about taking a more active role on the team, on the field and in the clubhouse. "You're a leader here," I said.

"Yeah, yeah," he said.

"No, Straw. Not that quick. No 'yeah, yeah.' I need you to come and do your work and get ready for the game. You skip batting practice too often and you rarely get to the ballpark early.

"I'm not going to be the manager that knocks on your door," I said. "I'm not going to be the manager that follows you around wherever you go. But when those things happen, when you skip BP and you show up late, I know about it. You need to get to the ballpark early and you need to be a little more professional about your work when you get here. That's the kind of leader you need to be. You can be a better outfielder; you've just got to work at it. If you do your work and you go oh for four, it's okay. But if you come in and you're just dillydallying around and doing nothing, and then you go oh for four, it's not okay."

I told him, "We all have our good and bad days, but come and get ready to play." I just talked to him. I wasn't mad at him or anything, and he understood that. He was a gifted player. He was really good in 1990, and then the next year he was gone.

Whenever I asked Strawberry to do stuff, he always agreed. I mean off-the-field stuff for charity. When I was coaching, I was involved with the Make-A-Wish Foundation, and I got Darryl involved, too. He'd make telephone calls to kids in the hospital and talk to them, or he'd take the time to talk with groups of sick kids that came to the game. Darryl would take his batting gloves off and give them to a kid. He was always generous that way.

One day I said, "Darryl, there's this kid John, he's a cancer kid and he's relapsed and in the hospital. Would you say hello to him?"

"Sure," Darryl said. No hesitation.

I called John in the hospital. "John, I have Darryl Strawberry here; he wants to talk to you."

I handed the phone to Darryl and went off to see if I could bring in and put any other players on the phone. Gooden was at his locker. I went to him and said, "Doc, I have a little cancer kid in the hospital. Would you say hello to him on the phone?"

"Oh, no," said Gooden. "I can't do that."

"Okay," I said, and I went looking for another player to put on the phone. I liked Dwight a lot. I never had a problem with him when I was a coach or manager. But I couldn't get him to talk on the phone to the kid in the hospital and that's okay. Maybe he couldn't deal with talking with a kid who might be dying. Maybe he was just shy. I can understand that. Strawberry was different. He never turned me down on a request like that.

After Gooden turned me down, I worked the room until I found another player who agreed to talk to John, and I took him to the telephone. And there was Darryl with the phone to his ear, still talking with John. He must have talked to him for thirty minutes. I thought, "This guy has a heart."

Darryl has a knack for getting along with people. And people respond to him. They seem to have forgiven Darryl for all his falls from grace. In 2006, when the Baseball Assistance Team commemorated the twentieth anniversary of the 1986 Mets World Series championship at their annual dinner, many of the members of that team attended, and Darryl got the loudest ovation and the most attention at the autograph session. Same thing when the Mets brought players back for the final game at Shea Stadium. Again, Strawberry got the loudest ovation.

Gooden was there. It was his first time at Shea since he'd retired, and he looked uncomfortable. Doc has always been shy. Strawberry never was.

The Mets are proud that Darryl has turned his life around. They use him as a spokesman. I run into Darryl a lot. I try to do as much as I can and make as many appearances for charity as I can fit into my schedule. I've been to a lot of places where I have run into Darryl. He's out there doing stuff. He hugs me whenever he sees me. He has some respect. He doesn't have to judge me as a manager and he doesn't. He judges me as a person.

Darryl does things for the March of Dimes, and through his sister-in-law he's become involved in the fight against autism. He understands his place in the world. He's energetic and dedicated. He says all the right things, such as how fortunate he is to have found religion, to be on the straight path, and to be able to give back to others because of his success in baseball.

Darryl has righted his ship. He's created a bunch of positives out of a tremendous amount of negatives. I'm proud of him.

CHAPTER 21

Anybody who has ever spent any time in a major league club-house has seen the sign—you can hardly miss it. It's spelled out in huge letters and its message is clear; it comes across in no uncertain terms without the slightest possibility of being misunderstood:

MAJOR LEAGUE RULES

(d) Betting on Ball Games.

(1) Any player, umpire, or Club or League official or employee, who shall bet any sum whatsoever upon any baseball game in connection with which the bettor has no duty to perform, shall be declared ineligible for one year.

(2) Any player, umpire, or Club or League official or employee, who shall bet any sum whatsoever upon any baseball game in connection with which the bettor has a duty to perform, shall be declared permanently ineligible.

I raise this issue now because over the years I have been asked many, many times if Pete Rose belongs in the Hall of Fame.

First let me say that I don't really have to answer the question because Pete's name has never appeared on the ballot. Besides, it wouldn't matter to me if his name did appear on the ballot because I don't have a vote. What I do have is an opinion, and over the years that opinion has changed almost as frequently as George Steinbrenner changed managers.

Because I don't have a vote, this is all hypothetical.

Does Pete Rose belong in the Hall of Fame?

Based solely on his playing record and his accomplishments over 24 seasons in the major leagues, whether Rose "belongs" in the Hall of Fame is a no-brainer.

Nothing stopped him. He was a little hit machine.

Who would ever argue against a player that played in more games (3,562) and got more hits (4,256) than anybody else in baseball history?

How could you deny someone who was a 17-time All-Star, a 2-time Gold Glove winner, and National League Rookie of the Year in 1963?

Who wouldn't vote for a player who had more than 200 hits in a season 10 times (2 other times he had more than 190 hits), won 3 batting titles, and hit over .300 16 times?

How could you overlook a player with a lifetime average of .303?

Who could ever ignore a player that played with such enthusiasm and élan that he earned the nickname Charlie Hustle, and who played with such daring and reckless abandon as to wreak havoc on the base paths.

Does Pete Rose belong in the Hall of Fame?

For so long, when I was asked that question, my answer was an unequivocal yes. But lately, I have flip-flopped, done an about-face, and changed my mind. Let me emphasize that my change of opinion is not based on vengeance because Pete and I had that confrontation around second base in Shea Stadium in the third game of the 1973 National League Championship Series.

Pete and I got past that. We were teammates with the Phillies; we have appeared together at card shows; we've exchanged autographed pictures of the brawl; and Rose came to a few games of the Long Island Ducks when I managed his son, Pete Jr.

I never had a problem with Pete Jr. when I managed him. Petey was easy to manage. He could play a little bit. He could hit. He was a tough out. He played 21 seasons in the minor leagues and independent leagues and wound up with 1,877 hits. One year, 1997, he batted .308 for Chattanooga, a Cincinnati farm team in the Class AA South Atlantic League. The Reds brought him up in September that year and he got in 11 games, came to bat 14 times, and had 2 singles. He was twenty-seven at the time and never got another chance, but he kept playing (it was in his genes) and didn't quit until he was a few weeks shy of his fortieth birthday.

It couldn't have been easy for Petey because of who his father is. People would inevitably make comparisons, and how can anyone measure up to comparisons with Pete Rose? Petey handled it okay, but he wouldn't sign autographs. Why, I don't know. It's probably something a psychologist would have to investigate to find out the reason.

There never were any hard feelings between Pete Sr. and me, and there are none now. What's done is done. What happened in 1973 was just part of the game. It was the way Pete played the game. It happened and then it was gone; it was gone right away, the next day.

I always liked Pete and I have always respected him for his work ethic, his hustle, and his tremendous career. To me, Rose has to be the greatest overachiever in baseball history, a guy with limited natural ability (he's not the fastest runner, the best defender, or the most powerful hitter) who reached superstar status with determination and hard work.

Yet, in this case, more has to be considered than merely the playing record.

That warning against gambling is posted in every major league clubhouse, a warning that Rose saw and read—or could have seen and read—3,562 times as a player and another 786 times as a manager.

Pete Rose broke the cardinal (also the Pirate, Phillie, Red Sox, Giant, and Dodger) rule; the one that's been on the clubhouse door forever. It just says gambling, that's all. It doesn't say you cheated on your wife, you beat your wife, you embezzled money, you're an ax murder, none of that stuff. It says if you gamble on baseball, you're banished for life.

Some guys were caught with marijuana, some had drug problems, some have police records, and were elected to the Hall of Fame. But Shoeless Joe Jackson of the Chicago White Sox was not elected, and he batted .408 in 1911 and had a career batting average of .356, the third-highest ever. *But,* he, along with seven of his teammates, was implicated in the "Black Sox" betting scandal in the 1919 World Series, accused of throwing the Series to the Cincinnati Reds; accused and never convicted but nonetheless banished from baseball for life by Commissioner Kenesaw Mountain Landis.

Rose voluntarily accepted a permanent place on baseball's ineligible list in return for an agreement by Major League Baseball not to make formal charges against him with regard to gambling allegations. His file was sealed, so we don't know what evidence baseball has against him, but the perception is that they have enough to make the suspension stick and keep him out of the Hall of Fame. I find it significant that guys that know him best, guys he played with that are in the Hall of Fame, Johnny Bench and Joe Morgan, have been outspoken in their belief that Pete does not belong.

This could all have been academic and Pete would probably be in the Hall of Fame today if he'd only come clean when the charges against him surfaced, admitted he bet on baseball, showed remorse and regret, and apologized for his transgression. We're a country that believes in forgiveness and second chances. We want to forgive our heroes. We would have forgiven Rose and given him another chance. But he never admitted his mistake. At least not right away. Pete did come clean years later in a book and in a television interview, but he insisted he bet on the Reds only when he was a manager, not as a player, and he bet on them only to win, never to lose. Unfortunately his confession was too little and too late.

Ego and arrogance have always motivated Rose. He seemed to believe he was bigger than the game, that he was bulletproof. But ego and arrogance probably are two reasons he was such a great player. Through the years, many great players, Hall of Famers, have had problems with alcohol or drugs, and people would say if so-and-so didn't drink or do drugs, just think how much greater he could have been. My answer to that is, maybe if they didn't drink or do drugs, they might not have been as great as they were.

I know one thing: you can't play this game drunk and you can't play this game high. But maybe some guys needed to drink to relax, just as some guys needed to smoke cigarettes to calm them. The drinking, the smoking cigarettes, the ego, and the arrogance all were part of the whole package, and the whole package made them great players. So when people say they wonder what certain players would have been like if they didn't drink or smoke or do drugs, I'd say, "Maybe you wouldn't have liked it. Maybe they wouldn't have been able to perform without those things."

Pete Rose's ego, his arrogance, his cockiness, helped make him the great ballplayer he was and were as much a part of him as his legendary will to win, his work ethic, and his hustle.

One of Pete's greatest attributes was his ability to concentrate no matter what else was going on his life or what was happening around him. He's never been someone that let any personal problem bother him or affect his play. In 1978, when he was chasing Joe DiMaggio's major league record of hitting in 56 consecutive games, Rose was involved in a paternity suit that would have distracted most players and affected them on the field. Not Pete.

Rose didn't catch DiMaggio, but he came as close as anybody else ever did, hitting in 44 straight games, 7 more than the National League record set thirty-three years earlier by Tommy Holmes of the Boston Braves. The streak was stopped on August 1 in Atlanta by Larry McWilliams and Gene Garber, who struck Pete out for the final out of the game.

There is a picture of Pete's and my contretemps around second base at Shea Stadium. Fans would show up at card shows with the picture and ask Rose to sign it. Apparently tired of signing all those pictures and of other people making money off it, Pete bought the rights to the photo, so now when somebody buys a copy of the picture, Rose gets a piece of the action.

At card shows, Pete gets $65 to sign the picture. I get $6 to sign the same picture. But if someone mails me the picture and encloses a self-addressed, stamped envelope, I'll sign it and mail it back, no charge. The one thing I won't do is put crazy stuff on it—you'd be surprised at what people want me to write. I won't do it. I just put *NLCS 10/8/73* and my signature.

People will take the picture, already signed by me, to card shows where Rose is appearing and pay the $65 for him to sign just his name. If they want something else under his name, that costs more.

One day when I was coaching for the Mets and we were in Cincinnati, Pete, who was the manager of the Reds at the time, sent word over to our clubhouse that he wanted to meet me on the field. I met him and Pete asked me to pose for a picture with him, which I did. The next thing I knew, copies of that picture started showing up at card shows and I never made a nickel off that picture.

Another time I was with Jerry Grote in Cooperstown at an autograph session and I found out that Rose was there, too (it had nothing to do with the Hall of Fame; he was hired by an independent merchant). I finished my signing and went to find Pete and say hello. I walk into this store and there's Pete at a table with this long queue of fans for his autograph. Before long I was sitting down next to him and putting my signature next to his.

That's Pete. Love him or hate him, you can't ignore him, and it's difficult to say no to him. You have to give him his due. Not only was he a great player, the guy is a charmer.

CHAPTER 22

My involvement and my love affair with baseball goes back more than a half century if you include Little League, high school, and college, and I can honestly say that after all that time, the love affair still burns passionately within me.

Does that mean I'm entirely pleased with the game as it is today? Not at all. Some changes have been made in the game I knew fifty years ago, some good, some not so good, but the bottom line is that the game on the field has not been dramatically altered from its beginnings more than 150 years ago.

I have some issues with today's game, but it's still the greatest game ever created by man—Abner Doubleday, Alexander Cartwright, Bobby Valentine, Tony La Russa, Tim McCarver, Bob Costas, or whomever.

The first thing that jumps out at me when I compare today's game with the game in my day is that players today are bigger, stronger, and faster—that suggests the steroid scourge in baseball, which I will get to later. Today's players have better diets, better equipment, better training facilities, and better instruction.

I played at five feet ten inches, between 145 and 155 pounds. Compare that with the size of today's shortstops:

Derek Jeter, 6-3, 195
Elvis Andrus, 6-0, 200

> J. J. Hardy, 6-2, 200
> Yuniesky Betancourt, 5-11, 210
> Jose Reyes, 6-1, 200
> Hanley Ramirez, 6-3, 230
> Troy Tulowitzki, 6-3, 215

I like to think that if I were playing today, I would have a chance to make it with guile, experience, hard work, and determination, but unquestionably I would be at a huge physical disadvantage to my peers.

Another difference is the salaries of today's players compared with those of the players in my day. The most I ever made was $90,000 a year. That's a week's pay for some of today's players. Take Jeter for example. The 2010 season was the last of a ten-year contract that paid him $189 million, or a mind-boggling average of $18.9 million a year. At $90,000 a year, I'd have had to play 2,100 years to earn $189 million, and except for Jim Kaat, I can't think of anyone that played 2,100 years in the majors.

I don't begrudge the money today's players make and I'm not bitter about it. Major leaguers being paid huge salaries was long overdue. I say more power to them for finally getting what they deserve. What I do regret is that in my day many players had to take off-season jobs to make ends meet; consequently they were not able to spend the off-season working out daily. Today's players don't have to work in the off-season, so they can spend the time working out and getting ready for the following season. In addition, most of the big-time, higher-paid players can afford to build houses big enough to include their own gymnasium.

Now the steroid issue. When people ask me whether players took steroids in my day, I tell them I hit 7 home runs so I must have taken steroids at least seven times.

Seriously—and I don't mean to make light of the situation because it is a serious matter—the steroid era is one of the darkest periods in baseball's otherwise glorious history. It stained the game for a time, but baseball is so strong and its appeal so solid that the steroid scourge could not bring the game down. The sad part is that only a small percentage of players have been implicated in the scandal, but it has cast suspicion on every player.

As long as the game has been played, players have always tried to get some kind of edge over their competition, either legally or illegally. That's why players have corked their bats and pitchers have scuffed the baseball. Steroids make you stronger. I'm not condoning their use, but the player that takes steroids to get stronger still has to swing the bat and hit the ball.

The good thing is that baseball, the commissioner and the Players Association working in concert, addressed the issue and seem to have a handle on it.

Perhaps the biggest change on the field in the last fifty years has been the philosophy of pitching.

Today pitchers regularly get four days off between starts. In my day, the top pitchers started every fourth day. Back in the early days, after the turn of the twentieth century, pitchers such as Christy Mathewson even would start with two days' rest.

Pitchers today are on pitch counts. The number of pitches they are allowed to throw in a game is monitored and limited. It starts in high school and goes right up through the major leagues. Most starters are limited to between 100 and 110 pitches in a game. I'm not sure what the reason is for limiting the number of pitches. Some say conventional wisdom preaches that the arm has only so many pitches in it, and overextending a pitcher will lead to serious arm trouble. But Nolan Ryan pitched a record 27 years in the major leagues, and Jim Kaat pitched 25 years, and neither of them ever had a sore arm. They both have been outspoken against the theory that throwing too many pitches results in a sore arm and, eventually, surgery. They maintain that the arm is a muscle, and you strengthen a muscle by using it, not resting it. Kaat proved his theory by throwing every day, if not in a game then in a bullpen side session.

In his career, Ryan had many games in which he threw 150 or 160 pitches or more. He made 35 to 40 starts and pitched 250 to 300 innings a season and pitched in the major leagues until the age of forty-six, still throwing upward of 90 miles an hour.

Teams today have seventh-inning and eighth-inning specialists, or setup men, and a ninth-inning man, or closer. In my day, pitchers finished what they started. Guys such as Sandy Koufax, Don Drysdale, Tom Seaver, Bob Gibson, and Juan Marichal were their own setup men and their own closers.

In 1965, when I first came up to the major leagues, Koufax led the National League in complete games with 27 and Mel Stottlemyre led the American League with 18.

In 2011, the leader in complete games in the National League was Roy Halladay with 8. The leader in the American League was James Shields with 11.

In 1965, 416 complete games were pitched in the ten-team National League and 323 in the ten-team American League.

In 2011, the sixteen-team National League had 80 complete games and the fourteen-team American League had 93. (The AL has the luxury of the designated hitter so pitchers never have to leave the game for a pinch hitter.)

I'm not sure how this business of pitch counts got started or why it became so popular. I don't know what's behind the theory. Is it insurance? If a team gives a pitcher a long-term contract and tries to have it insured, does the insurance company insist the team has to limit his workload?

Is it because managers are told by their front office, "We're paying our setup men $8 million a year and our closer $12 million a year, so you better use him"?

To me, negative thinking produces negative results. If you pull a pitcher after 100 pitches, how can you ever expect him to pitch longer than six or seven innings? What's going to happen when you need him to get out of a jam in the seventh inning?

I believe you have to build up pitchers. If a runner is training for a marathon, which is twenty-six miles, he doesn't get ready for that marathon by running twenty-six miles. He has to run thirty-five miles or forty or fifty, so that when he has to run twenty-six miles, it's like a sprint to him. The same goes for a pitcher. If you expect him to go nine innings, you can't get him ready for nine innings by taking him out of a game after 100 pitches.

It's much harder to manage today than it was in my time because if you're not building up your starters to go nine innings, to throw more than 100 pitches, then you're burning up your bullpen. If you don't bring in your setup man in the seventh and eighth inning, and your closer in the ninth inning with a 3-run lead—even though you believe your starter is the right guy to finish the job he started—and you blow the game, then you're going to be second-guessed by the fans, the writers, the talk show hosts, and your own general manager and owner, and you'll soon be out of a job.

I'm proud of Ryan, my old teammate, for having the courage of his convictions. He took over as president of the Texas Rangers and instituted a policy of ignoring pitch counts and making pitching decisions based on instinct and observation. What goes around comes around. Under this "revolutionary" (or retro) system, the Rangers' pitchers thrived, and Texas won the 2010 and 2011 American League pennant. Baseball people being superstitious and notorious mimics, Ryan's philosophy will likely catch on, and the future will see more pitchers finishing what they start.

The designated hitter, or DH, is another innovation that came along toward the end of my career, in 1973, but only in the American League, which I think is ridiculous. The National League didn't have it then and doesn't have it now. How can you have two leagues playing under different rules and then getting together in the World Series?

Since I played my entire career in the National League with the exception of one season with the Texas Rangers in 1980, I'm partial to National League baseball—that is, *without* the DH, as baseball was originally. I understand why the American League adopted the designated hitter. Their attendance was declining at the time, and their surveys indicated fans liked seeing home runs. I know the DH allows some big-name stars to stay around longer than they normally would, but I still like the National League style of play better. It requires more strategy, more bunting, more hitting-and-running, more pitching decisions—and results in more second-guessing of managers, which makes the game more interesting.

It seems that players and managers, such as Joe Torre and Mike Scioscia, who came from the National League and go to the American League and play National League baseball have usually been successful.

The game has gone through some changes, but it's really still the same game it's been for almost 150 years. It's still sixty feet six inches from the pitcher to home plate, and ninety feet between the bases. A batter still gets three strikes and four balls. A game is still nine innings, except for extra innings to break a tie, and there are still three outs for every half inning. And it's still the greatest game ever invented.

CHAPTER 23

Sometimes things work out for the best. Sometimes fate comes in, takes you by the hand, and guides you. In other words, as they say, even a blind squirrel will occasionally find an acorn.

I may have found my acorn when I was fired as manager of the Mets. As difficult as it was to take at the time, it might have been a blessing in disguise. One door closes and another door opens.

Part of my deal when I moved up from third-base coach to manager after Davey Johnson was let go was that if (when) I was fired, the Mets would keep me in the organization and give me a job (unspecified) for the same money I was making as manager. I had that in writing, and the Mets lived up to the terms of the contract. They made me a scout, a position I held for two years. Occasionally, I did some advance scouting for the big league team, but mostly my assignment was to visit our minor league affiliates and evaluate our farmhands. As an unplanned by-product of that assignment, I would stumble into the next (and current) phase of my baseball life: owner.

As a longtime resident of Long Island's Suffolk County, I had become acquainted with a Long Island businessman named Frank Boulton, who, among other things, was dabbling in the ownership of minor league baseball teams. He owned two minor league affiliates of the New York Yankees, the Albany-Colonie Yankees of the Class AA Eastern League and the Prince William Cannons of the

Class A Carolina League. From time to time I would run across Frank at golf outings and other Long Island functions because he was active in the area, and we formed a relationship. One day in 1991 I mentioned to Frank that I had done everything in baseball from playing to coaching to managing to scouting, and that I loved minor league baseball and would be interested in ownership of a minor league team.

Frank informed me that the owners of the Carolina League's Peninsula Pilots, a Seattle affiliate, were putting the team up for sale. I saw that as an opportunity to get my foot in the door of minor league ownership. The Pilots were located in Hampton, Virginia, across the water from Norfolk, home of the Mets' top minor league affiliate, the Tidewater Tides of the Class AAA International League. In my position as a scout for the Mets at the time, and earlier when I was a Mets roving instructor and visited all of their farm teams, I had spent a lot of time in Virginia, so I was familiar with the area.

I worked closely with Frank Boulton, who was helping to put together an investment group for me for the purpose of purchasing a minor league franchise. But when the lead investor dropped out, Frank jumped in and became the lead investor, and that's how we became partners. Frank arranged a meeting with the Pilots' two owners at their office in the World Trade Center. We made an offer to purchase the team and it was accepted.

When I got home that night, Kim, my wife, asked me what I did that day.

"I bought a baseball team," I said.

"How much did it cost you?"

"One million two hundred thousand dollars."

We took over ownership of the Pilots in 1992. I assumed the title of team president. My main function as president was to make periodic visits to Hampton and appear on local radio and television to try to drum up interest in the team.

At the time, the Pilots were playing in an old, antiquated

ballpark that had been built by Branch Rickey. It had light poles in playing territory and tool sheds that served as COLOREDS ONLY bathrooms. They hadn't been used in years, but they remained as a painful and chilling reminder of a regrettable and contemptible period in our nation's past.

Although we didn't make our plan known publicly, our group had no intention of staying in Hampton. We sought permission from the Carolina League to move the team to Wilmington, Delaware, where there was funding to build a brand-new ballpark. That plan didn't go over well with the officials of the Carolina League.

"You want to move the team where?" they said.

"Wilmington, Delaware!"

We were then told, politely but firmly, that Wilmington is north of the Mason-Dixon Line, and with Calvin Falwell (yes, a relative of Jerry) as the owner of the team in Lynchburg, Virginia, moving a Carolina League team from Hampton, Virginia, to Wilmington, Delaware, fourteen miles north of the Mason-Dixon Line, was not going to be a slam dunk.

Eventually, permission was granted by the league and the move was effected. We signed a working agreement with the Kansas City Royals and changed the name of the team to the Wilmington Blue Rocks.

Operating a team first in Hampton, Virginia, and then in Wilmington, Delaware, gave me the opportunity to find out how to run a minor league franchise and to learn how things work in the front office, etc., all the things I had never experienced in my years as a player, coach, manager, and scout. We operated the Blue Rocks for two years, then sold the team. I'm pleased to say they're still there, still in the Carolina League, and doing well.

All the while, Frank had been trying to move his Albany-Colonie Yankees to Long Island, but he was frustrated by the Mets, who invoked their territorial rights and blocked the move. No way did the Mets want a Yankees farm team in their area, less than an hour's drive from Shea Stadium. Had Frank's team been a Mets affiliate, he might have been given permission for the move.

With his grand plan shot down by the Mets, Frank went back to the drawing board. A book titled *Green Diamonds* by Jay Acton deals with minor league baseball. In one of the chapters, Frank Boulton is featured in a discussion about how to do a minor league baseball deal. As a result, Frank started getting phone calls from officials in various cities that were frustrated because they were being denied baseball. Affiliated baseball had claimed territorial rights in practically every area in the United States, thereby blocking any expansion.

Boulton got calls from officials in Atlantic City, Bridgeport, Connecticut, and other cities, and before long an idea was formulating in his mind. At the same time, with a Major League Baseball Players Association strike looming, there was a free agent camp for potential replacement players in Homestead, Florida. Frank and I took a trip to the camp and came across quite a few capable former major league players hoping to resurrect their careers and get one more chance at the big leagues.

Frank began to think about a league outside of affiliated baseball that would utilize players who had been dropped by teams for economic reasons, not because they couldn't play the game. Maybe they were a little older and they were being pushed aside by younger players. After all, only a limited number of jobs are available in the major leagues—and even in the minor leagues—and teams were cutting costs, so they tended to dump veteran players and replace them with younger, less costly players.

Boulton's ultimate goal was to bring professional baseball to Long Island, but that was still in the future. The first step was to form a league made up of the two hundred best available free agent players in the world that had major league, AAA, and AA experience. Frank was aware that independent league teams had been sprouting up around the country, but our area had no independent league. He solved that problem with the formation of the Atlantic League of Professional Baseball in 1998.

Charter members of the Atlantic League were the Somerset Patriots, Newark Bears, and Bridgeport Bluefish (still members of the league), the Atlantic City Surf and Newburgh Black Diamonds (both defunct), and the Nashua Pride (moved to the independent Can-Am League). Camden, Lancaster, Southern Maryland, and York came later. The teams are close enough geographically that travel in the league is decent. We travel by luxury bus for the most part.

The Long Island Ducks joined the Atlantic League in 2000. Our primary goal was to provide affordable family entertainment to Long Island in the form of professional baseball. It didn't have to be an independent league team. It could have been an affiliated team in the farm system of the Mets or the Yankees or any other major league team, it didn't matter. Since we were blocked from getting an affiliated team because of territorial rights, we wound up forming the Long Island Ducks. We're glad we did.

Our whole concept is that you can come to a Long Island Ducks game with your children and be entertained for about three hours without having to take out a loan to purchase tickets for the entire family.

We don't just stick a BASEBALL TODAY sign out and sit back and watch the people come through the gates. We're a year-round operation. We work hard at what we do. We have Fireworks Night every Friday and Autograph Day every Sunday, and we get involved in community events such as Thanksgiving Day parades and St. Patrick's Day. We try to stay in front of the people. We have a mascot, Quaker Jack, who not only is there at every game to keep the kids entertained and amused, but also goes into the schools and takes part in reading programs, recycling programs, how to be a team player in the classroom.

We planned our ballpark to be a fun place, and it is. It's a happening, and it's all families. People will come for the first time and fathers will say, "This is great; I have my kid on my shoulder and another one walking by my side." That's what it's all about. It's not about five guys coming to the game to drink beer. You can get beer at our ballpark, and it's not cheap. We don't want it to be cheap. We don't want you coming to our games for the beer. And we'll cut off the sale of beer in the seventh inning.

While entertainment is uppermost in our minds, and we have strived to fill our roster with names that are recognized by even the most casual baseball fans, we try never to lose sight of our endeavor to put the best possible team on the field.

Over the years, we have had such familiar names as Edgardo Alfonzo, Jose Offerman, Donovan Osborne, Bill Pulsipher, Mark Whiten, John Rocker, Pete Rose Jr., Carlos Baerga, Jay Gibbons, and Sidney Ponson on our roster.

I was the first manager of the Ducks, in 2000, and then I turned it over to younger men, including Hall of Famer Gary Carter and former major league pitcher Dave LaPoint. Sparky Lyle has managed in the league since its inception. Other familiar names that have managed in the Atlantic League are Tim Raines, Butch Hobson, Tommy Herr, Willie Upshaw, and Andy Etchebarren.

We like having marquee names among our players and we like to win, but we are just as pleased when players leave us and go to the major leagues, either going back or getting their first shot. Through the years a former Duck has signed with every major league franchise.

We won the Atlantic League championship in 2004 and made the play-offs every year from 2004 to 2009. I'm also pleased that in our first eleven years we presented our brand of baseball and family entertainment to just shy of 5 million fans, an average of more than 400,000 fans a year and more than 6,100 a game.

When I stepped down as manager after the first season, I didn't take the uniform off. I'm still there, at every home game, coaching first base, throwing batting practice, signing autographs. I love every part of it, everything about it. It's still a thrill just putting on the uniform. I've been doing it all for more than a decade, and I hope to do it for at least another decade, maybe longer.

Frank Boulton tells people that if there's someone on Long Island that doesn't have my autograph, he'd be surprised.

Well, if you are that person that doesn't have my autograph, come on out to a Long Island Ducks game at Citibank Park in Central Islip, Long Island, and I will be happy to correct that oversight.

EPILOGUE

I never played baseball for the money!

Don't get me wrong, I'm not complaining. I made a good living, supported my family, and have had a good life. I have traveled around the world, played with and against some of the greatest players in baseball history.

When I retired from baseball as a player, I began to think of all the people I'd met. I was with Casey Stengel. I was with Yogi Berra. I knew Mickey Mantle. I got to meet Joe DiMaggio and had the great joy of being able to introduce him to my father-in-law, who was born in Italy. I remember President Nixon, after he left office and was living in New Jersey, attending games at Shea Stadium and coming into our clubhouse. He'd stop by every locker and had something to say to everybody; he knew something about every player.

I met Presidents Reagan and Bush, the elder, when he was vice president. We were invited to the White House after we won the World Series in 1986, and Bush wined and dined the players and gave us golf balls with the vice presidential seal. I still have mine in my office.

I owe all of it to baseball. But it never was the money that motivated me.

To give you an example of baseball's pecking order, I was a career .236 hitter and I live all the way out on Long Island, in Suffolk County, a good fifty miles from downtown New York City. Ed

Kranepool, my old Mets teammate, was a .261 hitter and lives in Long Island's more exclusive Nassau Country within easy hailing distance of the Big Apple. Before moving back to California, my old buddy and roommate Tom Seaver, who is in the Hall of Fame, lived in the high-rent district, the exclusive and wealthy town of Greenwich, Connecticut.

I came from rather humble beginnings. We weren't poor, but we were far from rich; still, my childhood was happy. My dad worked hard and didn't make a lot of money, but there always seemed to be enough to feed and clothe us, with some left over for luxuries— modest and inexpensive family things such as boating and camping.

I signed with the Mets for a bonus of $13,500, and six years later I was the Mets' regular shortstop when we beat the heavily favored Baltimore Orioles to win the World Series. It was the culmination of a dream and of all the hard work I had put in, the many hours spent taking ground balls to improve my defense and in the batting cage as I was trying to become a switch-hitter.

I can still remember the feeling of pride and accomplishment I got when Cleon Jones caught Davey Johnson's fly ball to left field for the final out of Game 5 of the 1969 World Series, then dropped to one knee, as if genuflecting in triumph and thanksgiving.

I'm pleased that here it is, more than thirty years after I retired, and with all the changes that have been made in their ownership and front office, I still maintain a close relationship with the Mets. I wouldn't want not to be associated with them. I want that attachment. The Mets call me from time to time to make appearances for them, for which there is a fee. I've made it clear to them that I'm not doing it for the money, and whatever fee there is, it's given to my foundation.

Maybe someday I'll need the money, but fortunately right now I don't. The Long Island Ducks do well.

I try to share time between doing things for the Mets and my commitment to the Ducks, but the Mets know that the Ducks come first. You can find me at every Ducks home game, in the first-base coach's box when we're at bat, signing autographs before the game and often throwing batting practice to our hitters. I love all of it, going to the ballpark, coaching, meeting the fans, taking part in pregame practice, and I hope to never stop doing it.

I told Kim, my wife, that if there ever comes a time when I can't throw batting practice anymore, that will be the time to take me out back and shoot me.

INDEX

259

Index